Preparing for the 2022 California Clinical Social Work Law & Ethics Exam

Preparing for the 2022 California Clinical Social Work Law & Ethics Exam

Benjamin E. Caldwell, PsyD

First Printing: 2022

ISBN-13: 978-1-7348735-7-3

Ben Caldwell Labs
6222 Wilshire Blvd, Suite 200
Los Angeles, CA 90048

www.bencaldwelllabs.com

Ordering Information:

U.S. trade bookstores and wholesalers: Please contact Ben Caldwell Labs via email at support@bencaldwelllabs.com.

To you
You've got this
Pass

Contents

Acknowledgements

To you, using this book to prepare for your exam: Thank you for the good and important work you do. The path to becoming a clinical social worker is not easy, nor should it be. That you have chosen this path says a great deal about who you are, and how much you have to give to your community. I'm honored to be part of your journey.

Deep and profound thanks to Marcia Castro-Rohrer, Emma Jaegle, and Jeff Liebert, my current and former teammates here at Ben Caldwell Labs, without whom this book would not exist. My family have continued to provide their unwavering support and encouragement, including debating more practice questions than anyone should be subjected to. We have unusual dinner table conversations at my house.

My gratitude as well to all of those who used and provided feedback on earlier editions of this book. Your feedback found its way in here.

About the author

Benjamin E. Caldwell, PsyD is an Adjunct Professor teaching Law and Ethics for California State University Northridge in Los Angeles. He routinely advocates for prelicensed therapists at licensing board meetings, and has been directly involved in several important pieces of legislation in the past 15 years. His research papers have been published in the *Journal of Marital and Family Therapy*, *American Journal of Family Therapy*, *Journal of Divorce and Remarriage*, *Journal of Systemic Therapy*, and elsewhere. He regularly gives presentations on legal and ethical issues impacting therapy work.

Other books by Benjamin Caldwell:

Basics of California Law for LCSWs, LPCCs, and LCSWs,
    9th edition (2022)
Preparing for the 2021 California MFT Law and Ethics Exam
Saving Psychotherapy: How therapists can bring the talking cure back
    from the brink (2015)

For books and exam prep resources, visit bencaldwelllabs.com

Continuing education courses led by Benjamin Caldwell:

Visit simplepracticelearning.com

***Psychotherapy Notes* blog:**

Visit psychotherapynotes.com

Disclaimers

The information in this book is believed to be accurate at the time of publication (May 2022). However, mistakes can happen, and legal and ethical standards can change quickly. It is the responsibility of each individual therapist to make sure they are remaining current with legal and ethical standards of practice.

While this book discusses legal requirements for the practice of clinical social work, it is intended to be used exclusively in the study process for the California Clinical Social Work Law and Ethics exam administered by the Board of Behavioral Sciences. Defensible multiple-choice questions are often, by design and necessity, much less complex than real clinical situations. **No part of this book should be construed as legal advice or as a substitute for consultation with a qualified attorney.** If you need specific legal guidance, your professional liability insurer and your professional association may provide legal resources to you at no cost.

Neither this book, nor any book or test preparation program, can guarantee success on an exam. Your success on the test depends on your ability to learn and recall key knowledge, to apply that knowledge in the test setting across a wide variety of case vignettes, and to manage anxiety.

Introduction

First thing's first:
You've got this.

    The California Clinical Social Work Law and Ethics Exam is 75 questions over 90 minutes, and it is *absolutely* a test that you can pass. You've taken a graduate-level course in Law and Ethics that was probably pretty good, and probably not all that long ago. But even if it was a while back or a bit lacking in quality, you can catch up with current standards fairly quickly. Most people attempting the exam pass on their first attempt; of those who don't pass on their first attempt, most pass on their second.

    As licensing exams go, this exam focuses on a relatively narrow scope of knowledge. Later, when it comes time to take the ASWB Clinical Exam, you'll need to know the theory and interventions involved in many different models of treatment; you'll need to know more about assessment, diagnosis, and crisis care; and you'll need to know a wide variety of additional information on effective clinical care *in addition to* knowing the legal and ethical rules governing the profession. But **this first test is just about those legal and ethical rules.** In that way, it's actually a better test all around: It's shorter, it's more clearly geared to public safety, and on your side, it's easier to prepare for.

    You've got this.

About this book

This book is meant solely to help you prepare for the California Clinical Social Work Law and Ethics Exam. It aims to be as efficient as possible in providing the critical, current information you need to know to be successful on the test.

There are three main sources for the information covered in this book:

1) The *NASW Code of Ethics*, available at socialworkers.org
2) *Basics of California Law for LCSWs, LPCCs, and LCSWs, 9th edition*, available on amazon.com and at bencaldwelllabs.com
3) California statutes and regulations, a summary of which is available at bbs.ca.gov (complete California law is available at leginfo.legislature.ca.gov)

In addition to those sources, several other articles and books were used in the development of this book. This is similar to how the test itself is developed: Licensed Clinical Social Workers use source material common in the field, and develop questions assessing an examinee's knowledge of 128 "knowledge statements" outlined in the BBS Exam Plan for this test.

That Exam Plan is a public document. It's available at home.pearsonvue.com/cabbs for download, and is also included at the back of this book. Because it so clearly specifies what kinds of knowledge are needed for the test, the exam plan was also key to the development of this book: **Next to each header in the study guide, you will see small numbers that start with the letter K. These numbers indicate the knowledge statements, in the BBS Exam Plan, that are addressed in that section of the book.** As you'll see, this book covers all 128 knowledge statements necessary for the exam.

Of course, this book is not a substitute for a graduate-level Law and Ethics course, or for the textbooks used in such a course. For a deeper dive on state law for clinical practice, I would recommend *Basics of California Law for LMFTs, LPCCs, and LCSWs*. For more detailed texts on ethical issues for clinical social workers, I would recommend the following:

- ***Ethics in Psychotherapy and Counseling*** by K. S. Pope, M. J. T. Vasquez, N. Y. Chavez-Dueñas, & H. Y. Adames (6th edition, Wiley, 2021)
- ***Issues and Ethics in the Helping Professions*** by G. Corey, M. S. Corey, C. Corey, & P. Callanan (10th edition, Brooks/Cole, 2018)
- ***Social Work Values and Ethics*** by F. G. Reamer (5th edition, Columbia University Press, 2018)

All the information you need to know for the exam comes from sources in the field, including the NASW Code of Ethics, state law and regulation, and the same Law and Ethics textbooks (like my *Basics of California Law* text) commonly used in social work graduate courses in the state. What this book does is **organize and filter** that knowledge in ways that should be useful, and then give you practice **applying** that knowledge in vignettes that are built to approximate the actual exam.

About the Exam

Test basics

The California Clinical Social Work Law and Ethics Exam is a 75-item, 90-minute test. Of those 75 items, only 50 count toward your score. The other 25 items are being tested for possible inclusion as scored items in future test cycles. You have no way of knowing which 50 exam questions are scored and which are those 25 experimental items, so it is in your best interest to do the best you can on every item on the test. All questions are four-option, multiple choice questions where you are tasked with choosing the *best* response from the available options.

The test is administered via computer at testing centers around the state, and can be taken at some centers outside of California as well. You can see a complete list of test centers by going to home.pearsonvue.com/cabbs (Pearson VUE is an independent company the BBS contracts with for the administration of their exams) and selecting "Find a Test Center." No personal items are allowed into the test centers, and to keep the testing environment secure, they have strict rules about the clothing that examinees can wear. Some test centers have lockers where you can store personal items during your test.

You will be seated at a workstation where your exam has been preloaded into the computer, and you may be offered a set of earplugs or noise-cancelling headphones to use during the test if you wish. Some examinees find these very helpful for blocking out the sound of other computers in the room, while others simply find them uncomfortable. The Pearson VUE testing centers administer a wide variety of tests for federal and state government agencies as well as private businesses, so it is likely that the other examinees in the testing room with you will be working on several different kinds of tests. Once you've had the opportunity to get settled in and familiarize yourself with the computer you will be using, you follow the on-screen instructions to begin your exam.

Content

Considered as a whole (but without considering the 25 experimental items), the test will break down into the following proportions:

Topic Area	% of scored items	# of scored items (out of 50)
Law	**40%**	**20**
Confidentiality, privilege, and consent	14%	7
Limits to confidentiality, including mandated reporting	16%	8
Legal standards for professional practice	10%	5
Ethics	**60%**	**30**
Professional competence and preventing harm	18%	9
Therapeutic relationship	27%	13-14
Business practices and policies	15%	7-8

The exam is not separated into these sections; you will get questions from various categories in random order. These are merely overall proportions. Still, they can be helpful to know. For example, knowing that ethical issues surrounding the therapeutic relationship make up more than a quarter of the test, you may place an emphasis in your studying on this area.

These percentages also are helpful to keep in mind if you hear from other examinees that they had a surprising amount of questions on a particular topic area on their test. You shouldn't adjust your studying on the basis of such reports. Surprises like that usually result from *experimental* (that is, non-scored) items having emphasis in a particular content area on *that specific version* of the exam. Multiple versions can be in use at the same time, so another person's version of the test may not match yours. *Scored* items for all versions of the test will break down to the percentages above.

Scoring

Your score is based on the number of non-experimental items that you answered correctly, out of 50 total. Every item is worth one point – there is no weighting of items based on difficulty, complexity, topic, or any other factor. There is also no penalty for an incorrect response; it is counted as 0 points, just the same as if the item were left blank.

The passing score on the test varies from one test cycle to the next, and sometimes among different versions of the test being given within the same test cycle. Some versions of the test are more challenging than others, so the BBS conducts careful statistical analysis of each test – and of every *item* on each test – to make sure they set the passing score appropriately. While the BBS no longer publicly announces the passing score, they used to. During that time, the passing score cutoff was consistently *around* 35 out of 50 scored items (70%). To the best of my knowledge, there has never been a cycle where the passing score cutoff was above 37 or below 33. Since the practice exams here don't include non-scored items, and since the difficulty level of various versions of the real exam can vary, I recommend aiming for scores above 80% on practice tests, as this will provide a bit of buffer in addition to helping your confidence.

Accommodations

Accommodations are available for examinees with recognized disabilities. If you need accommodations, you will need to arrange for a letter to be sent from your health care provider documenting your disability. Common accommodations include a quiet room for testing, or additional time to complete the exam. It is Pearson VUE, and not the BBS, who determines accommodations for examinees with documented disabilities. More information about the process of applying for accommodations, as well as the forms that must be completed, are at home.pearsonvue.com/Test-takers/Accommodations.aspx

As a separate process, the BBS will also allow additional testing time for those who do not speak English as their native language. There are strict requirements to qualify for this additional time, however. The form to apply for this additional time is at www.bbs.ca.gov/pdf/forms/esl_specaccom.pdf

If you are considering applying for exam accommodations, it's important to plan ahead. All requests for accommodation should be received at least 90 days prior to scheduling your exam. Actual processing time varies based on time of year, application volume, staffing, and other variables.

While many examinees with disabilities report that it is beneficial to receive accommodations, I have also sometimes observed those who do *not* have recognized disabilities trying to receive accommodations to get extra time on the exam. You should note here that 1) test anxiety, in and of itself, is not a recognized disability; and 2) unless you have a history of benefiting from disability accommodations, you probably don't need accommodations for this exam. Remember that the majority of those who attempt this exam pass on their first try, and among those who don't, rarely does inadequate time come up as an issue.

Test-Taking Strategy

There are many different test-taking strategies that can help you perform well on the exam. Of course, no test-taking strategy will substitute for having detailed knowledge of the material you're being tested on, and being able to apply that knowledge across a wide variety of clinical situations. But strategies can help maximize your score by helping with items you don't know the answer to, and strategies can also help with time and anxiety management.

In general, I defer here to your knowledge of your own strengths and challenges. You probably already know how good of a test-taker you are, and you probably already know what strategies work best for you. (If you don't, it may be worth it to you to try the practice exams here in a couple of different ways, to see what strategies help you the most.) Just like for studying, the only bad strategy for test-taking is one that doesn't work for you.

If you're already clear on the strategies that help you the most on exams, you can safely ignore the rest of this section. If you're interested, here are some strategies specific to this exam that may help you. Note that these strategies are not mutually exclusive, and you can use as many as you like at the same time.

Timing

- **Take the easy ones first.** You can go forward and backward on the test as much as you like. Remember that you have a time limit and that items are not weighted, so a good way to start the exam (and possibly build some confidence) is to go through the whole test, marking the responses you are sure of. Then you can go back and spend more time on those items that you need more time to consider. You may find that in a very short time period, you already have half or more of the test completed – and that almost all of those answers are likely correct.
- **Don't get stuck in a rabbit hole.** You have 90 minutes to respond to 75 questions. That gives you a little more than 70 seconds per question. If you find yourself getting hung up on an especially difficult question, move on. Make a mental note (or, if you're using

the blank paper provided at the test center, an actual note) of the question you're struggling with and any responses you have ruled out, and then go on to other questions you may be able to answer more quickly.

Content

- **Pay close attention to what each item is actually asking for.** One way of eliminating wrong answers is to notice when a question is asking specifically for a *legal* response or specifically for an *ethical* one – that will allow you to eliminate any response choices that would fall into the other category. Similarly, when a question asks what action you would take *first* or *next* in a given situation, there may be multiple answers that reflect things you would do. The question is demanding that you *prioritize* those actions to focus on the most urgent, which often means action to protect the physical safety of clients or those around them.

  The line between legal concerns and ethical concerns isn't as clear in real practice as it is on the test. The phrase "in accordance with applicable law" or its equivalent is all over our codes of ethics, and the (legal) unprofessional conduct category known as "general unprofessional conduct" can make ethical violations into legal ones as well. But for the purposes of the test, the two are clearly distinguished – in ways that can help you succeed on the test, if you understand which issues fall into which category. The table on page 26 addresses where several common concerns **generally** lie: Legal, ethical, or both. There may be exceptions within each.
- **Use the process of elimination.** Even when you aren't certain of the *right* response on a particular question, there is a good chance you will be able to identify one or more of the response choices as obviously *wrong*. Eliminating wrong options greatly increases your chance of getting the question right, even if you're not ultimately sure what the best answer would be.
- **Don't overthink.** In my experience, when people struggle with the law and ethics exam, it's often not a knowledge issue. Quite the opposite. It's because they spend *too much* time pondering all of the possibilities hinted at by each question, rather than focusing simply on the limited information included in the question itself. As a general rule, you should not assume any "facts not in evidence,"

as a lawyer might say. Focus solely on the information presented in the question itself. If your initial response to a question is "it depends," that's a cue to refocus *just on what is presented in the question*.

- **Go ahead and guess.** Because there is no penalty for an incorrect response, if there are items you are truly unsure about, it is in your best interest to go ahead and mark your best guess. **Use the last few minutes of your test to mark your best guess on all remaining items you haven't already answered.** The worst thing you can do is leave an item blank, since that gives you a 0% chance of getting the point for it. Even if you're not able to eliminate *any* of the response choices from consideration, guessing at it gives you at least a 25% chance of getting it right.

Mindset

- **Stay confident.** You're likely to encounter some weird questions on the test – either things that just don't make sense to you, or items that are strangely worded. You may even see bad grammar, spelling, and sentence structure. Don't panic. These kinds of items may be the non-scored, experimental items being tested for possible inclusion as scored items on future tests. This is precisely why the BBS does that kind of experimentation: They need to weed out bad items. It's still worth it to answer them as best you can, but if you can't figure some items out, don't let that shake your confidence in your overall knowledge. If a question is confusing, it's probably *a problem with the question,* not a problem with you.
- **It doesn't matter.** If you believe that the test is some kind of a meaningful indicator of your value – as a clinician, or as a person – then you're at risk of sending yourself into an anxiety spiral, especially if you run into a few difficult questions in a row. This test *is not* a meaningful indicator of your clinical skills or your value of a person, and it should not be thought of as such. It's simply a step on the path to licensure. You will probably pass, but even in the unlikely event that you don't, you just wait 90 days and try again. If you find anxiety creeping up on you, remember that this exam is very small in the grand scheme of things. Your clients, friends, and family will all think of you the same way after the exam as they do before it.

Primarily legal, ethical, or both?

Legal	Both	Ethical
	Informed consent for telehealth	Informed consent for therapy or research
Privilege	Confidentiality	
Scope of practice		Scope of competence
Retaining records 7 years	Maintaining adequate records; Client access to records	Storage and destruction of records
Professional titles	Truth in advertising	Testimonials
Telehealth regulations; HIPAA compliance	Telehealth competence	
		Personal values, attitudes and beliefs
		Countertransference
Ownership of records	Client autonomy	
	Non-discrimination	Cultural competence
	Fees for referrals Fee disclosures	Bartering; Termination for overdue balance
Abuse reporting	Minors' consent	
Involuntary hospitalization	Crisis management	
Insurance parity	Accurate info to payors	Advocacy with payors
		Termination and non-abandonment
Therapy Never Includes Sexual Behavior brochure	Sexual relationships	Multiple relationships
	Monitoring self for impairment	Assisting impaired colleagues
Licensure requirements	Supervision	

Before the test

Weeks and months before

The material on which you will be tested is largely consistent with what you would have learned in graduate school, particularly what you learned in your Law and Ethics class. So a lot of your preparation will simply be re-familiarizing yourself with that material, and making sure you're caught up on any recent changes that have taken place in the legal and ethical rules governing the profession.

There are, of course, lots of ways to **study the material for the exam.** Do what you know works for you. The law and ethics exam does not contain trick questions, and there is no "secret" way to study. The only wrong way to study is a way that doesn't work for you. If you work well with flash cards, make them. If you're someone who does better with reading and rereading, well, hopefully this book is helpful! The point is, trust your instincts and experience when deciding how to study, and how much. Some will find that an hour a night is all they can handle, while others will want to take several-hour-long blocks of time to study. Similarly, some find it more useful to study with friends or colleagues who are also about to test, while others prefer to study on their own.

The most important thing to do several weeks before the test is to **schedule your exam.** Review the list of test centers on the Pearson VUE website and choose the one that is most convenient to you. While all of the test centers are designed to have ample parking and similar testing conditions, you might want to consult with others who have recently taken exams at locations close to you. They can prepare you for things like the friendliness (or lack thereof) of test center staff, which can make a big difference in your testing experience. Note that the center you choose to schedule might not be the one that is geographically closest to you; you might find there's one farther away that is easier to schedule on your preferred day and time, or in a neighborhood that you like to visit.

One thing you may find helpful once you have your test scheduled is to **clear your test day of other obligations.** Arrange to take the day off from work, and don't put any other appointments on your schedule. You will want to focus squarely on the test. And once it's over, you will not want to go back to work right away. If you pass, you'll want (and deserve!) a bit of celebration, and if you don't pass, you'll want some time to shake it off.

Another thing to address once your test is scheduled: **tell employers, supervisors, and loved ones about your upcoming test.** Part of this is simply pragmatic: They will need to know that you will be entirely unreachable, even in the event of an emergency, during the time you are taking the test. (Cell phones are, of course, not allowed in the testing room.) But part of it is also to shore up social support: It's good to go into a test knowing that a lot of people are cheering for you, and will be ready to celebrate with you once you pass.

The week before

Since you schedule your exam by phone or online, you may not be familiar with the specific location of the test center where you will take the exam. It can reduce anxiety on your test day if you actually **visit the test center** during the week before the test. Try to go to the center in advance around the same time of day that you'll be going for the actual test. This can help you get a feel for traffic, parking, and the like. Based on how long it takes you to get there, you can better plan your actual test day, making sure to give yourself ample time for unexpected delays.

The week before the test is also the time to **wrap up studying**. Hopefully by this time you're feeling confident and ready. If not, it's worth taking an honest look at *why* you're not feeling that way. Is it simple anxiety about the test, or is it a recognition that you don't know the material as well as you should? Anxiety can be managed through relaxation techniques, time with friends, and perhaps a visit to your own therapist. If there are parts of the material you are struggling with, you still have time to shore up your weak points before going into the exam.

The wrap-up process does involve studying, of course, but **take care of yourself** during this time. There is indeed such thing as too much studying: if it is interfering with sleep, your ability to care for your clients, or your relationships with loved ones, you may find that simply adding on more study time this late in the process will do you more harm than good.

Part of taking care of yourself can be to **adopt a mantra**, or a brief statement you can use repetitively to center yourself and calm your nerves. A mantra can be part of a larger spiritual or meditation practice, but it doesn't have to be. Here are a few you can choose from, or create one that is a good fit for you:

It's just a test. It doesn't define me as a person or as a therapist.
I am ready.
I've had good education, good supervision, and good preparation.
I will be the same therapist after the test that I am before it.
This is a milestone, just one checkpoint on a larger journey.
I will pass.
My friends and family will love me the same no matter what happens.
I know the things I need to know.

Occasionally, people find that they are really not ready for the test at this point, and may consider rescheduling it for a later date. That's fine, but before taking this step, consider whether it is truly about your readiness, or whether it simply reflects anxiety creeping up on you. If it's anxiety, putting off the test may just mean you repeat the experience a few weeks later.

The day before

The day before the test, spend time reviewing what you know and making sure you have everything ready for the next day. You may want to prepare a checklist of things to do and things to bring to the test with you, such as photo ID, paperwork confirming the test time and location, and the like. (Remember that test centers will not allow you to bring personal items into the exam room. Some test centers have lockers you can use to store personal items during the test, but not all do.) Make sure you eat well and get a good night's sleep the night before the exam.

The day of the test

Different people have different ideas about whether it is helpful to do some last-minute studying on the actual day of the test. Again, do what works best for you. Some find that reviewing material one last time increases their confidence, as they recognize material, get practice questions right, and generally go into the test feeling good about how much they know. Others find that continuing to review at the last minute only increases their anxiety.

The most important thing you can do on the day of the test is to keep your anxiety in check. Have a normal, healthy breakfast. (Food and drinks are not allowed in the testing room, so don't go in on an empty stomach.)

Get a pep talk from your partner or a close friend. If you've chosen a mantra, spend time repeating it to yourself.

Before you leave home or work for the test, make sure you have the documents you will need to get in: ID and the confirmation from Pearson VUE that includes the date, time, and location of your test. Without these materials, you may not be allowed to take the exam.

After the test

Unless you have a disability accommodation that requires paper-and-pencil testing, or there is some unusual circumstance that has led the BBS to do a review cycle at the beginning of a new cycle of the exam, you will find out immediately whether you passed the exam.

If you pass, congratulations! You will not need to go through another test until you complete your 3,000 hours of supervised experience for licensure and are sitting for the Clinical Exam. Spread the word about your success to friends, family, colleagues, supervisors, social media, or anyplace else you want to announce it so that people can join in celebrating your accomplishment. **Please also let us know:** An email to **support@bencaldwelllabs.com** to share your success story is always appreciated!

If you do *not* pass on your first try, but there is ample time left before your registration renewal, then failing is largely inconsequential. You can take the test again after a 90-day waiting period, and pass on that attempt. (If you start early, you could attempt the test three times before your renewal comes up.)

If there isn't time to attempt again before your renewal, you can still renew your registration; the requirement for renewal is that you have *attempted* the test at least once. You'll need to *attempt* the exam at least once in your next year of registration, and continue attempting until you pass.

The BBS will not allow anyone to register with a second associate number, or to sit for the Clinical Exam, until they have passed the Law and Ethics Exam.

2022 changes in law and ethics

There were several changes in California and federal law, and in professional ethics, affecting social workers and other psychotherapists in 2022. Among the changes that may be included in your exam:

- New California requirements when writing letters for clients seeking to use Emotional Support Animals
- New federal requirements for fee disclosures (Good Faith Estimates) for uninsured clients and those who do not intend to use their insurance to cover costs of treatment
- Updates to the NASW Code of Ethics focused on cultural competency and self-care

That updated NASW code calls out self-care as an ethical responsibility of social workers for the first time, mentioning it by name in the preamble and ethical principles. However, it does not appear in the ethical standards, which are the most specific and enforceable statements of ethical responsibilities. Self-care seems most likely to appear on your exam as a method of preventing or responding to impairment in your clinical work.

The ethical standard for cultural competence is more significantly updated. While social workers have long held strong standards about understanding and respecting client culture, the revised language calls on social workers to take even more direct action in this regard. It requires not just that social workers obtain knowledge about various cultures, but that they *demonstrate* that knowledge as guiding work with clients, and "take action against oppression, racism, discrimination, and inequities." It further requires social workers to seek to prevent potential barriers to clients' access to care via technology. Together, these revisions make clear that cultural competence is both internal (your knowledge, understanding, and appreciation of client culture, and your cultural humility) and external (demonstrating cultural competence through observable behavior).

The new NASW code can be read in full at www.socialworkers.org/about/ethics/code-of-ethics/code-of-ethics-english A highlighted review of the 2021 changes is available at www.socialworkers.org/About/Ethics/Code-of-Ethics/Highlighted-Revisions-to-the-Code-of-Ethics

The changes above are reflected in the study guide section of this book.

In addition, there were several other meaningful changes in state law and regulation that involve the supervision relationship. Supervisor qualifications and training standards have been updated, and there are new guidelines regarding substitute supervision, among other updates. Because supervision law is *not* included in the BBS Exam Plan for the Clinical Social Work Law and Ethics Exam, we do not believe that these changes are likely to appear on your exam. But of course, they can be highly relevant to your current and future work as an Associate Clinical Social Worker. If you're interested in learning more about these changes, visit www.psychotherapynotes.com/major-changes-california-bbs-supervision-2022/

Here we go!

The next section is a summary of information likely to be included on the exam. The BBS uses 128 "knowledge statements" outlining what they believe you need to know in order to practice therapy within your legal and ethical boundaries. They've been organized here in such a way that should make them easier to study and retain. I've kept the descriptions as brief and simple as possible.

This study guide is divided into subsections that correspond with the knowledge categories on the exam plan:

- **Law: Confidentiality, privilege, and consent**
- **Law: Limits to confidentiality, including mandated reporting**
- **Law: Legal standards for professional practice**
- **Ethics: Professional competence and preventing harm**
- **Ethics: Therapeutic relationship**
- **Ethics: Business practices and policies**

At the beginning of each subsection, you'll see the number of questions from that section you are likely to encounter on your actual exam, out of 50 total scored items. This should help you determine how much emphasis to give each section.

Throughout this book, Clinical Social Worker is often abbreviated as CSW. For the purposes of this book, unless otherwise specified, the terms "social worker," "CSW," "LCSW," and "therapist" are used interchangeably and refer to a Licensed Clinical Social Worker who is licensed by the California Board of Behavioral Sciences and is practicing within the state.

If you have questions about any of the explanations here, or want to dive deeper on any of the subjects covered in this book, you best first stop is the primary source material used in the development of this book. If you have additional questions, email our team at support@bencaldwelllabs.com and we'll be happy to assist.

You've got this.
Good luck!

Study Guide:
Key Principles

LAW

Confidentiality, Privilege, and Consent

Scored exam questions (approximate): 7

Understanding confidentiality K1-2

Laws about confidentiality. Unless a specific exception to confidentiality applies, CSWs are legally required to keep the content of therapy confidential. This means that they do not share any information about clients, including even the existence of a therapeutic relationship, with outsiders.

Social workers sometimes mistake this as meaning that simply the *identity* of a client is confidential. But the way the law is written, *all information learned in a confidential setting* is supposed to remain confidential unless an exception applies or the client has granted permission for information about their care to be shared.

Laws about disclosure. While confidentiality is the default state, a number of legal exceptions to confidentiality exist. In fact, there are more than 20 instances in state law where confidentiality can or must be broken, and information shared with outside persons or agencies.

In those instances where confidentiality *can* be broken, therapists will often err on the side of confidentiality unless otherwise required by law. However, there may be instances where a therapist breaks confidentiality because they legally *can* do so and they believe it is in the best interests of the client or the community to do so. For example, a therapist can, but is not required to, break confidentiality if there is a public health emergency (like, say, a pandemic) and the therapist is reporting a client as having the disease to local public health authorities. Therapists are also allowed, but not required, to share otherwise-confidential information for the purposes of obtaining payment for services.

More commonly, the times when a CSW breaks confidentiality are limited to those instances when the law requires it. These times can be generally broken down into five categories:

- Suspected child abuse
- Suspected elder or dependent adult abuse
- Danger to self or others
- Legal authorization, such as a court order or client release
- Other, less common instances where disclosure is required

The first four categories will be discussed in greater detail below. As a CSW, you need to be keenly aware of them. The fifth category – those less common instances where disclosure is required – includes an investigation by a board, commission, or administrative agency; a lawful request from an arbitrator or arbitration panel; a coroner's investigation of client's death; a lawfully issued search warrant; and a national security investigation, among others. These instances do not commonly come up in therapy, but they are still worth being aware of. In the event of a national security investigation, CSWs not only are required to turn over client records, but are legally prohibited from informing the client that they have done so.

Understanding privilege K3-6

Privilege refers to information that can be excluded from court proceedings. Normally, all communications between a therapist and their client are considered privileged communications, meaning that they cannot be used in court. Other examples of communication that is usually privileged include communication between spouses, and communication between an attorney and their client. Privilege is specifically a *legal* issue, outlined in California law.

This is particularly important in therapy. Clients need to be able to trust that information they have shared with their therapist about mental health symptoms or other emotional problems will not be used against them in court; if that risk exists, clients will understandably be less open with their therapists about struggles in the clients' lives.

Clients generally hold their own privilege. In other words, only the client can waive their own right to privileged communication in most instances. Even when the client is a minor, the client is usually considered the holder of their own privilege, although the minor may not be allowed to *waive* privilege on their own. A judge may block a minor (or an adult, for that matter) from waiving privilege if the judge believes that waiving privilege is not in the person's best interest. In any case, it is never up to the therapist to determine whether privilege should be waived. That is up to the client, the client's guardian, another court appointee, or a judge.

Release of privileged information. By definition, privileged information cannot be used in a court proceeding. Privileged information may only be released in court if the client has waived privilege, or if a judge has determined that privilege does not apply, based on one or more of the exceptions spelled out in state law (see "Exceptions to privilege" later in this guide).

Responding to a subpoena or court order. If a CSW receives a subpoena (a legal document requesting that the therapist produce records, appear in court, or both), there are specific steps the CSW is commonly advised to take. These include:

1. **Contact an attorney as soon as possible.** The CSW will benefit from legal guidance throughout this process.
2. **Assess the subpoena for its source and validity.** A subpoena *from a judge* is a court order – the CSW must obey it. A subpoena from a *private attorney* is different, and may be fought if the client chooses. Occasionally, your attorney may advise you to object to the subpoena, if there is something wrong with the subpoena itself or how it was delivered.
3. **Contact the client to determine their wishes.** Often, the client will freely authorize the CSW to release the records or appear in court. Sometimes, the client will prefer that the CSW assert privilege on the client's behalf, arguing that the therapist's records or testimony should not be made part of the court proceeding.
4. Unless the client has specifically waived privilege or a judge has determined that privilege does not apply, **assert privilege.** This is considered the appropriate default position for a CSW to take in the absence of other guidance from the client or the court.

Of course, if the client does waive privilege, or if a court determines that privilege does not apply, you must comply with the subpoena.

Treatment of minors K7

Treatment of minors. In most cases, parents provide consent for the treatment of their child. Anyone under age 18 is a minor under state law, and parents can consent for treatment on their child's behalf. If a minor has two legal parents, then typically either parent can provide consent for therapy for the minor.

If the minor's parents are divorced, consent becomes more complicated. In joint custody, typically either parent can provide consent on their own. If one parent has sole custody, typically only that parent can provide consent for the minor's treatment. If that parent refuses or withdraws their consent, the social worker should not treat the minor. However, the word "typically" is important there. In some instances, custody agreements create exceptions around health care generally or mental health care specifically. If there is any doubt or concern about who is legally able to provide consent for a minor's treatment, the social worker should request a copy of the custody order and review it themselves.

Other caregivers may sometimes bring a minor in for therapy. Another relative who lives in the same home as the minor may provide consent for the minor's treatment if they sign a "Caregiver's Authorization Affidavit." The necessary language of this document is specified in state law.

Minors as young as 12 may be seen *without* parental consent if the minor is mature enough to participate intelligently in treatment. That determination is made by the therapist. In these cases, the therapist still must either make an effort to contact the child's parents, or document why they believe doing so would be harmful. Parents do not have a right to access records for their child if the child consented independently, and parents cannot be forced to pay for services provided without the parents' consent.

Documentation K8-11

Documentation of services. Documentation of therapy is both a legal and ethical requirement. Neither state law nor professional ethical codes define the specific *content* that needs to be in treatment records, and there are many formats for things like assessments and progress notes. However, all CSWs are legally required to keep records that are consistent with "sound clinical judgment, the standards of the profession, and the nature of the services being rendered" (CA BPC 4992.3(w)). As we will see, there are some specific things that legally must be documented when they occur, such as client releases of information and specific consent for telehealth services.

Maintenance and disposal of records. Under state law, records must be maintained for at least 7 years following the last professional contact. If you are working with a minor, records must be maintained for at least 7 years after the minor turns 18.

During the time you are maintaining records, you must take reasonable steps to ensure they are secure and confidential. When the time comes to dispose of old client records, this disposal must also be done in a manner that protects security and confidentiality (and, if you're a HIPAA-covered entity, is HIPAA compliant). You should never just throw old files in the trash.

Client access to records. Clients generally have a legal right to access their records, though there are some limitations on this. Unless you believe that the release of records to the client would be harmful, you must comply with their request in a timely manner: Within 5 days if the client simply wants to inspect their records, and within 15 days if the client wants a copy of their record. You cannot refuse a client's request for records simply because they owe you money. You can, however, charge for reasonable costs associated with accessing and copying the client's file. You also can provide a summary of the file, rather than the full record, if consultation with the client reveals that this will fulfill the purposes of their record request. A summary typically must be provided within 10 days of the client's request. Any client who inspects their record and believes some part of it to be incomplete or incorrect can submit a brief statement to be included in the client file.

If you believe that releasing records to a client would be harmful to them, you may refuse to do so. If you refuse, you need to document the request and your reason for refusal. The client may then request that a third-party professional review the records to see whether that third party agrees with you that the record should not be released.

In the case of couple or family treatment, therapists get consent from all members of the treatment unit prior to releasing records.

Release of records to others. Records of treatment can be released to third parties if the client requests it or if there is some other appropriate legal authorization. Most commonly, clients request that their records be forwarded to another therapist or health care provider for continuity of care, or they request that records be provided to their insurance company for the purpose of receiving reimbursement.

When a client requests that their records be released to a third party, this request typically must be in writing, and it must be signed and dated by the client or their legal representative.

There are some instances when a specific authorization to release information is *not* required by law, such as when the information is needed by another active health care provider or health care facility to for the purposes of diagnosis or treatment (in an emergency, for example, there may not be time to gather written authorization), or when the information is required as part of a billing process.

As discussed previously, records are also sometimes released by court order, which is its own form of legal authorization.

Telehealth laws K12-13

Telehealth consent. Under California law, therapists who offer services via telemedicine are legally required to first obtain specific consent for telemedicine (the consent can be verbal or in writing) and document this in the client's file. Failure to do so is considered unprofessional conduct. While purely administrative contacts, such as scheduling sessions by phone or email, would likely not qualify as telehealth, actually providing therapy by phone, videoconference, or other technology certainly would. (Throughout this book, "telemedicine" and "telehealth" are used interchangeably.)

Telehealth delivery. California and federal laws govern the delivery of services by telehealth. When delivering services by telehealth, all of the laws regarding scope of practice, client confidentiality, and client rights to information and records continue to apply. CSWs must be particularly cautious when considering using telemedicine to treat clients located outside of California, as a California CSW license only governs services provided to clients who are physically located within the state at the time of service.

By regulation, California social workers wishing to conduct therapy via telehealth need to take several specific steps. *At the start* of engaging a client in telehealth, the social worker must:

- Get specific telehealth consent (as noted above)
- Inform clients of the risks and limitations of telehealth services
- Provide the social worker's licensure/registration information
- Document reasonable efforts to locate crisis resources local to the client

Regarding that last point: A low-risk client wouldn't require the same effort to locate crisis resources local to them as a high-risk client would. So based on your assessment of client risk, you may locate crisis resources local to them just in case they're needed. Whatever you do in this area, it should be documented.

In addition to the steps above, the social worker must do the following *at each instance* of telehealth:

- Obtain and document the client's full name and current location
- Assess whether the client is appropriate for telehealth (this may be based on their symptoms, and also may be based on the technology and privacy available to the client at that time)
- Use best practices for security and confidentiality

There are two reasons for obtaining the client's current location, which should be specific (i.e., an address, or as close to one as possible). One is that you know where to send crisis resources if it becomes necessary. The other is to ensure that you are practicing only with clients who are located in California (or any other places where you are qualified to provide services).

HIPAA. Under the Health Insurance Portability and Accountability Act (HIPAA), CSWs covered by the act have specific additional responsibilities to protect the privacy of client records. Among the requirements:

- Designating a privacy official
- Informing clients and staff of privacy policy and procedures
- Disciplining staff members who violate privacy or security rules
- Repairing harmful effects of privacy violations
- Maintaining safeguards against the release of private information
- Having complaint procedures for violations of privacy

- Ensuring confidentiality of electronic health information
- Protecting against threats to information security
- Notifying the department of Health and Human Services of breaches of unsecured health information
- Getting client permission before communicating via unsecured email

Rather than memorizing that list, it may work best to simply recall that under HIPAA, CSWs need to have and enforce specific policies to protect the security and confidentiality of health information, and that clients are to be informed of the relevant policies. Therapists covered under HIPAA provide clients with a Notice of Privacy Policies that outlines how private information is gathered and used.

There is a specific category of documentation that HIPAA calls "psychotherapy notes," which are different from typical progress notes. "Psychotherapy notes" are a therapist's notes documenting or analyzing conversation with a client that happens in a private psychotherapy session. Within this definition, psychotherapy notes cannot include information like session start and stop times, diagnosis, progress, treatment plans, symptoms, interventions, or prognosis. Psychotherapy notes, as defined under HIPAA, must be kept separate from the rest of the client file and are not considered part of the client record. However, under California law, these records may still be subject to subpoena.

Sample Questions
See the next page for answers and rationales

1. A former client calls the CSW who had treated her two years earlier. The former client verbally requests that the CSW forward her file to her new therapist in a different state. The former client confirms her identity using her social security number and is able to identify specific topics of the prior therapy, leaving the CSW confident in the identity of the caller. The CSW should:

    a. Take down the information for the new therapist and forward the file as the client requested

    b. Take down the information for the new therapist, contact that therapist, and have that therapist complete a written records request

    c. Take down the information for the new therapist, and inform the former client that she will need to request that the records be released directly to her. She can then forward the file to the new therapist if she so chooses

    d. Take down the information for the new therapist, and send the former client appropriate paperwork to request in writing that her file be released

2. A potential client with partial paralysis contacts a CSW and asks whether he may receive therapy by phone for his symptoms of depression. The CSW assesses the potential client by phone and determines he is appropriate for phone-based services. Legally, the CSW must:

    a. Obtain consent for phone-based services and inform the potential client of the possible risks and benefits

    b. Obtain consent in writing for phone-based services and inform the potential client that such services are currently considered experimental in nature

    c. Assess the client in person at least once before moving to phone-based services

    d. Assess the client in person and identify the closest hospital emergency room to the client, in case of emergency

Sample Questions: Answers and Rationales

1. A former client calls the CSW who had treated her two years earlier. The former client verbally requests that the CSW forward her file to her new therapist in a different state. The former client confirms her identity using her social security number and is able to identify specific topics of the prior therapy, leaving the CSW confident in the identity of the caller. The CSW should:

   a. **Incorrect.** Take down the information for the new therapist and forward the file as the client requested. *The client should provide permission in writing for the release of their records. This option does not leave the therapist with adequate documentation of the request.*

   b. **Incorrect.** Take down the information for the new therapist, contact that therapist, and have that therapist complete a written records request. *The request for records should come from the client, not from the new treatment provider.*

   c. **Incorrect.** Take down the information for the new therapist, and inform the former client that she will need to request that the records be released directly to her. She can then forward the file to the new therapist if she so chooses. *With the client's permission, records can be transferred directly to the new treatment provider. They do not need to first go through the client.*

   d. **CORRECT.** Take down the information for the new therapist, and send the former client appropriate paperwork to request in writing that her file be released. *The client should provide permission in writing for the release of their records.*

2. A potential client with partial paralysis contacts a CSW and asks whether he may receive therapy by phone for his symptoms of depression. The CSW assesses the potential client by phone and determines he is appropriate for phone-based services. Legally, the CSW must:

    a. **CORRECT.** Obtain consent for phone-based services and inform the potential client of the possible risks and benefits. *These are current legal requirements.*

    b. **Incorrect.** Obtain consent in writing for phone-based services and inform the potential client that such services are currently considered experimental in nature. *Consent for telehealth can be provided verbally under state law, and does not need to be in writing.*

    c. **Incorrect.** Assess the client in person at least once before moving to phone-based services. *While assessing the client in person first may be helpful, it is not currently a legal or ethical requirement.*

    d. **Incorrect.** Assess the client in person and identify the closest hospital emergency room to the client, in case of emergency. *While assessing the client in person first may be helpful, it is not currently a legal or ethical requirement.*

LAW

Limits of Confidentiality

Scored exam questions (approximate):	**8**

Exceptions to confidentiality:
Child abuse K18-19

Laws about reporting child abuse. California therapists are **mandated reporters** of suspected child abuse when serving in our professional roles. In other words, we are required to report abuse we observe or suspect while in the office, but are not required to report abuse we observe or suspect at the grocery store, at home, or in other non-professional settings.

Your mandated reporting responsibilities are triggered when, in your professional role, you develop **reasonable suspicion** that a minor has been abused. ("A minor" is important here. The victim does not need to have been your client, it can be *any* minor whose abuse you learn about in your professional role.)

Reasonable suspicion is a specific term with a specific meaning. As the law is written, if another therapist with similar training and experience, when presented with the same information, would reasonably suspect that abuse had taken place, then so should you. You do not need to be certain that the abuse happened in order to reasonably suspect it – for example, you do not need to have personally observed injuries to suspect physical abuse.

There are five types of abuse that *must* be reported:

- **Physical abuse.** Anyone who willfully causes an injury to a child or engages in cruel or unusual corporal punishment is committing physical abuse. There are exceptions to this definition for school employees and peace officers (such as police) trying to reduce threats or end conflict using a "reasonable and necessary" degree of force. There is also an exception for what the law describes as a "mutual affray between minors." Two children who both choose to fight may injure each other, and this is not child abuse.

- **Sexual abuse.** This category includes sexual assault, sexual exploitation, and what the law calls "lewd and lascivious acts." When minors engage in consensual, *heterosexual intercourse*, the therapist must consider their ages, using these two rules:

  The 14th birthday rule:
  If one partner is 14 years old or older, and the other is under 14, the therapist must report.

  The 21/16 rule:
  This rule can be thought of as the "drinking and driving" age rule: If one sexual partner is old enough to drink (at least 21), the other partner needs to be old enough to drive (at least 16). To put this another way, if one partner is *under* 16 and the other is 21 or older, the therapist must report.

  For any other age combinations, the therapist should consider the age and maturational levels of the partners in assessing their capacity to consent and the nature of the relationship (i.e., is it exploitive or otherwise abusive) when deciding whether to report. When minors consensually engage in *oral sex, anal sex, or object penetration,* the 21/16 rule applies, but the 14th birthday rule does not. Of course, non-consensual oral sex, anal, object penetration, or intercourse will always be reportable when a minor is involved. "Lewd and lascivious acts" may include non-penetrative sexual behaviors like fondling or stimulating another person, and are a mandated report if the minor is under 14 and the partner is any age, or if the minor is 14 or 15 and the partner is 10 or more years older than the minor.

- **Willful harm or endangerment.** Any person causing a child "unjustifiable physical pain or mental suffering," or any caregiver who allows it to happen, is committing child abuse.

- **Neglect.** Even if it happens by accident, children are being neglected if their basic needs for adequate food, clothing, shelter, medical care, or supervision are not being met. A child does not need to have suffered actual harm for a report of neglect to be made. Note that a parent's "informed and appropriate" medical choices, including choices to refuse medical treatment for their child based on religious belief, are not neglect. However, this only applies if the parents have taken the child to a physician for assessment; otherwise, the parent's medical choices may not be considered to be "informed and appropriate."

- **Abuse in out-of-home care.** This is given its own category for reporting purposes. It applies to minors who are physically injured or killed in child-care or school settings.

In addition to those types of abuse, **emotional abuse** operates on a *permissive* reporting standard, which means that you *can* report this if you choose to, but you are not required to. Emotional abuse is defined in law as "serious emotional damage or […] substantial risk of suffering serious emotional damage." Children who witness domestic violence are sometimes reported as victims of emotional abuse.

Once you have developed reasonable suspicion, there are specific **timeframes for abuse reporting** that must be followed. You must make a report by phone to your local child protective agency immediately and follow up with a written report within 36 hours. This timeframe does not change for nights, weekends, or holidays.

Indicators of child abuse. Since the reasonable suspicion standard relies on therapists having a shared understanding of the times when abuse should be reported, it is critical that social workers are aware of common physical and behavioral indicators of abuse, neglect, and exploitation. The National Children's Advocacy Center has compiled the following lists of indicators. While none of these indicators by themselves would lead to a conclusion of abuse, they should lead a therapist to *consider* whether abuse or neglect may be taking place. Common physical indicators include:

- Unexplained bruises, cuts, or fractures
- Unexplained burns
- Evidence of delayed or inappropriate treatment for injuries
- Multiple injuries in various stages of healing
- Injury or trauma to genital area
- Sexually transmitted disease
- Pain, swelling, itching, bruising, or bleeding in genital area
- Unattended medical needs
- Consistent hunger or poor hygiene
- Consistent lack of supervision

Notably, the law specifically states that the pregnancy of a minor, in and of itself, is *not* sufficient grounds to report suspected abuse. This remains true regardless of the age of the minor.

Common behavioral indicators of abuse and neglect include the following. As with all child and adolescent behaviors, a therapist must be especially cautious not to reach premature conclusions on the basis of behavioral indicators alone, as there are a number of potential causes for each of these that would *not* indicate abuse. However, these behaviors should get a therapist's attention:

- Sudden withdrawn behavior
- Self-destructive behavior
- Bizarre explanations for injuries
- Shying away from contact with familiar adults
- Sleep disturbances, including nightmares or flashbacks
- Substance use
- Anger and rage
- Aggressive, disruptive, or illegal behavior
- Frequent absence or tardiness from school or other activities
- Consistent fatigue or listlessness
- Stealing food
- Extreme need for affection
- Extreme loneliness

Exceptions to confidentiality:
Elder and dependent adult abuse K14-17

Laws about reporting elder and dependent adult abuse. Under California law, you must report any time you observe, suspect, or have knowledge of elder or dependent adult abuse. An elder is anyone age 65 or older who resides in California. There has been a great deal of confusion about that this year, because of a new law that changed the definition of an elder for a number of other purposes related to Adult Protective Services functioning. But that bill notably *did not* change the specific section of law that defines an "elder" for purposes of mandated reporting of elder abuse (Welfare and Institutions Code section 15610.27 – you should never need to know code section numbers on your exam, I just include this in case you'd like to review the language yourself). For mandated reporting purposes, as of the publication time of this book, the definition of an elder still begins at age 65.

A dependent adult is anyone age 18 to 64 who resides in California and has physical or mental limitations that restrict their ability to carry out normal activities or protect their own rights. Anyone admitted as an inpatient in a hospital or other 24-hour health care facility is, by definition, a dependent adult.

For both elders and dependent adults, note the "resides in California" piece of the definition. You are not mandated to report the suspected abuse of adults who are not residing in California, even if they would otherwise meet the definition of an elder or dependent adult. This is different from the standards for reporting child abuse, which do not include California residency in the definition of a minor.

Reportable types of elder and dependent adult abuse include:

- **Physical abuse, which includes willful over- or under-medication.** Be careful with this, though – an elder reporting that they are in pain does not mean they are being abused. As long as they are being given the correct amount of medication prescribed by their doctor, it would simply call for a referral back to the client's physician to make any necessary adjustments in medication dosage or type. Various forms of sexual abuse are also included here as physical abuse.

- **Financial abuse.** This category is not a form of child abuse, but does apply to elders and dependent adults.
- **Abduction.** Specifically, the law refers to an elder or dependent adult being taken *outside of California*, or prevented from returning, against their will.
- **Isolation.** Elders who are physically restrained from seeing visitors, or who are being prevented from receiving mail, phone calls, or visitors (when the elder wants to see the visitor), are being isolated. In rare instances, a health condition may make limitations on mail and phone calls clinically appropriate, but there should be good medical documentation for such a decision, and other normal contact should not be restricted.
- **Abandonment.** Caretakers accept responsibility for the adults in their care. Abandonment occurs when a caretaker deserts their patient or gives up on their caretaking responsibilities when a reasonable person would not have done so.
- **Neglect, including self-neglect.** This is reportable not so that the elder or dependent adult will be punished, but so that they can be moved to a higher level of care if it is appropriate to do so.

Unlike child abuse laws, elder and dependent adult abuse reporting laws include permissive reporting of any other form of abuse not otherwise defined in the law. This gives a clinical social worker broad latitude to report behaviors that the CSW considers to be abusive, even if those behaviors do not fit neatly into any of the categories listed.

Similar to child abuse reporting, you do not need to have heard a direct report of abuse from the victim in order to develop suspicion that abuse has taken place. However, unlike child abuse reporting laws, the laws on reporting elder and dependent adult abuse say that **if you do hear of abuse directly from the victim, you *must* report it.** There is only a very narrow exception, for when the person has been diagnosed with dementia or another form of mental illness, there is no other evidence of the abuse, *and* the therapist does not believe the abuse occurred.

The **timeframes for reporting** elder or dependent adult abuse are complex. If the abuse did *not* take place in a long-term care facility, then a phone report of the abuse must be made immediately to Adult Protective Services or another local agency authorized to receive adult abuse reports. You then must follow up with a written report within two working days. (If the abuse happened within a long-term care facility, the rules are more complicated, sometimes requiring duplicate or triplicate reporting, and with varied reporting timeframes.) Recent state law allows for elder and dependent adult abuse reports to be made via Internet, in which case the Internet report should be done immediately, and it replaces both the phone *and* written reports.

Indicators of elder and dependent adult abuse. Common indicators of elder abuse include the following. As is the case with child abuse, it may be inappropriate to conclude that abuse has occurred based solely on an indicator here, as each of these can be caused by incidents that would not qualify as abuse. However, they can contribute to the development of reasonable suspicion of abuse:

- Physical or sexual abuse
  - Unexplained bruises, welts, or scars
  - Broken bones, sprains, dislocations
  - Restraint injuries (marks on wrists)
  - Unexplained bleeding or injury to genitals
  - Sexually transmitted disease
  - Medication over- or under-dosing relative to prescription
- Abandonment or neglect
  - Unusual weight loss
  - Poor nutrition or dehydration
  - Poor hygiene
  - Unsanitary or unsafe living environment
  - Inappropriate clothing (e.g., inadequate for cold weather)
  - Lack of needed medical aids, such as glasses
- Financial abuse
  - Sudden changes in financial status
  - Valuable items or cash missing from residence
  - Unpaid bills when the person has money to pay them
  - Unusual financial activity, or activity the person could not have done (e.g., ATM withdrawal by hospital inpatient)
  - Sudden appearance of unnecessary goods or services
  - Signatures on checks do not match the person's
- Unusual caregiver behavior (can indicate risk of abuse of any type)
  - Threatening, belittling, or controlling behavior
  - Deserting
  - Burnout (can be evidenced by mental health symptoms, substance use, poor resilience, irritability, or resentment toward the person being cared for, as examples)

It is important for CSWs to be aware that stress and burnout are common among caregivers, and these indicate a risk of abuse, but may also simply mean that the caregiver needs some time away from their responsibilities. Caregiving is difficult, particularly if the person being cared for has severe illness or dementia, is socially isolated, is physically aggressive, or has a history of domestic violence. These factors place the person being cared for at greater risk of abuse.

Exceptions to confidentiality: Danger to self or others K20-25

Identifying need for hospitalization. Under state law, an individual can be hospitalized against their will if, because of a mental health condition, they are a danger to others, are a danger to themselves, or are gravely disabled. In such instances, the person is taken to a hospital or other county-designated facility for assessment for up to 72 hours, which you may know as a "72-hour hold" or a "5150."

While danger to self and others are explained in additional detail below, the term "gravely disabled" has a specific meaning in law. It refers to instances where, because of a mental condition, the individual is unable to meet their most basic survival needs for food, shelter, and clothing. Especially as California has dealt with a rising homeless population, many of whom struggle with mental health conditions, determining whether someone is gravely disabled has gotten more complex. A severe mental illness in and of itself is not enough grounds for such a determination, but if the illness causes the person to be unable to meet those survival needs, then they may be considered gravely disabled.

Legal requirements for initiating involuntary hospitalization. When a CSW believes hospitalization is necessary, having a client go voluntarily is usually preferable to the process of involuntary hospitalization. However, if the CSW believes the client has a mental disorder that is causing them to be a danger to themselves or others or is gravely disabled, and the client refuses voluntary treatment, the CSW can begin the process of involuntary hospitalization.

In order for a client to be hospitalized against their will, a therapist must be able to cite specific facts (client words, appearance or behaviors) supporting the dangerousness of the client, and the conclusions the therapist drew from those facts. The therapist must then find what the county considers an "eligible professional" to actually write the 5150 application. (Usually a police officer or other person designated by the county serves this role. Social workers can serve in this role, but may need to first go through additional training and certification.)

Ultimately, it is up to a professional at the facility designated by the county to receive involuntary holds to determine whether the client is to be involuntarily hospitalized. If that professional agrees, the client can be initially held for up to 72 hours. If the client remains dangerous to themselves or others, or gravely disabled, at the end of the 72 hours, they can be certified for an additional hold of up to 14 days for intensive treatment.

Laws about confidentiality in situations of client danger to self or others. Danger to self or others is commonly understood as an exception to confidentiality under the law. The *Tarasoff v. California Board of Regents* case established that danger to a reasonably identifiable victim outweighs client confidentiality. A social worker dealing with a client who poses an imminent danger of serious bodily harm to reasonably identifiable victims must take reasonable steps to resolve the threat, which typically include breaking confidentiality. When a client is suicidal, the *Bellah v. Greenson* case established that therapists have a responsibility to act to protect the client's safety, and this can involve breaking confidentiality if needed. If a client poses a general danger to others because of a mental health condition, *Tarasoff* does not apply, but the therapist still can move to have the client involuntarily hospitalized if necessary.

In each of these instances, the CSW can break confidentiality. The CSW shares information about therapy with others who are involved in resolving the immediate danger. Even in these situations, though, the CSW should share *only* the information necessary to resolve the immediate threat. Sharing unrelated information about the client's therapy may still be seen as a violation of confidentiality rules.

Sometimes, law enforcement and therapists work together in mental health crisis response teams. These teams must be supervised by mental health professionals. The therapists and law enforcement officers responding to mental health crises on these teams are not doing therapy, but may benefit from knowing some information about the potentially dangerous person. If you are providing information about your client to emergency responders, it is up to your judgment to determine what information is appropriate to share to resolve the threat, and not to share more than necessary.

If a *Tarasoff* situation arises where the therapist is able to resolve the immediate danger *without* notifying law enforcement, the CSW still must inform law enforcement of the threat within 24 hours. This relatively recent law was enacted to help law enforcement put potentially dangerous individuals into a database that would prevent them from buying guns.

Methods and criteria to identify when a client poses danger to self or others. There are good, brief ways of assessing clients who may pose a danger to themselves or someone else, including screening instruments and structured interviews. Assessments for suicide and violence to others tend to focus on the following factors:

- **Ideation (thoughts).** Is the person actively considering harming themselves or someone else? If suicidal, are they romanticizing what their death would be like, for them or others around them?
- **Planning.** Do they have a specific plan for how they would hurt themselves or someone else? Is it immediate?
- **Intent.** Does the person intend to commit violence? How sure are they? Some clients will fantasize about violence or death without any intent to ever act on these fantasies.
- **Access to means.** How easy would it be to carry out the plan? If they are considering suicide or homicide by gun, is there a gun in the house?
- **Past experience.** Have they attempted suicide or been violent with others before? How? Note that *previous suicide attempts* is the strongest risk factor for future attempts.
- **Protective factors.** What are the reasons the person has not hurt themselves or someone else so far? What would prevent them from suicide or violence in the future?

Demographic factors are also important to keep in mind, though these are not predictive of violence. While suicide is a leading cause of death among adolescents (because other causes of death are not common at this age), statistically, the highest risk for suicide is among the elderly (85+) and the middle-aged (45-64). Men are at higher risk than women. Whites and Native Americans have the highest suicide rates among racial groups. Military veterans and those who identify as LGBTQIA+ have heightened risk.

Duty to protect law. You are probably familiar with *Tarasoff v. California Board of Regents*, the court case that established a therapist's responsibility to act when a client poses an imminent danger of serious bodily harm to a reasonably identifiable victim or victims. In such instances, CSWs have a legal obligation known as "duty to protect." While this is not technically a duty to *warn* (and in rare instances, it might be inappropriate to warn the intended victim, such as times when doing so might trigger the victim to commit a violent act), the most common methods of protecting potential victims are to notify the victims and law enforcement of the threat. You also have additional protection from liability when you make reasonable efforts to notify both the victim and law enforcement.

The law does *not* require you to report or otherwise act on threats to property. Under California law, animals are a form of property, so you would not report threats that a client might make against a neighbor's pet, for example.

Indicators of intent to harm. Obviously, the strongest indicator of a client's intent to harm someone is when they tell you directly that they intend to harm someone. However, this is not the only indicator a therapist should be aware of. Third-party reports of a client intending to harm another person may be treated similarly to direct reports, if the therapist believes that the third party is a trustworthy reporter. Threats made in writing or by other means may be considered evidence of intent to harm. Indirect statements such as "after today, she won't be around any more" may also be reasonable indicators, based on the CSW's knowledge of the client. Threatening behaviors may also qualify. Clients who are actively using drugs or alcohol may present heightened danger to potential victims.

Exceptions to privilege K26-31

As noted earlier, privilege refers to information that can be excluded from court proceedings. Normally, all communications between a therapist and their client are considered *privileged communications*, meaning that they cannot be used in court. However, there are several exceptions to this rule defined in law. Information that would normally be privileged may be used in court if:

1) The client makes their mental or emotional condition an issue in a lawsuit.
2) The client alleges breach of duty by the therapist.
3) Evaluation or therapy is taking place by court order.
4) A defendant in a criminal case requested the evaluation or therapy to determine their sanity.
5) The client is under age 16 and is the victim of a crime, and the therapist believes that disclosing that information is in the child's best interests.
6) The therapist was sought out for the purpose of committing a crime or avoiding detection after the fact.

This list is worth memorizing. Each one of these exceptions gets its own Knowledge Statement in the BBS Exam Plan, so there is a strong likelihood you will be specifically asked to apply your knowledge of one or more of these on your exam.

Recall here that while clients can waive privilege, only a judge can determine whether an exception to privilege applies to a specific situation. That's never your determination to make. Even in situations where you believe a judge is likely to ultimately determine that an exception applies, if your client is asserting privilege, you should also assert privilege on the client's behalf until the judge makes that determination.

Sample Questions
See the next page for answers and rationales

1. The 59-year-old client of a CSW calls her therapist from the hospital for a planned check-in conversation. The client tells the therapist she has been hospitalized for a severe respiratory infection and is likely to remain as an inpatient in the hospital for at least another two weeks. She also expresses a belief that hospital staff are stealing her belongings. The CSW should:

    a. Maintain the client's confidentiality.
    b. Report the client's belief to hospital staff.
    c. Report the client's accusation as suspected dependent adult abuse.
    d. Presume the client's accusation is a side effect of the pain

2. An LCSW's client confesses to her that he is struggling with guilt over his involvement in three recent gang-related murders. Two adults were killed: one was a rival gang member, the other was an innocent bystander. The third victim was also a rival gang member, and was just 17 years old. The client tells the LCSW that he does not believe he or the others in his gang will be caught, but this is only worsening his guilt. How should the LCSW handle her legal obligations surrounding confidentiality?

    a. Break confidentiality for the three murders and work with law enforcement to warn other members of the rival gang
    b. Break confidentiality for the murder of the bystander and work with law enforcement to warn other members of the rival gang
    c. Break confidentiality for the murder of the 17-year-old, and otherwise maintain confidentiality
    d. Maintain the client's confidentiality for all past acts, and encourage him to consider self-reporting to law enforcement if necessary to resolve his guilt

Sample Questions: Answers and Rationales

1. The 59-year-old client of a CSW calls her therapist from the hospital for a planned check-in conversation. The client tells the therapist she has been hospitalized for a severe respiratory infection and is likely to remain as an inpatient in the hospital for at least another two weeks. She also expresses a belief that hospital staff are stealing her belongings. The CSW should:

   a. **Incorrect.** Maintain the client's confidentiality.
   b. **Incorrect.** Report the client's belief to hospital staff.
   c. **CORRECT.** Report the client's accusation as suspected dependent adult abuse.
   d. **Incorrect.** Presume the client's accusation is a side effect of the pain medication she is likely receiving, and take no further action.

Any inpatient in a 24-hour health care facility (such as a hospital) is automatically considered a dependent adult under state law. And unlike the rules for child abuse reporting, when an elder or dependent adult directly reports a behavior that would qualify as abuse, the therapist is generally obligated to report it. (There is a narrow exception in the law, described earlier in this section, which does not appear to apply here.) Because the client is making a direct accusation of financial abuse, this must be reported.

2. An LCSW's client confesses to her that he is struggling with guilt over his involvement in three recent gang-related murders. Two adults were killed: one was a rival gang member, the other was an innocent bystander. The third victim was also a rival gang member, and was just 17 years old. The client tells the LCSW that he does not believe he or the others in his gang will be caught, but this is only worsening his guilt. How should the LCSW handle her legal obligations surrounding confidentiality?

    a. **Incorrect.** Break confidentiality for the three murders and work with law enforcement to warn other members of the rival gang. *When the crime is not child, elder, or dependent adult abuse, LCSWs have no obligation to report past crimes, and doing so could be considered a breach of confidentiality.*

    b. **Incorrect.** Break confidentiality for the murder of the bystander and work with law enforcement to warn other members of the rival gang. *When the crime is not child, elder, or dependent adult abuse, CSWs generally have no obligation to report past crimes, and doing so could be considered a breach of confidentiality.*

    c. **CORRECT.** Break confidentiality for the murder of the 17-year-old, and otherwise maintain confidentiality. *Child abuse must be reported, and in this case the murder of the 17-year-old qualifies as child abuse. Child abuse must be reported even when it resulted in the death of the victim.*

    d. **Incorrect.** Maintain the client's confidentiality for all past acts, and encourage him to consider self-reporting to law enforcement if necessary to resolve his guilt. *The murder of the 17-year-old qualifies as child abuse. It must be reported, so the LCSW cannot legally maintain confidentiality for "all past acts."*

LAW

Standards for
Professional Practice

Scored exam questions (approximate): 5

Sexual relationships K32-33

Sexual relationship between therapist and client. Sexual behavior between therapist and client is specifically prohibited under California law. (Such contact is also specifically prohibited by the NASW Code of Ethics, which we will discuss in the Ethics section.) "Behavior" here is a broader term than intercourse.

Intimacy between therapist and *former* client. For former clients, state law prohibits sexual behavior for two years after the last professional contact. Sexual relationships with former clients after this time may still be problematic, and are further discouraged in the NASW ethics code. But they are not legally *prohibited* so long as two years have gone by since the last professional contact.

The *Therapy Never Includes Sexual Behavior* brochure. If your client informs you that they have had a sexual relationship with another therapist, you are required by law to provide for them the state-authored brochure *Therapy Never Includes Sexual Behavior*. (This was previously called *Professional Therapy Never Includes Sex*, which may be how your supervisor refers to it.) Failure to provide the brochure is considered unprofessional conduct. Many therapists keep a copy or two of the brochure readily available in their offices; it also can be downloaded and printed when you need it.

Scope of practice K34

Your scope of practice is set in state law. It specifies what someone with an LCSW license can legally do.

The CSW scope of practice allows you to work with individuals, couples, families, and groups. (The word "client" may refer to an individual, couple, or family.) The CSW scope of practice specifically allows you to use "counseling and [...] applied psychotherapy," making you a psychotherapist. And it allows you to use the training you received in your required coursework – which is key to understanding that CSWs can independently diagnose mental illness.

One of the most important pieces in understanding scope of practice is understanding its limits. **CSWs *cannot* provide legal advice, medical advice, or other forms of guidance that are outside the CSW scope of practice.** Recommending that a client take a certain medication, for example, would be outside of the CSW scope of practice. Social workers should refer to physicians to make determinations about medication use and dosage.

It is helpful here to understand the difference between scope of *practice* – which is set in state law, and is the same for every CSW in the state – and scope of *competence*, which is based on your specific education, training, and experience. Scope of competence varies by individual CSW, and is primarily an ethical issue.

Unprofessional conduct laws K35

State law currently defines 28 specific categories of unprofessional conduct. For our purposes, it's most important to know what unprofessional conduct *means*: It refers to **actions taken in a professional role that are below minimum professional standards**. Unlike criminal cases (where you could go to jail) or civil cases (where you might have to pay damages to someone you have wronged), unprofessional conduct rules apply to your professional role. "Unprofessional conduct" refers to those behaviors that can result in action being taken against your license or registration.

The types of conduct defined in state law as unprofessional conduct include the following. The language here is lightly edited from state law, and grouped into categories:

Sexual misconduct
Sexual contact with a client or former client
Committing a sex crime with a minor
Committing a sex crime
Sexual misconduct
Failure to provide *Professional Therapy Never Includes Sex*

Scope of practice and competence
Performing or offering services outside of scope

Impairment
Impairment due to mental or physical illness or drug dependence
Drug dependence or use with a client while providing services

Confidentiality
Failure to maintain confidentiality

Crimes and bad acts
Conviction of a crime
Committing a dishonest, corrupt, or fraudulent act
Discipline by another board or by another state

Fraud
Getting or attempting to get a license by fraud
Misrepresenting your license or qualifications
Impersonating a licensee
Aiding someone else's unlicensed activity

Testing
Violating exam security or integrity

Supervision
Improper supervision of a trainee or associate
Violations during or involving required hours of experience

Fees and advertising
Failure to disclose fees in advance
False, misleading, deceptive, or improper advertising
Paying, accepting, or soliciting a fee for referrals

Record-keeping
>Failure to keep records consistent with sound clinical judgment
>Failure to comply with client requests for access to records

Telemedicine
>Violating state telehealth standards

General misconduct
>General unprofessional conduct
>Gross negligence or incompetence
>Intentionally or recklessly causing physical or emotional harm

The category simply called "general unprofessional conduct" allows the BBS to act against you if you violate other law, professional ethical codes, or the professional standard of care while in your professional role. In this way, behaviors that are unethical can also be considered illegal, even if they aren't specifically designated as such in the law.

You do not need to memorize the entire list above. Most of it is simply what you would expect (and what is covered in this book). Knowing all of the categories will not be nearly as helpful to you as being able to determine whether a *particular behavior* qualifies as unprofessional conduct under the law.

When a therapist engages in unprofessional conduct with a client, the client may submit a complaint to the BBS. The BBS then has an investigations unit that assesses the complaint, determines whether it is actionable, and investigates if appropriate. During this time, the CSW has the opportunity to defend themselves. If the CSW is found to have committed unprofessional conduct, the BBS can levy fines, place the CSW's license (or registration, in cases involving CSW associates) on suspension or probation, restrict their practice, and in severe cases, revoke the CSW's license or registration. They also may require other actions, such as regular drug testing, while the CSW is on probation or in order to resolve the disciplinary issue. The disciplinary process is meaningfully different from a criminal trial or a civil lawsuit; the BBS only needs to find *clear and convincing evidence* that a violation occurred to issue a penalty.

Disclosing fees K36

Disclosing fees. Under state law, you must inform clients before treatment begins of (1) the fee they will be charged and (2) the basis upon which that fee was computed. If you're confused about that second part, think about the sliding-fee scales used at many training clinics: *Client income* is the basis on which the fee is computed. As other examples, some social workers charge more for couple or family sessions than they do for individual sessions, while others charge different rates based on time of day or day of the week. Those are both fine, but clients need to know about this before treatment starts. Failure to disclose fees and their basis prior to starting treatment is considered unprofessional conduct.

Third-party reimbursement K37-38

Third-party reimbursement rules. Health insurance coverage has expanded significantly since the passage of the Affordable Care Act. Of course, insurance is not the only form of third-party payment; employers, courts, nonprofit organizations, family members, and others may be the ones who are actually paying for client care. CSWs need to be aware of the rules surrounding third-party payment, including the limits on information that can be shared with third-party payers.

Some of the key legal rules regarding third-party payment include:

- **Freedom of choice.** Insurance companies typically must reimburse CSWs alongside other mental health providers. Associates do not have to be reimbursed, though some plans will pay for services provided by associates.
- **Mental disorder only.** Most insurers will only reimburse when there is a diagnosed mental disorder. Some will cover services when there is no mental health diagnosis, but plans are not legally required to do so.
- **Protests and complaints.** Providers can (and generally should) appeal denials of reimbursement. Consumers and providers both can complain to the state about insurance company practices. Depending on the plan, it may be governed by the state Department of Insurance or the Department of Managed Health Care.

One of the most important legal rules regarding third-party reimbursement is the prohibition against insurance fraud, which can draw criminal and civil penalties in addition to action against your license. Any falsification of diagnosis, procedure code, amount paid, or any other information for the purpose of receiving insurance payment is insurance fraud.

Parity laws. State and federal law require parity in insurance coverage for mental health. Co-payments, deductibles, and treatment limitations (like caps on visits or days of coverage) for mental health must be equal to or better than the limits placed on other medical coverage. Any plan language claiming to give the insurer "discretionary authority" to refuse coverage for medically necessary mental health or substance abuse treatment is considered invalid.

Advertising K39

Advertising laws. Essentially any public statement where you suggest that you offer therapy or counseling services to the public would be considered an advertisement – the law is purposefully broad on that. The only exception in the law is for bulletins within a religious setting, published only to members of that religious group.

State law is highly specific on the **licensure status** disclosures that need to be included in *any* advertisement of a CSW's services. A licensed CSW needs to include their name, their license number, and their title ("licensed clinical social worker") or an acceptable abbreviation ("LCSW"). An associate needs to include their name, their registration number, their employer's name, an indication that they are under licensed supervision, and their title ("Registered Associate Clinical Social Worker"). That title can be abbreviated "Registered Associate CSW."

LCSWs and associates can advertise themselves as **psychotherapists** and say that they perform psychotherapy, as long as they clearly list their licensure type, something the law already requires anyway.

LCSWs can advertise using **fictitious business names**, so long as those names are not misleading and clients are informed of the business owners' names and licensure status before treatment begins.

Ads making any kind of **scientific claims** must be backed by published, peer-reviewed research literature.

Any **fees** included in an advertisement must be exact; you cannot advertise fees in ways like "$95 and up." For this reason, many LCSWs and clinics choose not to list their fees in their advertising.

It would be unprofessional conduct for any CSW to advertise in a manner that is **false, misleading, or deceptive**. Any claims that would be likely to create unjustified expectations of treatment success are also prohibited by law.

Payment for referrals K40

Clinical social workers are both legally and ethically prohibited from giving or receiving payment for referrals. This includes payments to or from clients, payments to or from the professional you referred the clients to (sometimes called "kickbacks"), or payments to or from third parties. The idea here is that referrals should be made *solely* on the basis of what is in the best interests of the client. If you are receiving payments for referrals, there is at least the *appearance* of a conflict of interests, as you might make a referral based more on what will financially benefit you than what will clinically benefit the client.

Some CSWs participate in "networking groups," which are organizations of professionals who sell a wide variety of goods and services. Members join the networking group for the specific purpose of referring potential customers to one another. However, because these groups often operate in a structure where members are rewarded for the referrals they generate (the reward might be the *absence* of a fee that they would otherwise have to pay to participate), CSWs in such groups risk being disciplined for violating the standards against receiving payment for referrals.

Sample Questions
See the next page for answers and rationales

1. A clinical social worker with a new private practice is considering how to market his practice. He wants to operate on a sliding fee scale based on client income. How can he best fulfill his legal and ethical responsibilities?

    a. Develop a fee structure that is based on services provided, and not client income. Fee scales based on client income are prohibited in private practice settings

    b. Advertise that services are offered "as low as" the lowest fee on his scale and noting that not everyone will qualify for the lowest fee

    c. Make no mention of fees in his advertising

    d. Make his sliding fee scale a percentage of income, regardless of the income level

2. A famous actor contacts a CSW seeking help with his anxiety. Because he is so well-known, the actor expresses concern that the fact that he is in therapy could be "leaked" to the media, making it harder for him to be cast in desirable roles. He asks the CSW whether he can pay solely in cash so that the CSW will not have financial records, and he asks the CSW to keep records for treatment under a fake name that the actor would use when signing all treatment-related documents. How should the CSW respond?

    a. Refuse the requests

    b. Refuse the request to keep records under a fake name, but allow the client to sign all documentation using whatever fake name they choose

    c. Honor the request to keep treatment records under a fake name, but refuse the request to not keep financial records

    d. Agree to both requests to protect the client's privacy while otherwise maintaining the terms of treatment

Sample Questions: Answers and Rationales

1. A clinical social worker with a new private practice is considering how to market his practice. He wants to operate on a sliding fee scale based on client income. How can he best fulfill his legal and ethical responsibilities?

    a. **Incorrect.** Develop a fee structure that is based on services provided, and not client income. Fee scales based on client income are prohibited in private practice settings.

    b. **Incorrect.** Advertise that services are offered "as low as" the lowest fee on his scale and noting that not everyone will qualify for the lowest fee.

    c. **CORRECT.** Make no mention of fees in his advertising.

    d. **Incorrect.** Make his sliding fee scale a percentage of income, regardless of the income level.

Sliding scales are allowed in private practice, making (A) incorrect. An "as low as" advertisement (B) is considered misleading in state law, and it would likely still be considered misleading even if it includes a disclaimer that not everyone will qualify. And a scale that is a percentage of income *regardless of income level* (D) would likely be considered exploitive of high-income clients, considering the high fees that could result. Option C is the best answer here; while CSWs are allowed to state fees in their advertising, they are not required to do so. Since every other option is clearly incorrect, this approach – removing fees from advertising – is the best one of the choices available.

2. A famous actor contacts a CSW seeking help with his anxiety. Because he is so well-known, the actor expresses concern that the fact that he is in therapy could be "leaked" to the media, making it harder for him to be cast in desirable roles. He asks the CSW whether he can pay solely in cash so that the CSW will not have financial records, and he asks the CSW to keep records for treatment under a fake name that the actor would use when signing all treatment-related documents. How should the CSW respond?

    a. **CORRECT.** Refuse the requests. *CSWs are bound to keep treatment records that are accurate and reflect sound clinical judgment. The actor's requests would violate these standards.*

    b. **Incorrect.** Refuse the request to keep records under a fake name, but allow the client to sign all documentation using whatever fake name they choose. *This may violate the requirement that CSWs keep accurate records. It also would create difficulty if the CSW relied on those signed documents as evidence of an informed consent process.*

    c. **Incorrect.** Honor the request to keep treatment records under a fake name, but refuse the request to not keep financial records. *CSWs are bound to keep records that are accurate. Using a fake name would violate that requirement.*

    d. **Incorrect.** Agree to both requests to protect the client's privacy while otherwise maintaining the terms of treatment. *CSWs are bound to keep records that are accurate and consistent with the standards of the profession.*

ETHICS

Competence and Preventing Harm

Scored exam questions (approximate): 9

Scope of competence K41-45, K49

Understanding scope of competence. Your scope of competence is defined by your education, training, and professional experience. Your scope of competence is unique to you and can change over time. Scope of competence is primarily an *ethical* issue, though practicing outside of one's scope of competence is also considered unprofessional conduct in state law.

Knowing your own limitations. Just as it is important to be able to identify actions that would be out of your scope of practice, it is also critical to understand when issues come before you that are outside your scope of competence. You can't possibly have training and experience for every possible situation you will encounter in your practice, so acknowledging limitations in your scope of competence is not a weakness. It is good professional behavior.

Need for consultation. When a situation comes up in therapy that is outside of a CSW's scope of competence, a responsible CSW will consult with a supervisor, treatment team, or others to determine what appropriate next steps would be. In many cases, the therapist will work to expand their competence while continuing to work with the client.

Collaborating to determine need for referrals. It is up to the CSW to monitor their own scope of competence. However, the assessment of client needs, and determinations of whether referrals are clinically indicated, should be a collaborative process with the client. There is little point in providing clients with referrals or resources they do not believe will benefit them. Social workers commonly collaborate with clients to determine what the clients' needs and expectations are, and to provide referrals (where appropriate) that are relevant to those needs.

Protecting client rights in consultations. Of course, CSWs are encouraged to regularly consult with other professionals and community resources to promote quality client care. It is common for CSWs to collaborate and consult with physicians, teachers, social service providers, and other important persons in a client's life, on issues that are outside the CSW's scope of competence. CSWs are expected to be aware of colleagues' competence and expertise, so that when consulting is appropriate, the CSW can easily find a knowledgeable person. Ethically, the CSW should only seek consult from someone with appropriate knowledge or competence.

When doing such consultations, CSWs respect the confidentiality of their clients. Each member of the treatment unit (individual, couple, or family) must give their permission for clinical information to be shared with any outsider, unless an exception to confidentiality applies. Even when client permission or an exception to confidentiality is present, the CSW should only provide the information necessary for the consultation.

Expanding competence. If one's scope of competence is determined by education, training, and experience, then it makes sense that CSWs can expand into new areas of practice, or improve their competence in existing ones, by getting additional education, training, and experience.

Responsibility to remain current. The CSW field is constantly growing and changing, with new treatment models and new scientific developments occurring on a regular basis. The training and experience that make you competent to work with a certain problem today may be considered outdated and inaccurate 10 years from now. CSWs have an ethical responsibility to remain current with new developments in the profession, through education, training, and supervised experience. This is part of the reason why LCSWs are required to get continuing education hours in each license renewal cycle.

Self-awareness K46-48, 50-51

Impairments. Good social workers are keenly aware of their own limitations. Social workers are expected to continually monitor themselves for potential impairment. If you are struggling with a serious emotional problem, mental or physical illness, or substance use, it can interfere with your ability to provide effective services to clients. In addition, if you have a strong emotional reaction to a particular client – perhaps because their struggle mirrors one you have gone through, or because there is something in the client's behavior that you strongly dislike – you may not be able to provide effective services.

Responding to impairments. CSWs need to know the referrals and resources available in the event that the therapist is struggling with an impairment and needs to step away from client care, either temporarily or on a longer-term basis. (Knowledge of appropriate referrals and resources comes up multiple times in the BBS Exam Plan, as it is important in many different sets of circumstances. Obviously, the test will not ask what the closest hospital is, since the same test is being given across the state. But you may be asked about the *kinds* of referrals and resources that would be most appropriate to a given situation. Referrals should always be appropriate to the level and type of client need.)

For the social worker, seeking treatment is appropriate when the problem is a serious emotional problem, mental or physical illness, or substance use. For these and other forms of impairment, the CSW could also seek supervision and consultation, engage in self-care, and consider going to therapy. In whatever time it takes for the CSW to resolve their impairment, protecting the welfare of the client is the highest priority.

Methods to facilitate transfer. In some cases, the impairment of a CSW will lead to their needing to transfer clients to other therapists. If it is possible and appropriate, the CSW may have a termination session with the client, focused on transitioning them to a new provider. The CSW should provide appropriate referrals based on client need. The CSW and client should consider a Release of Information authorizing the transfer of client records to the new provider, and authorizing the old and new providers to communicate to ensure continuity of care. The CSW should follow up with the new provider to transfer the records and coordinate care appropriately.

Personal values, attitudes, and beliefs. CSWs are ethically prohibited from influencing client decisions on preferred treatment or outcomes based on personal values, attitudes, and beliefs. (Going forward, I'll just say "attitudes" to refer collectively to "values, attitudes, and beliefs.") Obviously, it is important for CSWs to be aware of their own attitudes and how they might impact the therapy process. Social workers allowing for their attitudes to influence them might pathologize the behavior of clients the social worker doesn't like, leading to incorrect diagnoses and poor treatment decisions. They might show bias toward one or more family members, impacting the effectiveness of couple or family work. They might become overly friendly (or overly hostile) with a client. They might place their own belief about a particular problem above current scientific knowledge in the field. Ultimately, the social worker is likely to miss or misinterpret important clinical information, decreasing the likelihood of effective therapy.

Managing the impact of therapist attitudes. So what happens, then, when a CSW becomes aware that they have personal attitudes that are entering into the therapy room? It depends on the nature of what is arising. If the therapist is experiencing judgment or bias toward the client based on personal attitudes, the therapist should carefully consider how those attitudes are impacting treatment. The therapist may seek out supervision or consultation to ensure quality of care, and may go to their own therapy to identify the source of the attitude, working to change it if appropriate. If the therapist attitude is likely to continue interfering in the therapeutic relationship, the therapist may consider referring the client to another therapist – but must be cautious to avoid client abandonment, and to ensure that the referral is not discriminatory in nature. If the therapist refers clients out based on personal attitudes about race, gender, or other protected characteristics, the therapist may be engaging in discrimination.

Multiple Relationships K52-56

A multiple relationship (or "dual relationship" -- the terms are used here interchangeably) occurs any time a CSW has a relationship with a client that is separate from being their therapist. Not all multiple relationships are unethical, and some can't be avoided, especially in rural areas or in work with more tight-knit communities. The NASW Code of Ethics clarifies that multiple relationships do not have to be simultaneous – a multiple relationship can still occur (and can still be problematic) when one type of relationship begins after the other has concluded.

Assessing multiple relationships. Not all multiple relationships can be avoided, especially if you are working in a rural area or with a highly-specific population. It is also true that not all multiple relationships are problematic. If a colleague tells you that you can't see a client because "that would be a dual relationship," they haven't adequately made their case.

Multiple relationships must be carefully examined to see whether they would **impair clinical judgment** or create **risk of client exploitation**. These two considerations are critical to determining whether a multiple relationship can be allowed. If you know and like someone in your community and they ask to see you in therapy, your liking of them would surely influence how you observe them clinically -- in other words, your pre-existing view of them would impair your clinical judgment. (Impairment can mean positive bias as well as negative.) Having a client who coaches your daughter's soccer team could create risk of exploitation, as you could use your knowledge of the client's personal secrets to push for more playing time for your daughter. The fact that you wouldn't actually do this does not eliminate the risk of it, nor does it take away your responsibility to protect clients from that risk.

Even when such risks exist, though, in some cases it may be appropriate to continue with the therapy. If you are the only provider in a rural area, for example, the best interests of the client might be better served by going ahead with therapy. You would then need to take specific actions to reduce the risk of impaired judgment or exploitation.

Prohibited multiple relationships. Sexual or romantic relationships with clients and those close to the client are expressly prohibited, and discussed in greater detail below. Social workers are also ethically prohibited from taking advantage of any professional relationship to further the social worker's personal, religious, political, or business interests.

Managing boundaries. CSWs commonly take steps to ensure the integrity and boundaries of the therapy relationship. This can be especially important when it appears that a client is becoming confused about the nature of the relationship, or is wanting more of a personal or social relationship than what therapy allows.

Some examples of methods for managing boundaries include having a conversation with the client to remind them of the boundaries of therapy;

maintaining a clear treatment plan with identified therapy goals; making sure all contact between client and therapist stays focused on therapeutic issues; starting and ending sessions on time; and, when clinically appropriate, limiting contact by phone or other means between scheduled session times.

Potential conflicts of interest. CSWs are ethically obligated to be alert to potential conflicts of interest as they arise. A potential conflict emerges any time a therapist engages in a non-therapist role, such as consultation, coaching, or behavior analysis, with people who are or have been clients in therapy. A potential conflict also emerges any time an outside interest may interfere with the CSW's ability to exercise impartial professional judgment.

In any instance of potential conflict of interests, CSWs have an obligation to clarify their roles, and to distinguish how any applicable non-therapist role is different from therapy. In order to avoid any risk to clients, it may be preferable to refer out for additional services that are different from those for which the CSW was initially hired.

One common example of a conflict of interests emerges when a CSW who has been serving as a *therapist* is then asked to also serve as an *evaluator* for the same client. The phrase "conflict of interests" can be quite literal here: If a CSW is asked to provide a recommendation in a custody case where they have been serving as a therapist, then the interests of the client (in maintaining a trusting bond with their therapist, and pursuing their goals related to custody or whatever else) *conflict* with the interests of the court (which would want as much information about the client, positive and negative, as they could obtain, in the interests of making an objective determination). CSWs can serve as clinicians or evaluators, but unless compelled by a court, typically should not serve in both roles at once.

The NASW code of ethics includes discussion of conflicts of interest that can emerge when social workers share personal information online. Such sharing is allowed, but social workers must understand the potential for boundary confusion and inappropriate dual relationships to result.

When a conflict of interests arises, social workers should seek to resolve the conflict in ways that place the best interests of the client as the highest priority. As the code notes, protecting client interests may require terminating the therapeutic relationship and making proper referrals.

Potentially damaging relationships. Sexual relationships, which are discussed at greater length below, are the best example of a relationship that can be damaging to the client. However, they are not the only example.

Other forms of multiple relationships can harm clients directly, through poor care or exploitation, or they may harm clients more indirectly, by reducing their overall confidence in therapy as an effective and worthwhile treatment. Social relationships between CSWs and clients can create confusion about the therapist's role, for example, and can hinder success in therapy by clouding the CSW's clinical judgment.

Social workers are ethically prohibited from terminating clinical services in order to pursue a social, financial, or sexual relationship with a client.

When multiple relationships can't be avoided. Some multiple relationships are unavoidable. For example, some level of multiple relationship is created any time a CSW gets a new client through a referral from an existing client. Another example occurs in a rural area, where a CSW may have regular interaction with many clients at community gatherings. In these and similar situations, the NASW Code of Ethics (standard 1.06(c)) requires CSWs to "take steps to protect clients and [be] responsible for setting clear, appropriate, and culturally sensitive boundaries."

In some cases, the precautions may be as simple as having a conversation with the client to reassure them of confidentiality and clearly separate roles. In other cases, more stringent precautions may be appropriate, like the CSW regularly consulting on the case with a colleague.

Sexual relationships K57-59

Risk of exploitation. The rules prohibiting sexual contact between therapists and their clients come from a fundamental understanding that because the therapist has power in the therapy relationship, because clients are often emotionally vulnerable, and because the therapy process happens behind closed doors, sexual relationships between therapists and clients are likely to be exploitive and ultimately harmful to clients.

This exploitation does not require sexual *intercourse*, and the ethical standards around sexual relationships are worded in such a way as to include sexual behavior generally, even if there has not been intercourse. The NASW code even includes "inappropriate sexual communications," either in person or via technology, as an ethical violation. (If you're working with a couple on sexual issues, that might require candid conversation about their sexual behavior; that's appropriate, as it is clinically relevant.)

Intimacy between therapist and client. As noted in the legal section, sexual conduct -- again, a purposefully broader term than intercourse -- between therapist and client is specifically prohibited under California law. Such contact is also specifically prohibited by the NASW code of ethics.

Intimacy between therapist and *former* client. For former clients, the NASW Code of Ethics *forever* discourages sexual relationships or sexual contact with former clients, due to the risk that such contacts will be exploitive and harmful to the former client. While state law has a prohibition against such contact that lasts for two years beyond the last professional contact, the NASW ethical standard has no time limit attached.

Intimacy between therapist and client's spouse, partner, or family member. State laws about sexual relationships with clients and former clients apply only to the clients themselves. Under ethical guidelines, the prohibition is broader: Therapists *also* may not enter into sexually intimate relationships with clients' spouses or partners, other family members, or anyone else with whom the client maintains a personal relationship, if there is risk of exploitation or harm to the client (and there typically is such risk). The NASW code makes no direct mention of sexual relationships with the partners, family members, or friends of former clients.

Therapy with former romantic partners. Just as it would typically be unethical to start having sex with a former client (subject to the rules noted above), it would also be unethical to accept a client in therapy who was a former sexual partner. This is expressly prohibited by the NASW Code of Ethics, considering the potential for harm to the individual and the likelihood that the prior relationship would make it difficult to maintain professional boundaries.

Sample Questions
See the next page for answers and rationales

1. An experienced LCSW working with clients from a variety of backgrounds is gently questioned by a supervisor after making comments that clients perceived as offensive and unwelcoming. The LCSW argues that she has completed more than 30 hours of training in working with different racial groups over the course of their career, and even gave talks on working with Black clients in the mid-1980s, shortly after she was first licensed. Considering her ethical responsibilities, the LCSW should:

    a. Update her knowledge on diversity and inclusion
    b. Apologize to the clients who were offended, and ask them to help her become more knowledgeable about their backgrounds
    c. Provide the supervisor a list of the diversity-related coursework she has taken throughout her career
    d. Avoid discussing client race or other demographics in future sessions

2. A client is aware of a local wellness center that is soon to be put up for sale. The client tells her therapist, a CSW, about the business and how much she would like to join the CSW in buying it. She presents a detailed proposal that would have them end their therapy relationship so that they could become investment partners. The CSW should:

    a. Carefully consider the risks and benefits associated with the potential investment
    b. Remind the client of the boundaries of the therapy relationship
    c. Inform the client that the CSW will only consider terminating therapy if it is clinically appropriate, and that any potential investment partnership could only be discussed once the therapeutic relationship has ended
    d. Thank the client for her consideration in bringing the opportunity to the CSW, and to protect the client from potential exploitation, offer to serve as an unpaid advisor for the buying process without investing any money

Sample Questions: Answers and Rationales

1. An experienced LCSW working with clients from a variety of backgrounds is gently questioned by a supervisor after making comments that clients perceived as offensive and unwelcoming. The LCSW argues that she has completed more than 30 hours of training in working with different racial groups over the course of their career, and even gave talks on working with Black clients in the mid-1980s, shortly after she was first licensed. Considering her ethical responsibilities, the LCSW should:

    a. **CORRECT.** Update her knowledge on diversity and inclusion

    b. **Incorrect.** Apologize to the clients who were offended, and ask them to help her become more knowledgeable about their backgrounds

    c. **Incorrect.** Provide the supervisor a list of the diversity-related coursework she has taken throughout her career

    d. **Incorrect.** Avoid discussing client race or other demographics in future sessions

Race and other demographic factors are key elements of client identity and experience, and should not simply be ignored. Here, the LCSW has taken some diversity training, but more than 30 hours of such training amounts to very little over what appears to be a 30-plus-year career, and the clients' complaints suggest that the LCSW's knowledge may be out of date. While apologies to the clients may be appropriate, it is not appropriate to ask clients to do the emotional labor of providing the LCSW with training on how to work effectively with diverse groups. It's the LCSW's job to get training on her own, and then to bring that knowledge and skill into session.

2. A client is aware of a local wellness center that is soon to be put up for sale. The client tells her therapist, a CSW, about the business and how much she would like to join the CSW in buying it. She presents a detailed proposal that would have them end their therapy relationship so that they could become investment partners. The CSW should:

   a. **Incorrect.** Carefully consider the risks and benefits associated with the potential investment. *While what is proposed in the question would be, technically, a business venture with a former patient, termination should be based on sound clinical judgment and not on a financial opportunity arising. The CSW should not accept this offer regardless of the balance of risks and benefits associated with the investment.*

   b. **CORRECT.** Remind the client of the boundaries of the therapy relationship. *Engaging in a business venture with a client is a problematic dual relationship, and ending therapy to engage in a business relationship is prohibited.*

   c. **Incorrect.** Inform the client that the CSW will only consider terminating therapy if it is clinically appropriate, and that any potential investment partnership could only be discussed once the therapeutic relationship has ended. *Ending therapy to engage in a business relationship is prohibited. Better for the CSW to remain in a clinical role here.*

   d. **Incorrect.** Thank the client for her consideration in bringing the opportunity to the CSW, and to protect the client from potential exploitation, offer to serve as an unpaid advisor for the buying process without investing any money. *While it may be well-intentioned, advising on this purchase would be out of the CSW's scope of practice and suggests a potentially problematic multiple relationship.*

ETHICS

Therapeutic Relationship

Scored exam questions (approximate): 13-14

Informed Consent K60-65

Informed consent. In order for a client to offer consent that is truly *informed*, they need a reasonable amount of *information* about the treatment process. CSWs have an ethical responsibility to provide clients with appropriate information about the treatment process, so that the client can make an informed decision about whether they want to participate. Because treatment plans and methods can change during therapy, informed consent for treatment is best understood not as a single event but as an ongoing process.

Facilitating client decisions about treatment. Professional ethics require CSWs to provide enough information to clients that the clients can make meaningful choices about whether to start therapy. The nature of this information may vary by therapist and by treatment type, but CSWs are specifically required to inform clients of:

- The purpose for all services provided
- Risks associated with those services
- Limits to services imposed by third parties
- Limits to confidentiality, and potential consequences of disclosure
- Uses of technology in service delivery
- Service costs
- Alternative services
- Clients' right to refuse or withdraw consent
- How long their consent is considered valid if not withdrawn

Couple, family, and group clients should be specifically informed of how the CSW or clinic handles confidentiality among members of the treatment unit – and that the CSW cannot guarantee that other members of that treatment unit will maintain confidentiality.

Social workers should obtain specific consent for creating audio or video recordings of sessions, or for conducting a digital search related to the client (except in cases of emergency).

All of this information is intended to help clients make well-informed decisions about their participation in treatment. Clients should always be given the opportunity to ask questions related to informed consent (this, too, is an ethical requirement), and if a client has doubts or hesitancies about treatment as a result of what is presented to them in the informed consent process, the CSW should focus on providing the client with any additional information that may help their decision-making, and not on simply trying to "sell" the client on the services the CSW provides.

Client autonomy in treatment decisions. Clients have the fundamental right to choose for themselves what kinds of mental health treatment they will participate in. While there are exceptions to this, such as for clients who present an imminent danger to themselves or others and thus can be involuntarily hospitalized, generally speaking, clients can choose their treatment type, treatment provider, and treatment goals as they see fit. (Some goals would be considered inappropriate for therapy, such as a parent bringing their child into therapy in hopes of changing the child's sexual orientation. While a parent is certainly free to pursue this goal, it would not be appropriate for a therapist to attempt to offer this treatment.) Consistent with this principle, clients can also discontinue treatment or change treatment provider at any time. Even when treatment is taking place by court order, clients typically are able to choose their provider. CSWs respect clients' rights to choose whether to start therapy and whether to leave it at any time. Of course therapists can and should discuss such decisions with clients, but CSWs cannot require a client to remain in therapy, or to remain in therapy with the specific clinician, if the client does not wish to do so.

Culturally and developmentally appropriate methods. CSWs should gain consent for treatment in a manner that is culturally and developmentally appropriate. If a client is illiterate, does not read English, comes from a culture that promotes deference, or is otherwise unable to make sense of the informed consent document, their signature on it may not truly reflect informed consent. The informed consent process would be better served with a verbal discussion in language that the client can understand. CSWs also should be aware of the possibility that clients may be attending therapy against their wishes, at the demand of a family member or someone else; in such instances, it is important for the CSW to determine whether the client is truly providing voluntary consent for treatment.

Guardians and representatives. When clients are unable to make informed decisions on their own, their guardians and legal representatives have the right and responsibility to make choices on the client's behalf. Most commonly, this happens when a parent or legal guardian consents to the treatment of a minor. However, it can also apply when a client under conservatorship is put into treatment by their conservator, or when a court-appointed *guardian ad litem* seeks treatment for minors involved in a custody dispute. In these and other instances, guardians and legal representatives are responsible for making informed decisions about treatment that will be in the best interest of the client.

Clients who can't provide voluntary consent. When a client is unable to provide voluntary consent for treatment, the CSW remains responsible for protecting client welfare. Clients may be unable to voluntarily consent for treatment if they are under the influence of drugs or alcohol, if they have been involuntarily hospitalized as a danger to themselves or others, or if they are a child brought to treatment by their parents, as a few examples.

In these instances, the CSW would still take steps to promote client welfare and facilitate the client's ability to make decisions about treatment to the degree possible. In the case of a client under the influence of drugs or alcohol, the CSW may simply take steps to keep the client safe until the influence of the drug has worn off and the client can voluntarily consent to further treatment. A more thorough informed consent process may take place at that point. If a client has been involuntarily hospitalized, the CSW may remind them of their remaining rights. In the case of a minor, a CSW may utilize an assent agreement, which spells out the purpose, risks, and benefits of therapy in a way that is developmentally appropriate to the child, and allows them to ask questions about the therapy.

Generally speaking, clients mandated to treatment by a court or other outside entity retain their right to choose their treatment provider and voluntarily consent to therapy. They may be required by a court to be in therapy, but typically, they don't have to be in therapy *with you*. CSWs working with mandated clients are ethically required to clarify the CSW's role and the limits of confidentiality that will apply to the mandated services. This clarification helps protect client rights, as they can choose whether to go forward in treatment under those rules.

Consultation and collaboration K66-68

Effects of concurrent treatment. When done well, concurrent treatment can maximize therapeutic gains. Coordinated care among multiple therapists can mean that family members receive individual therapy to work on their individual concerns at the same time they are receiving family therapy to address relational issues. This may speed improvement by addressing multiple levels of concern at once, and by reducing the homeostatic processes in family systems that can keep individual symptoms locked in place.

Concurrent treatment can also cause problems, however, especially when the multiple therapists involved are not in communication with one another. It is not in the best interests of clients to go to one therapist who encourages the client to create distance from the client's mother, and then to go to another therapist who is working to develop a closer relationship between mother and client. When multiple service providers are working with the same client and not coordinating their care, the different services may confuse the client or even actively work against one another.

Collaborating with other professionals. Social workers are not just encouraged but *expected* to participate in interdisciplinary teams and to establish collaborative professional relationships to further the welfare of the client. Establishing collegial relationships can be as simple as friendly outreach. Sometimes it requires multiple efforts, or proof that your client has authorized you to discuss their case. CSWs are expected to help clearly establish the professional and ethical obligations of each individual member of a treatment team.

These principles apply regardless of the role or location of the other service provider. CSWs successfully collaborate with physicians, schools, social services, nutritionists, alternative medicine practitioners, and many others both inside and outside of the world of mental health care. If the client is working with another professional of any kind, and there is potential benefit from the CSW and the other professional coordinating their efforts, the CSW should be proactive in seeking to do so, obtaining releases from the client for such collaboration when appropriate.

Once your role on a treatment team has been clearly established, you are expected to contribute to the team's work in order to support the client. CSWs are ethically expected to "participate in and contribute to decisions that affect the well-being of clients by drawing on the perspectives, values, and experiences of the social work profession" (standard 2.03(a)). This, of course, requires that the CSW be familiar with those current professional perspectives, values, and experiences.

Occasionally, a decision made by a treatment team will raise ethical concerns for a CSW. In those instances, the CSW should try to resolve the issue through appropriate channels. If that fails, the CSW should seek out additional means of addressing their concerns to support the client. This doesn't mean that the CSW should use *in*appropriate means to resolve the issue, but rather that the first option is always to try to resolve the issue directly with the team. If that doesn't work, then the CSW may make use of other systems to support the client as well as possible.

Protecting client rights in consultation and collaboration. Of course, CSWs are encouraged to regularly consult with other professionals and community resources to promote quality client care. It is common for CSWs to collaborate and consult with physicians, teachers, social service providers, and other important persons in a client's life. CSWs are expected to be aware of colleagues' competence and expertise, so that when consulting is appropriate, the CSW can easily find a knowledgeable person. Ethically, the CSW should only seek consult from someone with appropriate knowledge or competence.

When doing such consultations, CSWs respect the confidentiality of their clients. Each member of the treatment unit must give their permission for clinical information to be shared with any outsider, unless an exception to confidentiality applies. Even where permission has been given, the CSW should disclose the minimum amount of confidential information necessary to fulfill the purpose of the consultation.

Involvement of multiple clients or third parties K69-73

Identifying the "client." CSWs are ethically obligated to clarify at the beginning of therapy which person or persons are considered clients, and the nature of the relationship the therapist will have with each person involved in treatment. There is a meaningful difference between a partner or family member *visiting* treatment, where they might offer input or moral support to a client's problem, and being a *client*, where they may be directly involved in therapeutic interventions. Whether someone is a client or not will impact the social worker's responsibilities to that person. If work with a family creates the potential for a conflict of interests, the CSW should take steps to minimize that conflict.

Confidentiality. When working with couples or families, confidentiality becomes a key concern. If a client calls between sessions and informs the therapist of a secret, does the therapist have the right to bring that information up in a couple or family session?

The NASW Code of Ethics requires that CSWs inform clients of applicable policies regarding the handling of individual confidences. Some CSWs and agencies support a no-secrets policy, where individual confidences will *not* be upheld. Others prefer a limited-secrets policy, believing this is better for accurate assessment of the couple or family. In either case, the CSW should ensure that all individuals in the couple or family being treated are aware of the policy, and the CSW should then stick to that policy.

In couple, family, or group therapy, CSWs should seek agreement among participants as to their responsibilities to each other. Such clients should be warned that others participating in treatment with them may not honor those agreements. Some CSWs ask group members to sign an agreement that they will respect the privacy of the group.

Preserving the therapeutic relationship. Of course, it would not be possible to list all of the factors that can influence the therapeutic relationship in couple, family, or group therapy. Nor is that necessary for an exam about legal and ethical practice. Lots of things can influence the relationship, not all of which are foreseeable. If the CSW keeps client welfare and the preservation of the therapeutic relationship paramount, the CSW will be able to manage most of these factors easily.

Consider two examples: In the first example, a CSW doing couple therapy begins to feel hostility from one of the partners, and is not sure why. The CSW asks the other partner whether it would be ok to meet alone with the hostile partner for a few minutes, and the other partner agrees. During this time, the hostile partner reveals that she is concerned the therapist is siding with her spouse over her. While this was not the CSW's intent, the

CSW is able to change behavior moving forward, and offers an apology to the hostile partner.

In the second example, a CSW doing family therapy with a mother, father, and their two adolescent girls assesses that the girls' acting out behavior appears to be related to conflict in the parental subsystem. The CSW discusses with the family the possibility of changing the treatment modality to focus on couple work. While the CSW reminds the family that he enjoys having them all come in, he believes the girls have done their job, and now it is time for him to do his in treating the family's core issue.

In each of these cases, the therapist took steps to support client welfare and the therapeutic relationship, when it would have easily been possible for therapy to go down an unproductive path. A CSW should be able to address therapeutic issues related to their role, the modality of treatment, and the involvement of outsiders openly with clients.

Potential conflicts in concurrent treatment. When a CSW is providing concurrent therapy to multiple people in the same family system – for example, when the CSW is seeing members of a couple both individually and as a couple – conflicts can quickly emerge. Individuals in the same couple or family may have competing and even incompatible needs. An individual may want to talk with the CSW privately about something they don't want their family to know. More practically, scheduling and costs can become difficult in these situations. While this kind of concurrent treatment is not prohibited, CSWs are ethically obligated to carefully consider potential conflicts in these situations, and to take steps to avoid or minimize those conflicts. Good ways to do so include having a clearly identified "client," maintaining a clear policy on individual secrets, regularly addressing confidentiality issues, and following a clear treatment plan.

Treatment involving multiple systems or third parties. The NASW Code of Ethics encourages CSWs to revisit discussions of confidentiality with clients when appropriate. This is especially important when treatment involves multiple systems or third parties. In some cases, providing services to an adolescent may mean involving their teacher, their religious leader, their doctor, and others. Everyone involved should be clear about what the CSW's role is and what the third parties' roles are in the treatment, and how information may be shared among treatment providers and others. Managing privacy and confidentiality in these situations can be a complex task. Of course, clients should give permission before third parties are brought in to treatment, and should be made aware that they can revoke this permission at any time.

Managing confidentiality K74-75

Ethical standards. The NASW Code of Ethics requires social workers to specifically inform clients of the limits of confidentiality at the beginning of treatment. Of course, this is not the only time when it may be relevant to discuss confidentiality. The code notes that therapy may require multiple discussions of confidentiality and its limits.

In addition, throughout the course of therapy there are multiple standards that relate to social workers' responsibility to keep information from therapy private. Consultations, recordkeeping, telemedicine, supervision, teaching/presentation, and preparation for moving or closing a practice are *all* to be done in ways that protect client confidentiality, unless a specific exception applies or the client has granted permission for their information to be shared.

Managing the impact of confidentiality issues. When it is possible and appropriate to do so, CSWs are expected to discuss disclosures of confidential information with clients *before* the disclosure is made. This discussion should include considerations of the potential consequences of that disclosure.

Particularly if a social worker has been required to share information from therapy, a discussion with the client about what information was shared, with whom, and why can help minimize negative impacts on the therapeutic relationship. Such a discussion can also serve to remind the client of the limits of confidentiality, and of the therapist's commitment to protecting the safety of any others involved. For example, if a report of suspected child abuse has been made, the CSW may want to discuss the role that the CSW plays in larger society in protecting vulnerable populations from suspected abuse. Ultimately, a conversation like this can refocus client and therapist on the therapeutic process and (hopefully) repair any harm done to the therapeutic relationship.

Such discussions are not always appropriate or even possible. But they can often be helpful if the CSW has been required to share information from the therapy without a specific authorization from the client to do so.

Managing crises K76-78

Methods for assessing risk. Thankfully, there are good, brief ways of assessing clients who may pose a danger to themselves or someone else. Assessments for suicide and violence to others tend to focus on the factors listed previously (page 57). Direct client expressions of intent to harm should of course be taken seriously. More often, clients present with some combination of risk and protective factors, which must be weighed to make a determination of risk. All sources of information that the CSW deems trustworthy can be used in making this determination: Screening instruments; direct observation of client behavior; client statements; information from family members, friends, and others, when available; consultation with colleagues, supervisors, or others involved in the client's care; and client history, especially when that history suggests a pattern of risky behavior.

Ethical obligations for protecting safety. The first standard in the NASW Code of Ethics defines social workers' primary responsibility as promoting the well-being of clients. Many other ethical standards logically stem from this responsibility. For example, CSWs normally recognize and respect a client's right to self-determination. However, the CSW may limit clients' right to self-determination if the CSW believes that the client poses (or would pose) a risk to themselves or others. As another example, confidentiality is not to be protected when disclosure would prevent a serious and foreseeable harm.

In addition to this responsibility to individual clients, social workers also have a responsibility to the larger community and society. CSWs are expected to provide appropriate professional services in public emergencies, and to actively work for the general well-being of society.

Procedures for managing safety needs. As a general rule, safety needs should be addressed through the *least intrusive means* necessary to resolve the concern. You wouldn't hospitalize a mildly depressed patient, after all. Here are a few procedures for managing safety needs, ranging from the least to the most intrusive. This is not a complete list, and the options here are not mutually exclusive; it may be appropriate to develop a safety plan *and* increase the frequency of contact with a client, for example.

- **Continue to assess.** In the absence of any specific safety concerns, the therapist would simply continue assessing for safety in future interactions with the client.
- **Consult with the treatment team.** If you are participating on an interdisciplinary treatment team and have appropriate authorization to share information, it may be helpful to consult the team for their assessment of risk and to collaborate on methods for continued assessment and intervention.
- **Conduct more detailed assessment.** If a client suggests that their depression is deepening or that their hostility to others is increasing, but does not discuss any specific danger or threat, the therapist should assess the area of concern in more detail.
- **Develop a safety plan.** If a client has a history of safety issues, or is currently showing non-specific safety concerns (for example, a client with mild passive suicidality, but no plan or intent to harm themselves), a therapist may develop a safety plan. This plan lays out specific steps the client can take if their symptoms worsen. Steps usually follow a progression if early steps are unavailable or do not solve the problem. Steps may include contacting loved ones, contacting the therapist, contacting another on-duty therapist, and if these steps are unsuccessful, contacting a 24-hour crisis hotline or calling 911.
- **Increase frequency of contact.** If you have been seeing a client weekly and you begin to have concerns about their safety, but those concerns do not rise to the level where more immediate intervention is needed, you may ask to see them more often, or for the client to check in by phone more regularly. You may also choose to increase the frequency of collateral contacts (with probation officers, family members, or others in the client's life).
- **Refer to a higher level of care.** Clients whose symptoms get worse or who become dangerous during outpatient psychotherapy may be better served through inpatient treatment.
- **Use voluntary hospitalization.** Clients who pose an imminent danger to themselves or others and are willing to be assessed and treated voluntarily at a hospital will not be held there against their will. When a therapist is firm with a client that hospitalization is necessary, most clients will choose voluntary hospitalization over involuntary hospitalization.
- **Use involuntary hospitalization.** If a client presents a major safety risk and is not willing to be hospitalized, a CSW may initiate

the process of involuntary hospitalization. While most CSWs cannot invoke involuntary hospitalization, they can demand that a client be evaluated for a possible 72-hour hold.

Of course, if the safety concern is that the client poses an immediate danger of severe bodily harm to a reasonably identifiable victim, the appropriate procedure would be to notify the victim and law enforcement.

Best interests of the client K79-81

How legal and ethical obligations impact therapy. Our legal and ethical obligations as mental health professionals exist primarily to protect the best interests of clients. They can have the side effect of protecting therapists, by setting clear standards of professional behavior (and thus protecting us from accusations of being unprofessional when we are not), but they fundamentally exist to protect clients *from* us.

Sometimes, our legal and ethical obligations can create an inconvenience for therapist and client alike. Clients may not read every word of a long informed consent document, and therapists may not want to spend time in therapy discussing the limits of confidentiality. However, failing to meet our obligations can place clients at risk in a variety of ways. We fulfill these obligations because it is good for clients, even when it isn't convenient.

Social workers are instructed in multiple ways through the NASW Code of Ethics to inform clients when legal and ethical standards of the profession will limit the client's rights or change the therapist's role. For example, the ethics code requires that CSWs advise clients of those instances (such as child abuse reporting) where the therapist's responsibility to the larger society supersedes the therapist's responsibility to the client.

Conflicts between legal and ethical obligations. There are many times when there is not a direct conflict between law and ethics, but they set different standards. For example, the law may offer a stricter standard than the ethics code, or vice versa. In these instances, a CSW should follow the stricter standard, regardless of which set of rules it comes from.

If there is a direct conflict between the code of ethics and the law – that is, if the law says that you *must* do one thing, while the code of ethics says that you *must* do something that is different from and incompatible with what the law requires – the law wins. CSWs should follow the law, and practice in accordance with the code of ethics to the greatest extent possible.

Conflicts between agency and ethical obligations. It is also common for CSWs to work in settings where ethics codes conflict with workplace policy. The NASW code requires CSWs to make their commitment to ethical standards known to the organization, and to take reasonable steps to resolve the issue in a way that allows the social worker to practice in keeping with their ethical responsibilities. Social work administrators have an additional ethical responsibility to work within their roles to change any policies that might conflict with, or otherwise discourage compliance with, the ethics code. The overriding principle is clear: Agency policy does not provide an excuse for CSWs to ignore their ethical duties.

Diversity and nondiscrimination K82-85

Ethical standards for non-discrimination. The NASW code of ethics states that social workers shall not "practice, condone, facilitate, or collaborate with any form of discrimination" in professional services based on the following factors:

- Race
- Ethnicity
- National origin
- Color
- Sex
- Sexual orientation
- Gender identity or expression
- Age
- Marital status
- Political belief
- Religion
- Immigration status
- Mental or physical ability

In addition, social workers are expected to hold institutions accountable for cultural competence, and to "take action against oppression, racism, discrimination, and inequities, and acknowledge personal privilege."

Among major mental health professions, social workers have the greatest ethical duty to actively work toward social justice, in the therapy room and beyond.

Diversity factors in therapy. Social workers are specifically called upon to recognize the strengths that exist in all cultures, and to work toward reducing discrimination and exploitation on societal levels. CSWs understand the impact of culture on human behavior. This can mean, for example, recognizing when a behavior is culturally appropriate and thus should not be diagnosed as a mental illness, even if it otherwise meets diagnostic criteria.

Virtually any area of difference between client and therapist has the potential to impact the therapy process. While discussions of diversity in the US tend to center on issues of race, ethnicity, sexual orientation, and gender identity, a wide variety of other factors can impact a client's identity and cultural norms. In addition to all of the factors listed in the non-discrimination standards above, therapy can be impacted by differences between client and therapist in urban versus rural setting, educational level, regional identity, and many more.

Ethical standards for providing services to diverse groups. Social workers are ethically obligated to be mindful of all forms of historical and social prejudice, as this prejudice can lead to misdiagnosing clients or pathologizing culturally-accepted behavior. In addition, CSWs "obtain education about and demonstrate understanding of the nature of social diversity and oppression with respect to" all of the factors listed in the non-discrimination standard. Social workers should be able to demonstrate competence in providing services that are sensitive to client culture and to cultural differences. The services social workers provide should be "culturally informed services that empower marginalized individuals and groups."

Improving knowledge, skills, awareness, and sensitivity. So what can a CSW do when approached by a client who is different from the therapist in ways that impact the therapy process? While postmodern models of therapy encourage CSWs to allow clients to inform the therapist about the client's life and circumstances, it is likely to be inadequate for a CSW to take no other action to improve their knowledge and skills around the relevant diversity issues. The social worker could:

- Attend a continuing education training on working with the client's population
- Seek consultation or supervision from other therapists who identify as part of, or regularly work with, the client's population
- Seek out greater exposure to the client's population
- Read articles and other literature on the client's population
- Attend their own therapy to address issues of bias

Client self-determination K86-88

Client right to self-determination. Clients have a fundamental right to self-determination (also commonly referred to as autonomy). As discussed in the context of informed consent, this means that they alone can choose whether to participate in treatment, what the goals of treatment should be, and what provider to use.

This same principle applies to making major life decisions. Clients are free to determine for themselves what goals to pursue and how to best pursue them. Social workers may collaborate with clients in the process of determining those goals, but should not impose their own ideas about what may be best for the client. Treatment should be a collaborative process to the degree possible. Social workers only limit clients' right to self-determination in situations of "serious, foreseeable, and imminent risk" to the client or others.

Facilitating client decisions about treatment. As discussed in the section on informed consent, the NASW code of ethics requires CSWs to provide enough information to clients that the clients can make meaningful choices about whether to start therapy. The nature of this information may vary by therapist and by treatment type. Clients should be given the opportunity to ask questions about their treatment. If the client is receiving services involuntarily (as happens with court-mandated clients, as one example), they still should be informed about the relevant consent issues, and the extent of their right to refuse service. Specific consent should be obtained for any third-party observation or for any audio or video recording of services. All of this information must be given in clear and understandable language.

When clients are wrestling with decisions about treatment, including whether to engage in treatment (either starting or terminating), social workers should provide whatever information may be necessary and helpful in the client reaching an informed and appropriate decision. It may also be useful to discuss alternatives to treatment, and the potential risks, benefits, and other consequences of various treatment options available to the client.

Methods to assist clients in making decisions and clarifying goals. Moving beyond the immediate treatment context to consider client decisions more broadly, there are many ways a social worker can assist a client in decision-making without interfering with the client's autonomy in making those decisions. The social worker can help the client list various courses of action they could take in a difficult time, often expanding the possibilities beyond those the client may see on their own. The social worker can help the client foresee possible consequences of each of the possible courses of action, using current research as well as the social worker's knowledge of the client's specific context. The social worker can assess the client's readiness to act. The social worker can reflect and validate the client's excitement about some possibilities and anxiety about others. Each of these tasks facilitates the client making an important decision on their own, with the social worker's guidance and support.

Multidisciplinary teams K89-90

Methods for establishing collaborative relationships. Just as social workers should engage in outreach to develop collaborative relationships with outside professionals serving the same client, social workers should also be proactive in developing collaborative relationships on a multidisciplinary team. They should treat colleagues with respect and actively participate in team discussion and decision-making. Clear guidelines for the treatment team should be established, including defining the obligations of the team as a whole and each of its members individually.

Additional ethical standards. Treating colleagues with respect includes representing colleagues' opinions, qualifications, and responsibilities fairly and accurately.

CSWs should avoid unwarranted criticism of colleagues, especially criticism on the basis of demographic factors such as race, age, gender identity, immigration status, or disability. This does not mean that CSWs are prohibited from ever criticizing colleagues, just that such criticism should be focused on the topic at hand, and should seek to represent the colleagues' views fairly. It should not include personal criticism or attacks.

CSWs should draw on the values, experiences, and perspectives of the profession when contributing to team decisions that impact client well-being.

When a treatment team makes a decision that raises ethical concerns for the social worker, the social worker should seek to resolve the dispute through appropriate channels. If that is ineffective at resolving the issue, the social worker should seek other ways to resolve their concern, placing the well-being of client(s) as the highest priority.

Improving access to care K91-94

Evaluating client ability to advocate for themselves. Many clients can effectively advocate for themselves with third-party payors and with others involved in their care, but some clients struggle to do so. A key component of removing barriers to care is determine when clients can advocate on their own behalf, and when they need assistance.

Social workers should assess clients' ability to advocate for themselves. This can include examining their advocacy efforts to date, and seeing what has been effective compared to what has not; considering their current mental and emotional state (obviously, clients who are overwhelmed or in crisis may have more difficulty advocating on their own behalf than clients who are more stable); and broadly assessing their resource needs. This evaluation process can also help the social worker assess the client's overall level of need for the social worker's services.

Interaction with third-party payors. CSWs are ethically obligated to be truthful and accurate in documentation submitted to third-party payers. Additional ethical rules that can be applied to CSWs' interactions with third-party payers include:

- Do not "participate in, condone, or be associated with dishonesty, fraud, or deception"
- Ensure that billing practices accurately reflect the services provided, including the identity of service providers
- Do not disclose confidential information to payers without a specific release to do so
- Inform clients of limits to services imposed by third-party payers

Interaction with other service delivery systems. Standards applying to interactions with other service delivery systems include:

- Protect confidentiality unless authorized to share information
- Do not give or receive payment for referrals
- Ensure an orderly transfer of responsibility for the client
- Discuss whether consultation with prior providers is warranted

Enhancing clients' abilities to meet their own needs. Where it is possible to do so, teaching clients to advocate on their own behalf can have broader and more lasting positive impacts than simply advocating on behalf of the client. CSWs can raise client awareness of specific resources, empower and encourage clients to connect with those resources, walk clients through the process of advocating with third-party payors or with others, and engage clients in motivational approaches designed to help clients better meet their own needs going forward.

Termination and referrals K95-101

Ethical considerations with interrupting or terminating. There are times when interrupting or terminating therapy is appropriate or necessary, even when the goals of therapy have not been reached. You may become seriously ill, or need to step away from your practice to care for loved ones. The client may suddenly be called to a military deployment or a new job out of state. Your clinic may lose its funding. While we all hope these situations will not occur, the reality is that they sometimes do, and a CSW is ethically required to be ready for such abrupt shifts. A CSW also must take appropriate steps when this kind of situation does happen.

CSWs are ethically required to take reasonable steps to ensure continuity of services in the event that they become suddenly incapacitated or otherwise unavailable. These procedures may include emergency contact numbers where clients may reach the therapist or others able to take over client care. CSWs in private practice commonly have what is called a *professional will*, which lays out issues like who will take over client care in the event of the therapist's serious injury or death. The person assigned to take over client care must be given access to records so that they can contact clients to let them know of the change; for this reason, many CSWs include an authorization in their informed consent agreement letting clients know that a professional will exists and having clients agree that their records may be forwarded when necessary.

Having these plans in place minimizes the harm that may come to clients when a therapist is suddenly unavailable. However, treatment interruptions or sudden terminations are not always due to something happening to the therapist.

Whenever treatment must be interrupted or terminated, regardless of whether it is because of something happening to the client, the therapist, the clinic, or the larger social context, CSWs have ethical responsibilities to *non-abandonment* and appropriate *continuity of care*. Non-abandonment simply means that clients in need of continued services typically should not be left to fend for themselves; if treatment with the current CSW must be interrupted or ended, the CSW still has a responsibility to ensure that crisis needs are addressed and that any potential for harm due to the change in treatment is minimized. Continuity of care means that the client is able to receive continued care with another provider appropriate to their needs; most commonly, this means providing referrals that are local to the client, within their financial means, and able to treat the client's specific problem type and severity.

Social workers in fee-for-service settings may terminate care with a client when the client is unable to pay an outstanding balance. However, several specific elements must all be in place before such a termination is considered ethical: (1) The financial contract must have been made clear to the client (this often is addressed in the initial informed consent process); (2) the client must not pose an imminent danger to themselves or others; and (3) the consequences (clinical and otherwise) of the current outstanding balance must have been discussed with the client. So, a social worker who has been clear with a client about the client's financial commitment, has assessed a client for danger and found none, and who has discussed the consequences of an outstanding balance with the client is free to terminate.

As mentioned previously, social workers are ethically prohibited from terminating services in order to pursue a social, financial, or sexual relationship with a client.

Knowledge of referrals/resources to provide continuity of care. In order to make referrals when necessary, a CSW must be aware of local resources that can provide continuity of care to clients if therapy is suddenly stopped. Many CSWs maintain referral lists that include local hospitals and crisis resources, low-fee clinics, psychiatrists, other providers whose services are similar to those of the CSW, and other community resources.

Methods to facilitate transfer. There are several steps social workers can take to ensure that the transfer of a client does not result in that client being abandoned or otherwise falling through the cracks. These methods can generally be categorized as providing good referrals, ensuring client follow-through, and collaborating with their new service provider.

The social worker begins by being proactive when it comes to providing appropriate referrals: Ensuring that referrals provided are appropriate to client needs and are accepting new clients. If necessary, the social worker might even aid the client in making the initial appointment with a new provider. The social worker can create a "warm handoff" by inviting the new provider of the client's choice to join the social worker in the social worker's termination session. The social worker can ask the client to sign a release of information allowing the social worker to transfer treatment records to the new provider, and to discuss the client's case with the new provider to answer any questions the new provider may have. Similar releases might also allow the CSW to communicate with the client's partner or other close family members, to ensure that the client is able to connect with other providers.

Indicators of need to terminate or refer. The clearest indication that it is time to terminate therapy is, of course, when it is clear that the client has reached their treatment goals, and no new goals have emerged. Even in the absence of having reached the goals of treatment, if a client regularly comes in appearing to no longer be in distress, this can indicate that the client is ready to be done with therapy. Ongoing, careful monitoring and discussion with clients about their changing needs can help determine whether and when termination or additional referrals may be necessary.

The CSW should also refer out, or terminate existing services, if:

- The CSW is not able to provide competent services due to impairment
- There is risk of a conflict of interests
- There is a dual relationship that is likely to create risk of exploitation or impair the CSW's clinical judgment

Of course, referrals are appropriate for addressing client needs that the CSW cannot immediately address. Client reports of medical symptoms suggest a need for a referral to a physician. Other needs that the CSW cannot meet, but that appear relevant to the client's functioning, may be best met through appropriate referrals.

Client is not benefiting. Even if the goals of therapy have not been reached, it is appropriate to terminate therapy if it is clear that the client is not benefiting from treatment. Further deterioration of functioning is a clear indication of treatment failure. A lack of improvement in symptoms may or may not indicate a lack of benefit from treatment; if a client entered therapy on a downward trend, simply stabilizing them and keeping them out of hospitalization can be considered a benefit. Ultimately, though, clients should experience a benefit from being in therapy. If, by their own report or by therapist or other observation of client behavior, they are not improving, termination should be considered – with referrals given if symptoms still warrant treatment.

Managing termination. It is generally understood that a good termination process starts at the *beginning* of services, with therapist and client reaching clear agreement on what the goals of the services are and what improvements will lead to a determination that services can end. Discussions of progress toward termination should be a regular part of therapy. Once it is clear that termination is appropriate, a responsible CSW will provide advance notice of termination, and in one or more termination sessions, the CSW will take steps to prevent a relapse of symptoms, recognize the gains the client has made in therapy, and provide appropriate referrals for any additional needed care.

Preventing abandonment or neglect. A termination process that is done too quickly or without appropriate referrals can be considered client abandonment. There may be times when a therapist needs to end therapy abruptly, either due to a medical illness, client job transfer or deployment, or for other reasons. In such circumstances, the CSW (or, in the case of the CSW's illness, someone designated by the CSW) should offer as much advance notice of termination as possible, make appropriate referrals, and follow up to ensure the clients are able to obtain continued services.

Notably, the obligation to prevent client abandonment does not mean that a client can effectively hold a CSW hostage by refusing to accept referrals. When termination is appropriate, the social worker is obligated to provide appropriate referrals and to take reasonable steps to ensure that crisis needs are addressed.

Sample Questions
See the next page for answers and rationales

1. An associate CSW has been struggling with a difficult family case. The associate's supervisor suggests that the associate record video of future sessions so that the associate and supervisor can together review what happens in session. The associate is reluctant to record sessions, fearing that the parents in the family might feel embarrassed. The associate CSW is required to:

    a. Remind the clients that, because the associate is under supervision, video recording of sessions is a common and accepted practice

    b. Obtain specific consent for recording from each adult family member prior to recording sessions

    c. Comply with the supervisor's request even if the family would prefer to not be recorded, as the associate is working under the supervisor's license

    d. Remind the clients of the limits of confidentiality prior to recording sessions

2. A CSW is involved on a treatment team for a county social service agency. The CSW grows frustrated that the CSW's suggestions are rarely implemented by the team. An appropriate course of action would be for the CSW to:

    a. Seek advice from colleagues about handling treatment team dynamics

    b. Temporarily stop providing input into team decisions until the CSW can better understand why previous suggestions have not been implemented

    c. In the interest of transparency, directly inform clients of the CSW's recommendations, including those that the team has rejected

    d. Demand that the team implement the CSW's suggestions to promote the well-being of clients

Sample Questions: Answers and Rationales

1. An associate CSW has been struggling with a difficult family case. The associate's supervisor suggests that the associate record video of future sessions so that the associate and supervisor can together review what happens in session. The associate is reluctant to record sessions, fearing that the parents in the family might feel embarrassed. The associate CSW is required to:

   a. **Incorrect.** Remind the clients that, because the associate is under supervision, video recording of sessions is a common and accepted practice. *While this may be a common and accepted practice, pushing the clients in this way may lead them to believe that they do not have the ability to refuse recording.*

   b. **CORRECT.** Obtain specific consent for recording from each adult family member prior to recording sessions. *This is required by the NASW Code of Ethics.*

   c. **Incorrect.** Comply with the supervisor's request even if the family would prefer to not be recorded, as the associate is working under the supervisor's license. *Consent for taping cannot be forced upon the clients. They should be fully informed of the risks and benefits, and choose on their own.*

   d. **Incorrect.** Remind the clients of the limits of confidentiality prior to recording sessions. *While doing so may be helpful, it is not required.*

2. A CSW is involved on a treatment team for a county social service agency. The CSW grows frustrated that the CSW's suggestions are rarely implemented by the team. An appropriate course of action would be for the CSW to:

    a. **CORRECT.** Seek advice from colleagues about handling treatment team dynamics. *The NASW Code of Ethics encourages CSWs to seek advice when such consultation is in clients' best interests.*

    b. **Incorrect.** Temporarily stop providing input into team decisions until the CSW can better understand why previous suggestions have not been implemented. *Social workers are ethically obligated to be actively involved in interdisciplinary treatment teams. Stopping participation, even temporarily, would violate this standard.*

    c. **Incorrect.** In the interest of transparency, directly inform clients of the CSW's recommendations, including those that the team has rejected. *This could undermine treatment decisions made by the team, and places clients in a difficult position. It does not live up to social workers' requirement to work collaboratively with colleagues. To the degree that the CSW seeks to have clients take the CSW's side, this could be considered exploitation of the client.*

    d. **Incorrect.** Demand that the team implement the CSW's suggestions to promote the well-being of clients. *It is not collaborative for one member of a treatment team to make demands. Even if the team's decisions raised ethical concerns – which is not indicated by the question stem – making demands of the team is unlikely to resolve those concerns effectively.*

ETHICS

Business Practices and Policies

Scored exam questions (approximate): 7-8

Advertising K102-104

Accurate representation. Ethically, you can only advertise those degrees or credentials you have actually earned, and which are relevant to the practice of clinical social work. If you have a master's degree in social work and a doctorate in English, you could not include your doctorate as a professional qualification. Even though you do have a doctorate, it would be a misrepresentation of the credentials you hold relative to your clinical work.

Similarly, any other professional qualifications or competencies that you advertise must be accurate. If others misrepresent your qualifications or credentials, you should take reasonable steps to correct the information. You also must accurately represent the services you provide and the results to be achieved. Any time you speak on behalf of an organization, you should accurately represent the official position of the organization.

Testimonials. The NASW Code of Ethics prohibits seeking testimonials from current clients or anyone else who might be subject to undue influence. Clients and others may feel pressured by such requests. This issue has gotten more complicated in the age of Yelp, Angie's List, HealthGrades, and similar web sites designed for patients to share their experiences with a variety of professionals. Clients sometimes provide testimonials on such sites without being prompted to by therapists. CSWs should be aware that *responding* to any online testimonial may be considered a breach of client confidentiality, even when the client is openly discussing their treatment.

Affiliations. As you would expect, CSWs cannot advertise themselves as being employees, members, partners, or associates of a group that they don't actually belong to. Any representation of employment or professional affiliations must be accurate. Social workers are also expected to be particularly cautious about recruiting clients when those clients are currently being served by other providers. Social workers should discuss the clients' needs, possible benefits and risks of receiving services through a new provider, and whether consultation with the other provider will be helpful.

Social workers are ethically prohibited from charging a private fee for services that the client is entitled to receive through the social worker's employer or agency. In other words, you cannot use an employer's marketing and recruitment efforts to then steer potential clients toward your own private practice.

Maintaining records K105-108

Generating records. Professional ethics demand that treatment records be accurate and reflect the services provided. Documentation should also be completed in a timely manner to ensure continuity of care. When a CSW is suddenly unavailable, due to illness or any other reason, accurate and up-to-date records ensure that clients can be adequately cared for until the CSW is able to return.

The NASW Code of Ethics *specifically* demands that CSWs document the following:

- Informed consent for evaluation or research
- Client requests for records and, where applicable, reasons for refusing access to part or all of those records

Many other elements of documentation can be reasonably inferred from the code, even though they are not stated outright. For example, the code requires that CSWs *obtain* informed consent for therapy. While this consent does not specifically need to be in writing (and indeed, there are times when a written informed consent document may be inadequate), it is reasonable to assume that consent should be documented in some form.

The NASW code also addresses information that does *not* belong in a client's record. Documentation should only include information that is directly relevant to the services being provided. This helps to protect the privacy of clients.

Protecting the confidentiality of records. CSWs should protect the confidentiality of client records while services are being delivered and after the services have been completed. Possible methods for protecting the confidentiality of records include but are not limited to:

- Keeping paper records in a secure, locked file cabinet
- Keeping electronic records in a secure, encrypted format
- Carefully controlling who has access to client files
- Shredding paper files to dispose of them

Maintenance of records. Under state law, records must be maintained for at least 7 years following the last professional contact. If you are working with a minor, records must be maintained for at least 7 years after the minor turns 18. The NASW Code of Ethics reinforces this legal standard.

CSWs have an ethical responsibility to store records in ways that allow reasonable future access to them. At the same time, you should take reasonable steps to ensure they remain secure and confidential. When the time comes that you dispose of old client records, this disposal should also be done in a manner that protects security and confidentiality. A CSW should never simply throw old client files in the trash.

Client access to records. Clients generally have a legal and ethical right to access their records, though there are some limitations on this. They may request that records be released to themselves or to a third party. Unless you believe that the release of records to the client would be harmful, you must comply with their request in a timely manner, as described in the Law section.

If you believe that releasing records to a client would be harmful to them, you may refuse to do so. If you refuse, you need to document the request and your reason for refusal. Recall from the Law section that the client may then request that a third-party professional review the records to see whether that third party agrees with you that the record should not be released.

Couple, family, and group treatment present challenges when one client requests records but the others involved in treatment are either unaware of the request or do not agree to it. The NASW Code of Ethics requires CSWs to seek clarity, as early as possible, about policies for confidentiality from all participants in couple, family, or group therapy.

When clients are given access to records that identify or discuss other individuals, the CSW should act to protect the confidentiality of those other individuals. This may involve releasing a treatment summary as allowed by law. Note that a summary is typically not appropriate for removing records of one family member's participation in couple or family based treatment; all adult family members who participated in therapy should consent before such records are released.

Social workers have a specific ethical responsibility to develop and inform clients about policies related to the use of technology to give clients access to their records.

Helping clients and others understand records. Because clients are typically not trained mental health professionals, it may be easy for them to misunderstand or misinterpret the information contained in their records. CSWs can minimize this risk by using clear language in their documentation, going through the record with the client upon release, explaining diagnoses and other clinical decisions, and providing the client the opportunity to ask questions about their records if they wish.

Other professional roles K109-110

Clarifying roles. Because social workers serve clients in a variety of ways and in a variety of contexts, it is important to clarify the CSW's role at the beginning of services. This includes clarifying what services will be provided and who is considered the client. While not all dual relationships are avoidable, especially in rural settings, where the potential for a dual relationship exists the CSW should clarify their role and take steps to reduce the risk of exploitation or impaired judgment. Clarifying their role can be part of that process.

Engaging in conflicting roles. Generally, CSWs should avoid situations that amount to a conflict of interest, as discussed previously. However, in some situations it may become unavoidable for the CSW to engage in conflicting roles. For example, the CSW may be compelled by a judge to testify in a court case involving a client. When such instances occur, the CSW should clarify their role with all parties involved, and take steps to minimize conflicts of interest.

Technology and social media K111-113

Potential for harm. Technology has proven indispensable during the COVID-19 pandemic, as most mental health services have been provided through telehealth platforms. Such technologies offer clients convenience and access to care that may not have been achievable without the technology. However, social workers' use of telehealth platforms, social media, and other technology also carries risks.

Let's first look at client care provided via telehealth. When a client goes into crisis or has some other form of emergency in a CSW's office, the CSW knows what to do, whom to call, and where to send the client for immediate help. Over telehealth, that may not be the case. Clients may go into crisis without the CSW being aware of the client's location or where to send them – or even that the crisis is happening. When a CSW fails to respond in a timely manner to a client in crisis, damage to the therapeutic relationship can be lasting, and of course the client may remain at risk for suicide without the risk being addressed until the CSW makes contact.

When social workers post personal information online that is later discovered by clients, or when social workers engage clients in personal relationships on social media or other digital platforms, a number of harms can result. Clients may become confused about the CSW's role or the nature of their relationship. Professional boundaries become more difficult to uphold. Ultimately, an inappropriate dual relationship may result, damaging client confidence in the CSW and in the services being provided.

As it relates to clients' information, CSWs who fail to meet their responsibilities to protect client data may expose that data to hackers or others who could use information from social work services to blackmail the client or steal their identity. They also could simply make the information public, which could itself cause the client significant harm.

Ethical standards. Technology-specific obligations operate *on top of* all of the regular ethical requirements for social work, not in place of them. CSWs providing services via telemedicine are ethically obligated to:

- Be aware of cultural and economic barriers to technology-based care, and work to reduce those barriers
- Inform clients of the risks and benefits specific to telemedicine
- Discuss policies regarding the use of technology
- Verify the identity and location of clients

- Assess client appropriateness for telehealth
- Identify alternate service methods for clients who prefer not to utilize telehealth
- Comply with all applicable legal standards for practice in the location where the social worker is *and* the location where the client is
- Avoid using technology for personal or non-work related communications with clients
- Protect confidentiality of technological communication and electronic records
- Notify clients of any breaches of confidential data

Risks and limitations. While current scientific research is generally finding mental health services provided via technology to be as effective as care provided in-person, there remain some specific risks and limitations associated with the use of technology in service delivery. Some examples of these risks include:

- Technology failure or inconsistent performance
- Added difficulty in clinical assessment or observation
- Data breaches

In addition, some CSWs may experience telehealth as hindering their ability to connect with some clients. It is common for clinicians to express challenges in working with children, couples, and families online, for example.

One key limitation of technology in all of its forms is that it is not accessible to everyone. While telehealth has certainly increased access to care in rural or isolated areas, clients need access to a relatively recent computer or smart phone with a camera, as well as sufficient internet access, to participate in video-based services.

Fees K114-119

Determining fees. There are many factors you can consider when setting fees, such as a client's income, the fees generally charged for services in your area, your own qualifications, and so on. There are three particular things you *can't* do when determining fees:

- You can't enter into an agreement with other independent practitioners or clinics to set a common fee (or common minimum fee) in your area. This would be a violation of antitrust law.
- You can't set different fees based on race, national origin, or any other protected class in anti-discrimination rules.
- You can't set fees that are exploitive (i.e., high fees that take advantage of clients' vulnerability or wealth).

Fees must be fair, reasonable, and aligned with the services that clients are paying for. You can raise or lower fees whenever you wish, even for existing clients. You simply need to make sure that your fee changes are within the rules listed above.

Payment for referrals prohibited. As noted in the Law section, CSWs are both legally and ethically prohibited from giving or receiving payment for referrals. Referrals should be made solely on the basis of what is in the best interests of the client.

Bartering. Bartering – that is, exchanging clinical services for some other product or service, rather than money – comes with a lot of potential problems. There is risk of exploitation if the market value of the goods or services the client offers as payment exceeds the usual fee the CSW charges. There is also the risk that the therapy relationship will be impacted, if the therapist particularly likes or dislikes the goods or services received, or if they hold strong sentimental value for the client.

In spite of those problems, bartering is not completely prohibited. The NASW Code of Ethics allows CSWs to "explore and […] participate in bartering only in very limited circumstances" (standard 1.13(b)). Under the NASW code, bartering is only acceptable if *all* of these conditions are met (reformatted here into a list):

"(a) such arrangements are an accepted practice among professionals in the local community,

(b) considered to be essential for the provision of services,

(c) negotiated without coercion, and

(d) entered into at the client's initiative and

(e) with the client's informed consent."

As a general rule, you should not enter into a bartering arrangement with clients. If bartering ultimately presents a problem, the burden is on the

CSW to show that the bartering arrangement was not detrimental to the client. However, under the limited circumstances described above, there may be rare instances when bartering for services is preferable to interrupting or discontinuing treatment.

Collecting unpaid balances. While the collection of debts is not specifically addressed in the NASW Code of Ethics, based on existing standards it appears to be ethical to use collection agencies for the purposes of collecting unpaid balances. It would be reasonable to conclude that a CSW who uses such agencies should clarify in their informed consent documentation that they do so. And of course, any client information provided to a collection agency should only be the minimum information necessary to collect the balance, and should not include any details about the treatment itself.

Continuation of treatment. The NASW Code of Ethics goes so far as to specifically *allow* termination of therapy based on non-payment of fees, as long as the client does not pose an immediate danger, their financial responsibilities were made clear to them, and the impact of nonpayment has been discussed. When a CSW is unable or unwilling, for any reason, to provide continued care to a client, the CSW must assist the client in making appropriate arrangements for continuation of treatment.

Providing services paid for by third-party payors. When services will be paid for by a third party, such as an insurance company, CSWs are obligated to inform clients of the requirements of that payor that might limit services. (For example, insurers commonly cover individual therapy to treat a diagnosed mental health disorder, but may not cover therapy to treat conflict in a couple or family relationship.) In addition, CSWs should only provide information to the third-party payor when the client has provided specific authorization for the information sharing.

Gifts K120-121

While some professional standards have gotten stricter over time, the standards around giving and receiving gifts have actually grown more flexible. This is due largely to increased recognition of the cultural significance of gifts in many populations. Refusing a small gift may be culturally insensitive. The current NASW Code of Ethics does not mention gifts at all, though the existing standards around non-exploitation would prohibit a CSW from placing their own interests above the client's in deciding whether to accept a gift. CSWs commonly consider the effect of giving or receiving the gift on the client, and the potential impact of the gift on the therapy process.

Giving a gift to a client, or accepting a gift from a client, does come with some risks. The client might perceive that the gift changes the nature of their relationship with you to a more personal one. They might hold an expectation that any gift should be reciprocated. They might expect preferential treatment in scheduling or other elements of therapy. In each of these instances (and surely many others you could come up with), the integrity of the therapeutic process can be impacted. Whether you accept or reject a client gift, it is good practice to document your decision-making on the issue. You might consider factors like the cost, nature, and meaning of the gift, how it fits within cultural norms, and its potential impact on therapy.

Research ethics K122-125

Procedures for safeguarding research participants. The most important safeguard for research participants is the process of informed consent. Just as a client should be fully informed of the processes, risks, and potential benefits of therapy, a research participant should be fully informed of the processes, risks, and benefits of their participation in a study. Most studies are overseen by some form of Institutional Review Board, which reviews the protocols and protections the researchers have in place.

Necessary disclosures to research participants. Under the NASW Code of Ethics, research participants need to be informed of potential risks and benefits from participating. They should also be clearly informed of what participation entails: What is being asked of them, and for how long? Participants should be informed of the limits to confidentiality that apply to their participation, the steps being taken to preserve their confidentiality, and how long records of the research will be retained before being destroyed. Finally, participants must be informed that they can withdraw their consent and end participation at any time, without penalty.

Some forms of research, like naturalistic observation or archival research, do not involve informed consent processes. The NASW code notes that these methods should only be employed without informed consent when "a rigorous and responsible review" has found the research worthwhile, and when alternatives that involve informed consent are not feasible.

Client rights when participating in research. In addition to the right to be informed about the research they are participating in, clients also have the right to decline or withdraw their participation in a study at any time. They have a right to confidentiality unless they sign a waiver specifically authorizing the release of information from their participation. (If the study is a study involving therapy services, the same limits of confidentiality would apply as ordinarily apply in therapy, and the clients should be informed of this as part of the informed consent process.) Under the NASW code, they have the right to be protected from unwarranted danger or distress.

Confidentiality of research data. Unless clients provide a written waiver, CSWs consider any information they learn about a research participant to be confidential, subject to the exceptions to confidentiality outlined earlier. If others may be able to gain access to a participant's research data, the CSW should explain this possibility at the beginning of the study and share their plan for protecting confidentiality.

Unethical or incompetent colleagues K126-127

CSWs not only need to be able to recognize when their own ability to provide therapy is compromised. They also must be aware of times when a *colleague's* ability to provide ethical and effective therapy is compromised.
Situations that can impair the integrity or effectiveness of therapy include multiple relationships (subject to the boundaries previously described); therapist substance abuse, mental illness, or emotional disturbance; bias or discrimination by the therapist; exploitation; and many more.
Unlike some other states, California does not have any rules allowing clinical social workers to directly report colleagues who are behaving in unethical or incompetent ways. If a client tells you about bad behavior on the part of their previous therapist, you are required to keep this information confidential, subject to the same rules as any other confidential information. Reporting it to the board yourself, or directly confronting the colleague, would be a breach of confidentiality. If a client grants permission for you to talk with the other therapist (through a written release of information), you

could then address the other therapist, but it would be important to avoid taking the client's report at face value. There are often two very different sides to such stories, and social workers treat each other with respect.

If you learn of another therapist's unethical or incompetent behavior *directly from that therapist*, you may have more options. For example, if you learn that a colleague in your clinic is struggling with an alcohol abuse problem, you could encourage your colleague to seek treatment and to discontinue seeing clients until the problem is under control. The NASW Code of Ethics encourages CSWs to **offer assistance to colleagues who are impaired** and need to take remedial action. Doing so would certainly be in the best interests of their clients. If the other therapist refuses, you must carefully balance competing standards. The NASW code generally requires social workers avoid unwarranted criticism of colleagues. At the same time, the code demands that social workers who become aware of a colleague's impaired, unethical, or incompetent behavior attempt to consult with and assist that colleague (subject to the normal legal limitations surrounding confidentiality). If those efforts fail, you should take action through appropriate channels, if it is feasible to do so.

What is most important in a situation like this is that you take appropriate action to promote the welfare of clients. While confidentiality laws may prevent you from reporting it yourself when a client tells you that another therapist is behaving unethically or incompetently, you can (and often should) encourage the client to report that behavior themselves. You can't *require* the client to make that report – that would be putting your wishes above the client's – but you can encourage it.

Supervision K128

Supervisors have a number of specific responsibilities defined in the NASW Code of Ethics. In brief, supervisors are required to:

- Have the necessary skills and knowledge to supervise, getting consultation when needed
- Set clear, appropriate, and culturally sensitive boundaries
- Avoid multiple relationships where there is risk of impaired judgment or exploitation
- Evaluate supervisee performance in a manner that is fair, respectful, and based on clearly established criteria

- Ensure clients are aware when services are being provided by students (this ethical standard applies to fieldwork instructors)

1. An LCSW is being interviewed for a podcast. The interviewers ask about her training and clinical work, and repeatedly refer to her as "Doctor," even though her highest degree is a master's degree. The LCSW should:

    a. End the interview and ask that it not be released
    b. No action is called for, as the interview does not qualify as advertising
    c. Continue the interview, and afterward, remind the interviewer of her proper title
    d. Politely correct the interviewers, and ensure that the correction is included on any edited version of the interview used in the podcast

2. A social worker has been working with a family for several sessions and plans a session where the entire family will participate in a ceremony relieving the oldest daughter of the responsibility she has taken on as a co-parent. Shortly before the session, the mother informs the CSW that she will be away on a business trip and asks whether she can participate in the session by phone or videoconferencing. The mother's frequent absences are part of the reason why the daughter felt obligated to take on parenting tasks. The social worker should:

    a. Contact the BBS to see whether the CSW can include the mother in session while she is on her trip
    b. Include the mother in the session and in the ceremony via phone or videoconference, and clarify that her involvement is consultation rather than therapy
    c. Refuse the mother's request and reschedule the ceremony for a time she can attend in person
    d. Contact the other family members to see whether they believe including the mother would be legally and ethically appropriate

Sample Questions: Answers and Rationales

1. An LCSW is being interviewed for a podcast. The interviewers ask about her training and clinical work, and repeatedly refer to her as "Doctor," even though her highest degree is a master's degree. The LCSW should:

   a. **Incorrect.** End the interview and ask that it not be released. *Ending the interview would be a drastic and probably unnecessary step.*

   b. **Incorrect.** No action is called for, as the interview does not qualify as advertising. *Because the interview discussed her clinical work, the interview may be considered advertising. A correction is needed to ensure listeners are not misled as to the LCSW's education.*

   c. **Incorrect.** Continue the interview, and afterward, remind the interviewer of her proper title. *Reminding the interviewer afterward of her proper title might mean that the incorrect title is used many more times during the recording, misleading listeners.*

   d. **CORRECT.** Politely correct the interviewers, and ensure that the correction is included on any edited version of the interview used in the podcast. *The NASW Code of Ethics requires social workers to correct misinformation about their qualifications.*

2. A social worker has been working with a family for several sessions and plans a session where the entire family will participate in a ceremony relieving the oldest daughter of the responsibility she has taken on as a co-parent. Shortly before the session, the mother informs the CSW that she will be away on a business trip and asks whether she can participate in the session by phone or videoconferencing. The mother's frequent absences are part of the reason why the daughter felt obligated to take on parenting tasks. The social worker should:

a. **Incorrect.** Contact the BBS to see whether the CSW can include the mother in session while she is on her trip. *The BBS does not provide legal advice, and even asking the question may require providing information that is confidential.*

b. **Incorrect.** Include the mother in the session and in the ceremony via phone or videoconference, and clarify that her involvement is consultation rather than therapy. *Simply calling the mother's involvement consultation does not make it something different from therapy. This is especially true considering that the entire purpose of her presence in session is to be involved in a therapeutic intervention that the CSW designed.*

c. **CORRECT.** Refuse the mother's request and reschedule the ceremony for a time she can attend in person. *CSWs are required to carefully assess whether telemedicine services are appropriate in a given case. Here, the mother's absence would likely have a major impact on the planned ceremony; having her participate by phone or videoconference rather than in person appears likely to impact the effectiveness of the intervention.*

d. **Incorrect.** Contact the other family members to see whether they believe including the mother would be legally and ethically appropriate. *While the family may be able to offer useful clinical feedback on this question, it is not the role of the family to resolve the CSW's legal and ethical concerns.*

Mini-Mock Exam

Introduction to the Mini-Mock

The exam itself will not simply ask you to recount facts from the preceding pages. Instead, it will ask you to *apply and integrate* the legal and ethical standards that govern the field. That's why the sample questions in this book, like the questions on the real exam, take the form of case vignettes instead of simple memorization. Over the next few pages, you'll get some more practice, in the form of a 25-question mini-mock exam.

What makes these questions a bit different (and, indeed, a bit tougher) from the ones you've seen already is that 1) you don't know which areas of knowledge you're being tested on for each item, and 2) items may ask you to combine multiple areas of knowledge when determining the correct answer. You may need to pull from several content areas to rule out incorrect responses and determine the correct one.

In each question, assume you are an LCSW acting within your professional role. Remember that, as is the case on the test itself, questions may be complex, and they may require careful reading – but they aren't designed to trick you. There's a single, best answer for each question.

Items on this mini-mock exam are proportioned correctly based on the actual exam. In other words, just like the real thing, this mini-mock exam includes 40% Law questions (10 out of 25) and 60% Ethics questions (15 out of 25).

California LCSW Law & Ethics Mini-Mock Exam

1. ____	8. ____	15. ____	22. ____
2. ____	9. ____	16. ____	23. ____
3. ____	10. ____	17. ____	24. ____
4. ____	11. ____	18. ____	25. ____
5. ____	12. ____	19. ____	
6. ____	13. ____	20. ____	
7. ____	14. ____	21. ____	

1. A 57-year-old Armenian woman has been diagnosed with a psychotic disorder by an LCSW working at a community clinic. The client has an extensive history of risk-taking behavior in manic phases, followed by periods of relative stability. She calls the LCSW to let the social worker know that she has been stable long enough that she has chosen to discontinue her medication. When asked about risk-taking, the client acknowledges having gone cliff diving, climbing to the top of a carnival's ferris wheel, and almost getting into a knife fight, all within the past 36 hours. She says she's "doing much better without help than I ever did with it." How should the social worker proceed?

    a. Ask the client to come into the office for a full assessment as soon as possible

    b. Ask the client for permission to contact her physician and discuss her medication decision

    c. Ask the client for her current location, and begin the process of involuntary hospitalization

    d. Ask the client to self-assess her own current functioning to develop insight around her risk level

2. A 31-year-old male client is on probation for assault, and one condition of the probation is that the client attend therapy to address anger and substance use concerns. Six months into therapy, the client informs the LCSW providing treatment that the client wishes to discontinue. The client reports believing he has "gotten everything out of it that I can," and that he is growing frustrated with the expense. He notes that he has not had any angry outbursts in the past three months. Considering the LCSW's ethical obligations, how should the LCSW proceed?

    a. Encourage the client to remain in treatment

    b. Offer to write a letter to the court describing the client's successful completion of mental health treatment and encouraging the court to release the client from their remaining obligation

    c. Inform the client of the potential consequences of discontinuing treatment, including the possibility that their probation may be revoked

    d. Consult with the probation office about how to proceed with a treatment mandate when treatment is no longer warranted

3. A social worker in private practice has been working with a well-known movie actor who has talked publicly about his struggles with mental illness and sobriety, even mentioning the social worker by name when discussing his treatment. The actor dies of an unexpected heart attack, and while the death is under investigation, the social worker begins receiving requests from newspapers and other media outlets to provide more information on the actor's recent mental health and substance use. Considering the social worker's ethical responsibilities, the social worker should:

    a. Provide a treatment summary, under the public-interest exception to confidentiality

    b. Provide a treatment summary, under the death exception to confidentiality

    c. Contact the actor's family to determine who controls privilege now that the actor has died

    d. Refuse all media requests for information

4. An LCSW is working for an agency that contracts with a local private school to provide mental health services. The social worker is called to the school to assess a 9-year-old girl who has been falling asleep in class. The girl's teacher tells the social worker that the teacher is concerned in part because the girl recently wrote a story as part of a class assignment, and in the story a young girl wasn't allowed to sleep when she got into trouble at home. During the assessment, the girl repeatedly asks whether she can take a nap, and refuses to answer any questions about the story she wrote. Asked how things are at home, the girl will only say, "I got in trouble. I'm always getting in trouble." The girl is being raised by a single mother, and the school nurse says that the girl is otherwise in relatively good health, but that her grades have been dropping and her behavior in class has been increasingly disorganized. How should the social worker proceed?

    a. Contact the mother to inform her of the child's behavior and the school's concerns

    b. Contact the child's physician to request a medical assessment

    c. Report suspected child abuse

    d. Ask the child directly whether she is being physically abused or neglected

5. An LCSW is distressed to learn that a former client has posted a detailed account of the client's therapy online in the form of an article. While the article is mostly positive, it mentions the LCSW by name and includes some incorrect information about the LCSW's qualifications. The LCSW notices that it is possible to leave comments on the article. The LCSW should:

    a. Post a comment in response to the article, thanking the author while also correcting the errors

    b. Contact the site owners to ask that the article be taken down, without specifying whether the writer was actually a client

    c. Contact the former client directly to encourage them to correct the article

    d. No action is called for

6. An adult client tells a CSW that the client's 89-year-old mother is in hospice care. The client goes on to say that the hospice staff have been screening the mother's mail and phone calls, as they are concerned that she would fall prey to financial scammers who target the elderly. The client tells the CSW that the mother has severe dementia and that the client believes the screening of mail and phone calls is appropriate. The client also says the staff has never refused him access to his mother. The CSW should:

    a. Obtain a release from the client, contact the hospice directly, and gather more information about the mother's diagnosis and the need for mail and calls to be screened

    b. Report suspected elder abuse

    c. Maintain the client's confidentiality

    d. Empower the client to gather more information on the mother's diagnosis and the need for mail and calls to be screened, and ask the client to bring that information to a future session for the client and the CSW to review together

7. A CSW is surprised to see that her new client did not complete the CSW's standard informed consent paperwork in the waiting room prior to their scheduled session. The CSW brings the client into her therapy office, where the client says that he can only read and write in Spanish. He speaks English fluently, and says he prefers that his therapy sessions be in English. The CSW only speaks and writes in English. Ethically, the therapist should:

    a. Have a verbal conversation to establish informed consent, and have the client sign the informed consent document
    b. Have a verbal conversation to establish informed consent, and document that conversation in session notes
    c. Provide a Spanish translation of her informed consent documents as soon as possible, for the client to read and sign
    d. Have a verbal conversation about informed consent, and offer to provide a Spanish language translation of her informed consent documents as soon as possible

8. A 20-year-old client who identifies her family background as Chinese starts therapy with an LCSW. The client describes herself as a social media influencer with about 1 million followers, and says that she posts about 20 minutes of video online each day. She tells the LCSW she is coming to therapy after family members expressed concern that she may be depressed. She tells the LCSW in session "I feel like such a faker with every video I post." Considering their ethical responsibilities, the LCSW should:

    a. Anonymously review the client's public social media posts, without commenting on them
    b. After session, contact the family members to learn more about their concerns
    c. After session, digitally request to be added as a "friend" or "follower" on the client's social media accounts, so that the client can make an informed choice as to whether to do so
    d. In session, ask the client's permission to review their public social media postings

9. During an unusually tense family session, a mother confronts a CSW on the CSW's recent filing of a written report of suspected child abuse. The mother feels violated and reports that she can no longer trust the CSW. Other family members attempt to calm the mother, but share her concerns. The CSW should:

    a. Discontinue treatment, as the therapeutic relationship has been irreparably compromised

    b. Remind the family of the limits of confidentiality, and seek to regain the family's trust

    c. In the interest of full disclosure, inform the mother that follow-up reports to the local child protective service agency may be necessary

    d. Ask to speak to the other family members without the mother present, to determine whether there is an appropriate path forward for therapy

10. A client mandated for treatment by his county probation office returns to therapy after a six-month absence. He informs the CSW that he needs records of his progress in treatment sent to his probation officer before his next court date, and provides a Release of Information allowing those records to be sent. The CSW assesses the client and determines he is not in crisis. However, he carries a balance due of more than $500 from sessions he attended but did not pay for prior to being absent from therapy. The CSW should:

    a. Continue with treatment at a reduced fee, and refuse to turn over records until at least a portion of the balance is paid

    b. Continue with treatment at a reduced fee, and refuse to turn over records until the outstanding balance is paid in full

    c. Consider terminating the client if he will be unable to pay his balance, and turn over records to the probation officer

    d. Consider terminating the client if he will be unable to pay his balance, and notify the probation officer of the outstanding balance

11. A 14-year-old client consented to her own treatment at a nonprofit agency, which agreed to treat her for $5/session. The client tells the therapist (an LCSW) that the client has been abusing a friend's prescription painkillers. Legally, the LCSW should:

    a.   Notify the local child protective service agency
    b.   Notify the client's parent or guardian, as the behavior is considered high-risk
    c.   Work with the client to develop a plan to gradually reduce dosage and ultimately stop the client's drug use
    d.   Document the discussion and refer the client to a physician

12. After a family session where a family's 15-year-old daughter believed the CSW sided with the mother instead of the daughter, the daughter comes to the next session wearing earbuds she refuses to take out, and demanding an apology from the CSW. The CSW should:

    a.   Consider whether the daughter is correct, and if appropriate, offer an apology
    b.   Side with the mother again, reinforcing the appropriate power hierarchy in the family
    c.   Refuse to go on with therapy until the 15-year-old removes her earbuds
    d.   Demand an apology from the 15-year-old

13. A CSW is running a therapy group for adults abused as children. Given the sensitive nature of the group, the CSW wants to begin with a discussion about privacy. Group members ask the CSW whether they can share information they learn in the group with their significant others at home. The most appropriate course of action would be for the CSW to:

  a. Remind group members of their legal obligation to keep information confidential
  b. Discuss with the group why privacy is important to the success of the group process
  c. Remind group members of their ethical obligation to keep information confidential
  d. Discuss with the group what they believe the appropriate rules should be around such disclosures, as well as the consequences for violations of those rules

14. A walk-in client at a local counseling center presents with moderate suicidal ideation and racing thoughts. The front desk worker at the clinic tells an available CSW that the client should be seen immediately, and that the clinic manager has approved skipping the usual intake paperwork to get the client in to see the CSW as quickly as possible, as the client has verbally agreed to be seen. Legally, the CSW must:

  a. Inform the client of the fee for services, and the basis on which the fee is computed, prior to beginning treatment
  b. Demand that the client complete the full standard intake paperwork for the clinic prior to beginning treatment
  c. Inform the client of the limits of confidentiality prior to beginning treatment
  d. Demand that the clinic manager provide approval in writing for skipping the usual intake paperwork, in order to reduce the CSW's potential liability

15. An adult struggling with substance abuse seeks treatment from an LCSW who specializes in Substance Use Disorder. During the intake session, they both realize that they had a brief sexual relationship 20 years earlier. The client laughs and says, "It looks like you've done well for yourself. I've had a harder time, as you can see." The LCSW asks whether the client is concerned about saying more, given their prior relationship. "No, it's fine," the client says. The LCSW should:

    a. Assess for crisis, discontinue the session and provide appropriate referrals

    b. Assess for crisis, continue treatment, and seek consultation

    c. Assess for crisis, and provide the client with a copy of the brochure *Therapy Never Includes Sexual Behavior*

    d. Assess for crisis, continue with initial assessment, and plan to ask again about the client's comfort level at each session

16. A CSW is conducting and researching a group therapy process for adolescents who have been victims of child abuse. The parents of one of the members of the group ask to have their 16-year-old child removed from the group and from the study, noting that they believe the group is making the child's trauma symptoms worse. The parents had been informed of this risk prior to agreeing to put their child in the study. The CSW should:

    a. Remind the parents of the agreement they signed outlining the risks of the research, and attempt to convince them to keep their child in the group

    b. Remind the parents of the agreement they signed outlining the risks of the research, and leave the decision about participation up to the child

    c. Remove the child from the group, and take steps to resolve any negative impacts the group caused for the child

    d. Take steps to resolve any negative impacts the group caused for the child, and keep the child in the group based on the parents' initial agreement

17. A CSW working in a middle school setting is confronted by a mother who is upset that the CSW has not filed a child abuse report over the bullying her daughter has faced. The daughter is regularly taunted by other girls at the school and has been injured in some shoving matches. Though the daughter has sought to avoid these fights and does not fight back, the CSW defends herself by noting that in each case the girl has been fighting with other girls around the same age and size. The daughter is a regular client of the CSW, and the mother has attended some sessions. The CSW must:

    a. Contact her local child protective service agency to report the mother for failing to protect her child
    b. Contact her local child protective service agency to report physical abuse of the daughter
    c. Contact the school principal to discuss the mother's concerns
    d. Calmly explain to the mother why her daughter's injuries are not considered problematic

18. An LCSW begins a therapeutic relationship with a local schoolteacher. Several months later, the LCSW's daughter starts 3rd grade, and the daughter's class is taught by the client. There is only one teacher for the grade level at that school. How can the LCSW best address their obligations in this situation?

    a. Clarify therapeutic boundaries and transfer the daughter to a different school for the year
    b. Acknowledge the risk of exploitation, clarify therapeutic boundaries, and seek regular consultation
    c. Clarify therapeutic boundaries and request that the client carefully document conversations outside of therapy about the daughter, to ensure that no abuse of power is occurring
    d. Assess the client's comfort level, and do not attend any school events for the year

19. A CSW receives a subpoena from the attorney for an Italian restaurant where a client of the CSW formerly worked. The subpoena requests the client's complete clinical record, and notes that the client is suing the restaurant over the client's firing. The client claims that the firing was discriminatory and caused damage to her mental health. How should the CSW respond to the subpoena?

   a. Contact the client, determine her wishes, and encourage her to allow the records to be released now since the situation is an exception to confidentiality.
   b. Contact the client, and assert privilege if she desires.
   c. Contact the court, assert privilege, and do not respond directly to the attorney since a private subpoena is not a court order.
   d. Contact the court, assert privilege, and respond to the subpoena by saying that records cannot be released without the client's signed consent.

20. A group therapy client informs other group members that she has opened a bakery, and is willing to provide the other group members with a discount on purchases there. The client extends this offer to the CSW who facilitates the group, and clarifies that this is simply a way of saying "thank you" for running the group; the client does not expect any special treatment in return. The CSW should:

   a. Politely refuse the offer
   b. Consider the clinical and cultural implications of accepting or rejecting the offer
   c. Determine whether the value of the discount would be more than $25
   d. Discourage group members from using the discount they have been offered

21. Two clients in a therapy group have become friends outside of the group. They often arrive to group together and appear to share inside jokes during the group. Other group members express concern to the CSW running the group that they are being made fun of or that what they share in the group may come up between these two friends outside of group. The CSW should:

    a. Encourage concerned members to express their concerns in the group
    b. Reassure concerned members that ethically the two friends cannot share information from the group outside of the group context
    c. Remove one of the two friends from the group and refer them to another group
    d. Demand that the two members who have become friends explain to the group the nature of their friendship and any group-related conversations they have had outside of the group

22. A female CSW finds herself becoming increasingly blunt and even harsh with a client who is overweight and experiencing depression. The CSW realizes she is judging the client for the client's weight and her apparent lack of interest in resolving any of the personal or relational struggles that the CSW believes are perpetuating the client's depressive symptoms. The client continues attending therapy and reporting attempts to complete homework assigned by the therapist, but without improvement. The CSW should:

    a. Seek consultation and attempt to repair the therapeutic relationship
    b. Seek consultation and refer the client to a therapist who does not share the CSW's weight bias
    c. Refer the client out and seek additional training to recognize and not blame the client for common correlates to depression
    d. Refer the client out as it does not appear that therapy has a reasonable likelihood of success

23. An LCSW in private practice has a new adult client, who describes a variety of troubling experiences in prior therapy with another local LCSW. As the client describes it, the prior therapist pressured the client for advance payment for sessions, raised the client's fees frequently and without warning, and at one point asked the client for a significant loan. To address their ethical responsibilities, the LCSW now seeing this client should:

    a.   Report the colleague to the BBS based on the client description
    b.   Confront the colleague on their behavior, without revealing how they learned about it
    c.   Inform the client that descriptions of unethical or unprofessional behavior are an exception to confidentiality
    d.   Inform the client of the process for reporting the prior therapist's behavior

24. A military family in treatment with a CSW for four months comes into session appearing dazed, as the mother has learned she will be deployed to Germany in a matter of weeks. The family will be moving with her and will need to discontinue treatment upon their moving date, they say, even though the treatment is incomplete. The CSW should:

    a.   Discuss the transition, consider increasing the frequency of sessions in the remaining weeks, and encourage the family to continue therapy with a local provider during the deployment
    b.   Empower the mother to delay the deployment, discuss the possibility of transition, and consider adding individual sessions with the mother
    c.   Assess for substance abuse, discuss the transition, and offer to provide online therapy during the deployment
    d.   Consider the deployment a "pause" rather than an ending of therapy, and encourage the family to continue treatment once they return

25. A clinical social worker in a cash-pay private practice notices that several clients have unpaid balances. Some of those with unpaid balances attend the same religious service as the CSW. As the CSW considers how to resolve the unpaid balances, how can the CSW best address their legal responsibilities?

    a. Forgive the balances of those in the religious group, and consider it a donation to that group
    b. Terminate the clients with unpaid balances above $250, refusing to release records or provide other documentation or referrals until the balance is paid
    c. Work with each client with an unpaid balance to develop a payment plan
    d. Charge fees for unpaid balances, to discourage clients from carrying balances in the future. Inform all clients of the new fee and how much, if any, they additionally owe

- STOP HERE -
END OF TEST

Mini-Mock Exam:
Answers and Rationales

Mini-Mock Exam: Quick Answer Key

1.	C	8.	D	15.	A	22.	A
2.	C	9.	B	16.	C	23.	D
3.	D	10.	C	17.	B	24.	A
4.	C	11.	D	18.	B	25.	C
5.	C	12.	A	19.	B		
6.	C	13.	D	20.	B		
7.	B	14.	A	21.	A		

1. A 57-year-old Armenian woman has been diagnosed with a psychotic disorder by an LCSW working at a community clinic. The client has an extensive history of risk-taking behavior in manic phases, followed by periods of relative stability. She calls the LCSW to let the social worker know that she has been stable long enough that she has chosen to discontinue her medication. When asked about risk-taking, the client acknowledges having gone cliff diving, climbing to the top of a carnival's ferris wheel, and almost getting into a knife fight, all within the past 36 hours. She says she's "doing much better without help than I ever did with it." How should the social worker proceed?

   a. **Incorrect.** Ask the client to come into the office for a full assessment as soon as possible
   b. **Incorrect.** Ask the client for permission to contact her physician and discuss her medication decision
   c. **CORRECT.** Ask the client for her current location, and begin the process of involuntary hospitalization
   d. **Incorrect.** Ask the client to self-assess her own current functioning to develop insight around her risk level

The client's current risk-taking is dangerous, and even potentially fatal, to her. This risk-taking is a direct result of her mental health condition. She does not appear interested in receiving help on a voluntary basis. Of the options presented, beginning the process of involuntary hospitalization is the most appropriate.

2. A 31-year-old male client is on probation for assault, and one condition of the probation is that the client attend therapy to address anger and substance use concerns. Six months into therapy, the client informs the LCSW providing treatment that the client wishes to discontinue. The client reports believing he has "gotten everything out of it that I can," and that he is growing frustrated with the expense. He notes that he has not had any angry outbursts in the past three months. Considering the LCSW's ethical obligations, how should the LCSW proceed?

    a. **Incorrect.** Encourage the client to remain in treatment

    b. **Incorrect.** Offer to write a letter to the court describing the client's successful completion of mental health treatment and encouraging the court to release the client from their remaining obligation

    c. **CORRECT.** Inform the client of the potential consequences of discontinuing treatment, including the possibility that their probation may be revoked

    d. **Incorrect.** Consult with the probation office about how to proceed with a treatment mandate when treatment is no longer warranted

The client may believe they have gotten as much as they could from treatment, but the question does not specify whether the goals of treatment (in particular, those around substance use) have been met. As such, it would be premature for the social worker to declare that treatment is complete or no longer necessary. The social worker can best support the client's autonomy by informing them of the potential consequences of discontinuing at this stage.

3. A social worker in private practice has been working with a well-known movie actor who has talked publicly about his struggles with mental illness and sobriety, even mentioning the social worker by name when discussing his treatment. The actor dies of an unexpected heart attack, and while the death is under investigation, the social worker begins receiving requests from newspapers and other media outlets to provide more information on the actor's recent mental health and substance use. Considering the social worker's ethical responsibilities, the social worker should:

    a. **Incorrect.** Provide a treatment summary, under the public-interest exception to confidentiality
    b. **Incorrect.** Provide a treatment summary, under the death exception to confidentiality
    c. **Incorrect.** Contact the actor's family to determine who controls privilege now that the actor has died
    d. **CORRECT.** Refuse all media requests for information

There is no public interest or death exception to confidentiality in the NASW code of ethics. Quite the opposite. Social workers are specifically directed by the code to protect client confidentiality when receiving information requests from members of the media. (Privilege is a legal issue, not an ethical one, making the privilege response incorrect.)

4. An LCSW is working for an agency that contracts with a local private school to provide mental health services. The social worker is called to the school to assess a 9-year-old girl who has been falling asleep in class. The girl's teacher tells the social worker that the teacher is concerned in part because the girl recently wrote a story as part of a class assignment, and in the story a young girl wasn't allowed to sleep when she got into trouble at home. During the assessment, the girl repeatedly asks whether she can take a nap, and refuses to answer any questions about the story she wrote. Asked how things are at home, the girl will only say, "I got in trouble. I'm always getting in trouble." The girl is being raised by a single mother, and the school nurse says that the girl is otherwise in relatively good health, but that her grades have been dropping and her behavior in class has been increasingly disorganized. How should the social worker proceed?

a. **Incorrect.** Contact the mother to inform her of the child's behavior and the school's concerns
b. **Incorrect.** Contact the child's physician to request a medical assessment
c. **CORRECT.** Report suspected child abuse
d. **Incorrect.** Ask the child directly whether she is being physically abused or neglected

The child's statements and behavior are enough to reasonably suspect that she is being kept from sleeping at home as a punishment. While the social worker does not have certainty, such certainty is not required to develop reasonable suspicion. A report here (under the category of "Willful harm or endangerment") is appropriate.

5. An LCSW is distressed to learn that a former client has posted a detailed account of the client's therapy online in the form of an article. While the article is mostly positive, it mentions the LCSW by name and includes some incorrect information about the LCSW's qualifications. The LCSW notices that it is possible to leave comments on the article. The LCSW should:

a. **Incorrect.** Post a comment in response to the article, thanking the author while also correcting the errors. *Clients do not give up their right to confidentiality even when they voluntarily discuss their therapy. Acknowledging the social worker-client relationship in the absence of a release to do so can be considered a breach of confidentiality even if the client has already discussed the therapy publicly.*

b. **Incorrect.** Contact the site owners to ask that the article be taken down, without specifying whether the writer was actually a client. *While the LCSW should correct the errors, asking that the article be taken down is overstepping. Respecting client autonomy includes respecting their right to share their experiences in therapy as they see fit. There is nothing here to indicate that taking down the article would be necessary or helpful.*

c. **CORRECT.** Contact the former client directly to encourage them to correct the article. *LCSWs have an ethical obligation to correct misinformation about their qualifications once they discover it. In this case, contacting the former client directly appears to be the most appropriate means to do so.*

d. **Incorrect.** No action is called for. *While the LCSW must be respectful of the client's autonomy and their right to share therapy experiences as they see fit, the LCSW also has an obligation to take reasonable steps to correct misinformation about their qualifications.*

6. An adult client tells a CSW that the client's 89-year-old mother is in hospice care. The client goes on to say that the hospice staff have been screening the mother's mail and phone calls, as they are concerned that she would fall prey to financial scammers who target the elderly. The client tells the CSW that the mother has severe dementia and that the client believes the screening of mail and phone calls is appropriate. The client also says the staff has never refused him access to his mother. The CSW should:

    a. **Incorrect.** Obtain a release from the client, contact the hospice directly, and gather more information about the mother's diagnosis and the need for mail and calls to be screened. *Even if there were evidence of abuse, the CSW should not take on an investigator role.*

    b. **Incorrect.** Report suspected elder abuse to the CSW's local adult protective service agency. *There is no evidence of abuse here.*

    c. **CORRECT.** Maintain the client's confidentiality. *It appears to the client, and as presented to the CSW, that the hospice's actions in screening mail and phone calls are appropriate. Further, they are not refusing the client access to his mother.*

    d. **Incorrect.** Empower the client to gather more information on the mother's diagnosis and the need for mail and calls to be screened, and ask the client to bring that information to a future session for the client and the CSW to review together. *There does not appear to be reason for the CSW to suggest concerns to the client, nor is there reason for the CSW and client to investigate together.*

7. A CSW is surprised to see that her new client did not complete the CSW's standard informed consent paperwork in the waiting room prior to their scheduled session. The CSW brings the client into her therapy office, where the client says that he can only read and write in Spanish. He speaks English fluently, and says he prefers that his therapy sessions be in English. The CSW only speaks and writes in English. Ethically, the therapist should:

a. **Incorrect.** Have a verbal conversation to establish informed consent, and have the client sign the informed consent document. *There is no requirement or ethical preference that informed consent be provided via signature; it is enough to document informed consent in session notes.*

b. **CORRECT.** Have a verbal conversation to establish informed consent, and document that conversation in session notes. *Informed consent can be provided verbally and documented appropriately.*

c. **Incorrect.** Provide a Spanish translation of her informed consent documents as soon as possible, for the client to read and sign. *While a Spanish language version of the informed consent may be useful to have, since the CSW does not read in Spanish, there may be issues with translation that the CSW would not be aware of. The client may then have a different understanding of what they have consented to than the therapist would.*

d. **Incorrect.** Have a verbal conversation about informed consent, and offer to provide a Spanish language translation of her informed consent documents as soon as possible. *Since the client understands English well, the conversation is likely to be sufficient. Since the CSW does not read in Spanish, there may be issues with translation that the CSW would not be aware of. The client may then have a different understanding of what they have consented to than the therapist would.*

8. A 20-year-old client who identifies her family background as Chinese starts therapy with an LCSW. The client describes herself as a social media influencer with about 1 million followers, and says that she posts about 20 minutes of video online each day. She tells the LCSW she is coming to therapy after family members expressed concern that she may be depressed. She tells the LCSW in session "I feel like such a faker with every video I post." Considering their ethical responsibilities, the LCSW should:

    a. **Incorrect.** Anonymously review the client's public social media posts, without commenting on them

    b. **Incorrect.** After session, contact the family members to learn more about their concerns

    c. **Incorrect.** After session, digitally request to be added as a "friend" or "follower" on the client's social media accounts, so that the client can make an informed choice as to whether to do so

    d. **CORRECT.** In session, ask the client's permission to review their public social media postings

Even when clients' web sites or social media profiles are public-facing, social workers are expected to seek permission to review this information unless there is "compelling clinical reason" to do otherwise. Here, there's no reason why the LCSW couldn't ask permission in session, and they should do so. Social workers should not become "friends" with clients on social media, and should not contact family in the absence of permission to do so or an applicable exception to confidentiality, neither of which appears to be present here.

9. During an unusually tense family session, a mother confronts a CSW on the CSW's recent filing of a written report of suspected child abuse. The mother feels violated and reports that she can no longer trust the CSW. Other family members attempt to calm the mother, but share her concerns. The CSW should:

a. **Incorrect.** Discontinue treatment, as the therapeutic relationship has been irreparably compromised. *While there may have been damage to the therapeutic relationship, attempts to repair are appropriate before deciding that therapy is a lost cause.*

b. **CORRECT.** Remind the family of the limits of confidentiality, and seek to regain the family's trust. *The ethics code reminds CSWs that circumstances may require multiple discussions of the limits of confidentiality.*

c. **Incorrect.** In the interest of full disclosure, inform the mother that follow-up reports to the local child protective service agency may be necessary. *When written reports are filed, the therapist has discharged their responsibility by filing the report, and does not need to file follow-up reports unless new instances of abuse emerge.*

d. **Incorrect.** Ask to speak to the other family members without the mother present, to determine whether there is an appropriate path forward for therapy. *Speaking to other family members without the mother present would likely only further her distrust of the CSW and harm the therapeutic relationship.*

10. A client mandated for treatment by his county probation office returns to therapy after a six-month absence. He informs the CSW that he needs records of his progress in treatment sent to his probation officer before his next court date, and provides a Release of Information allowing those records to be sent. The CSW assesses the client and determines he is not in crisis. However, he carries a balance due of more than $500 from sessions he attended but did not pay for prior to being absent from therapy. The CSW should:

a. **Incorrect.** Continue with treatment at a reduced fee, and refuse to turn over records until at least a portion of the balance is paid. *Ethically a CSW must provide reasonable access to records. It is likely to be considered unethical to refuse to turn over records simply because the client owes money.*

b. **Incorrect.** Continue with treatment at a reduced fee, and refuse to turn over records until the outstanding balance is paid in full. *Ethically a CSW must provide reasonable access to records. It is likely to be considered unethical to refuse to turn over records simply because the client owes money.*

c. **CORRECT.** Consider terminating the client if he will be unable to pay his balance, and turn over records to the probation officer. *Termination for non-payment of fees can be ethical. The client has requested and authorized the release of records.*

d. **Incorrect.** Consider terminating the client if he will be unable to pay his balance, and notify the probation officer of the outstanding balance. *The probation officer is not involved in the payment agreement between therapist and client; disclosing the client's balance is not necessary or in the client's best interests.*

11. A 14-year-old client consented to her own treatment at a nonprofit agency, which agreed to treat her for $5/session. The client tells the therapist (a CSW) that the client has been abusing a friend's prescription painkillers. Legally, the CSW should:

    a. **Incorrect.** Notify the local child protective service agency.
    b. **Incorrect.** Notify the client's parent or guardian, as the behavior is considered high-risk.
    c. **Incorrect.** Work with the client to develop a plan to gradually reduce dosage and ultimately stop the client's drug use.
    d. **CORRECT.** Document the discussion and refer the client to a physician.

Drug use, in and of itself, is not considered child abuse (a). No such report is needed. Since the client consented to treatment on their own, the parents do not have a right to the client's records; even a high-risk behavior would not be disclosed (b) unless doing so was to prevent imminent danger. Advising the client on reducing prescription drug dosage would be considered giving medical advice and is out of an CSW's scope of practice. A referral to a physician (d) is appropriate.

12. After a family session where a family's 15-year-old daughter believed the CSW sided with the mother instead of the daughter, the daughter comes to the next session wearing earbuds she refuses to take out, and demanding an apology from the CSW. The CSW should:

   a. **CORRECT.** Consider whether the daughter is correct, and if appropriate, offer an apology.
   b. **Incorrect.** Side with the mother again, reinforcing the appropriate power hierarchy in the family.
   c. **Incorrect.** Refuse to go on with therapy until the 15-year-old removes her earbuds.
   d. **Incorrect.** Demand an apology from the 15-year-old.

Remember that this test is asking about your *legal and ethical responsibilities,* not your clinical skills. (Those will be tested in the Clinical Exam.) This question is about preserving the therapeutic relationship with each individual client in a family system. That may mean offering an apology to a client who feels wronged. There may be clinical reasons in support of the other response choices, but only option A addresses the ethical need to manage conflicts that can arise when working with more than one family member in the room.

13. A CSW is running a therapy group for adults abused as children. Given the sensitive nature of the group, the CSW wants to begin with a discussion about privacy. Group members ask the CSW whether they can share information they learn in the group with their significant others at home. The most appropriate course of action would be for the CSW to:

    a. **Incorrect.** Remind group members of their legal obligation to keep information confidential.
    b. **Incorrect.** Discuss with the group why privacy is important to the success of the group process.
    c. **Incorrect.** Remind group members of their ethical obligation to keep information confidential.
    d. **CORRECT.** Discuss with the group what they believe the appropriate rules should be around such disclosures, as well as the consequences for violations of those rules.

Group members do not have legal or ethical obligations particular to being a client (A and C). Clear guidelines are needed, but the group can come up with their preferred guidelines with the therapist's guidance. Simply discussing why privacy is important (B) would not answer the group members' question about whether sharing information in a limited context with a trusted partner would be allowed.

14. A walk-in client at a local counseling center presents with moderate suicidal ideation and racing thoughts. The front desk worker at the clinic tells an available CSW that the client should be seen immediately, and that the clinic manager has approved skipping the usual intake paperwork to get the client in to see the CSW as quickly as possible, as the client has verbally agreed to be seen. Legally, the CSW must:

a. **CORRECT.** Inform the client of the fee for services, and the basis on which the fee is computed, prior to beginning treatment. *Informing the client of the fee and the basis on which it was computed are legal obligations. While the client is experiencing moderate suicidal ideation, there is no further evidence in the vignette to suggest that the CSW could not take the minimal amount of time needed to fulfill these obligations, or that doing so would somehow be dangerous.*

b. **Incorrect.** Demand that the client complete the full standard intake paperwork for the clinic prior to beginning treatment. *This may not be necessary, as the standard paperwork may include a great deal of information gathering that is not legally or ethically required and that may be reasonably deprioritized to assess for safety.*

c. **Incorrect.** Inform the client of the limits of confidentiality prior to beginning treatment. *This is an ethical, rather than a legal, obligation.*

d. **Incorrect.** Demand that the clinic manager provide approval in writing for skipping the usual intake paperwork, in order to reduce the CSW's potential liability. *While the CSW should document their permission from the clinic manager, and to have it in writing might be particularly helpful, this is not a legal requirement, and placing such a demand ahead of caring for the client is to place the CSW's interests ahead of those of the client.*

15. An adult struggling with substance abuse seeks treatment from an LCSW who specializes in Substance Use Disorder. During the intake session, they both realize that they had a brief sexual relationship 20 years earlier. The client laughs and says, "It looks like you've done well for yourself. I've had a harder time, as you can see." The LCSW asks whether the client is concerned about saying more, given their prior relationship. "No, it's fine," the client says. The LCSW should:

    a. **CORRECT.** Assess for crisis, discontinue the session, and provide appropriate referrals

    b. **Incorrect.** Assess for crisis, continue treatment, and seek consultation

    c. **Incorrect.** Assess for crisis, and provide the client with a copy of the brochure *Therapy Never Includes Sexual Behavior*

    d. **Incorrect.** Assess for crisis, continue with initial assessment, and plan to ask again about the client's comfort level at each session

Regardless of how long ago the relationship occurred or how brief it was, the social worker cannot engage in therapy with a prior sexual partner. The social worker should discontinue the session and provide appropriate referrals.

16. A CSW is conducting and researching a group therapy process for adolescents who have been victims of child abuse. The parents of one of the members of the group ask to have their 16-year-old child removed from the group and from the study, noting that they believe the group is making the child's trauma symptoms worse. The parents had been informed of this risk prior to agreeing to put their child in the study. The CSW should:

    a.   **Incorrect.** Remind the parents of the agreement they signed outlining the risks of the research, and attempt to convince them to keep their child in the group.

    b.   **Incorrect.** Remind the parents of the agreement they signed outlining the risks of the research, and leave the decision about participation up to the child.

    c.   **CORRECT.** Remove the child from the group, and take steps to resolve any negative impacts the group caused for the child.

    d.   **Incorrect.** Take steps to resolve any negative impacts the group caused for the child, and keep the child in the group based on the parents' initial agreement.

One of the rights of research participants is the right to withdraw participation at any time; with minors, this includes the right of parents to withdraw their child's participation. The fact that the parents signed an agreement at the beginning of the study, indicating that they understood the risks of the study, does not change their right to withdraw their child.

17. A CSW working in a middle school setting is confronted by a mother who is upset that the CSW has not filed a child abuse report over the bullying her daughter has faced. The daughter is regularly taunted by other girls at the school and has been injured in some shoving matches. Though the daughter has sought to avoid these fights and does not fight back, the CSW defends herself by noting that in each case the girl has been fighting with other girls around the same age and size. The daughter is a regular client of the CSW, and the mother has attended some sessions. The CSW must:

    a. **Incorrect.** Contact her local child protective service agency to report the mother for failing to protect her child. *It is not the mother's job to protect the child while the child is at school.*

    b. **CORRECT.** Contact her local child protective service agency to report physical abuse of the daughter. *While there is an exception to the physical abuse reporting standards when children engage in willful mutual combat ("a mutual affray between minors," according to section 11165.6 of the Penal Code), the fact that the girl here is seeking to avoid these fights is critical. It means that they cannot accurately be described as mutual. Even when the combatants are of similar age and size, if one is being pushed into combat against their will, it can qualify as physical abuse under the law.*

    c. **Incorrect.** Contact the school principal to discuss the mother's concerns. *This would raise confidentiality concerns and would not resolve the CSW's reporting responsibility.*

    d. **Incorrect.** Calmly explain to the mother why her daughter's injuries are not considered problematic. *This would not resolve the CSW's reporting responsibility (see the rationale above for response B).*

18. An LCSW begins a therapeutic relationship with a local schoolteacher. Several months later, the LCSW's daughter starts 3rd grade, and the daughter's class is taught by the client. There is only one teacher for the grade level at that school. How can the LCSW best address their obligations in this situation?

a. **Incorrect.** Clarify therapeutic boundaries and transfer the daughter to a different school for the year
b. **CORRECT.** Acknowledge the risk of exploitation, clarify therapeutic boundaries, and seek regular consultation
c. **Incorrect.** Clarify therapeutic boundaries and request that the client carefully document conversations outside of therapy about the daughter, to ensure that no abuse of power is occurring
d. **Incorrect.** Assess the client's comfort level, and do not attend any school events for the year

With any dual relationship, social workers are required to assess the risk of exploitation and the potential for impaired clinical judgment. Both are present here, but not to high degrees. The risk of exploitation comes from the possibility that the social worker could use what she learns in therapy about the teacher to push for special treatment for the social worker's daughter. The potential impairment of clinical judgment stems from the possibility that their interactions surrounding the daughter's behavior in school will influence how the social worker treats the client in session. All of that said, monitoring this situation and seeking consultation are better than the other options here. Transferring the daughter or refusing to attend school events may raise questions for the daughter and others, and might even reveal the therapeutic relationship. Asking the client to document conversations about the daughter is improper as it makes the client responsible for the social worker's ethical compliance.

19. A CSW receives a subpoena from the attorney for an Italian restaurant where a client of the CSW formerly worked. The subpoena requests the client's complete clinical record, and notes that the client is suing the restaurant over the client's firing. The client claims that the firing was discriminatory and caused damage to her mental health. How should the CSW respond to the subpoena?

    a. **Incorrect.** Contact the client, determine her wishes, and encourage her to allow the records to be released now since the situation is an exception to confidentiality. *As described earlier in this guide, an exception to privilege does exist in law for when someone sues another party and makes their mental or emotional state an issue in the lawsuit. However, advising the client on a legal matter such as this would likely be considered outside the CSW's scope of practice.*

    b. **CORRECT.** Contact the client, and assert privilege if she desires. *An exception to privilege may apply because of the lawsuit, but that is for a judge to determine if the client objects to the records being released.*

    c. **Incorrect.** Contact the court, assert privilege, and do not respond directly to the attorney since a private subpoena is not a court order. *While a private subpoena is indeed not the same as a court order, simply failing to respond may land the therapist in trouble with the court. It would be better to respond by asserting privilege, if that is the client's desire -- and knowing the client's wishes would require first contacting the client, not the court.*

    d. **Incorrect.** Contact the court, assert privilege, and respond to the subpoena by saying that records cannot be released without the client's signed consent. *It is the client, not the court, that should be contacted first. You can then act in accordance with her wishes, at least until the court makes a determination as to whether an exception to privilege applies. The remainder of this option is also incorrect as there are exceptions to privilege (including one that likely applies here) that would allow records to be released absent the client's consent, if a judge determines this to be appropriate.*

20. A group therapy client informs other group members that she has opened a bakery, and is willing to provide the other group members with a discount on purchases there. The client extends this offer to the CSW who facilitates the group, and clarifies that this is simply a way of saying "thank you" for running the group; the client does not expect any special treatment in return. The CSW should:

  a. **Incorrect.** Politely refuse the offer. *The CSW is not prohibited by state law or professional ethical codes from accepting the gift. The word "must" in the question is key – the CSW **may** refuse the offer if they choose, but they do not have to.*
  b. **CORRECT.** Consider the clinical and cultural implications of accepting or rejecting the offer. *The NASW Code of Ethics does not directly mention gifts at all, but these considerations would still be vital to determining whether the therapeutic relationship would be compromised.*
  c. **Incorrect.** Determine whether the value of the discount would be more than $25. *Current ethical guidelines do not limit a CSW's ability to receive gifts based on the monetary value of the gift.*
  d. **Incorrect.** Discourage group members from using the discount they have been offered. *While the CSW may be wise to have a discussion with the group to clarify that there is no expectation of a return favor, the CSW is not obligated to discourage the group from using the discount they have been offered.*

21. Two clients in a therapy group have become friends outside of the group. They often arrive to group together and appear to share inside jokes during the group. Other group members express concern to the CSW running the group that they are being made fun of or that what they share in the group may come up between these two friends outside of group. The CSW should:

    a. **CORRECT.** Encourage concerned members to express their concerns in the group. *This best preserves client autonomy and the integrity of the group process. It also would invite a conversation about how group members should handle confidentiality among each other.*

    b. **Incorrect.** Reassure concerned members that ethically the two friends cannot share information from the group outside of the group context. *Ethics are the responsibility of the therapist running the group. While social workers should discuss client roles and obligations to one another early in the group process, clients do not have an inherent ethical responsibility to each other. The CSW also cannot guarantee that group members will respect the rules of the group.*

    c. **Incorrect.** Remove one of the two friends from the group and refer them to another group. *This would be punitive and could do more harm than good. It would be an overreaction to the situation of two group members becoming friends.*

    d. **Incorrect.** Demand that the two members who have become friends explain to the group the nature of their friendship and any group-related conversations they have had outside of the group. *Forcing client disclosure to other group members goes against client autonomy and could be considered a misuse of the therapist's power. Clients have the right to disclose only that information they want to disclose to the group.*

22. A female CSW finds herself becoming increasingly blunt and even harsh with a client who is overweight and experiencing depression. The CSW realizes she is judging the client for the client's weight and her apparent lack of interest in resolving any of the personal or relational struggles that the CSW believes are perpetuating the client's depressive symptoms. The client continues attending therapy and reporting attempts to complete homework assigned by the therapist, but without improvement. The CSW should:

a. **CORRECT.** Seek consultation and attempt to repair the therapeutic relationship. *The client's continued efforts suggest that the therapeutic relationship has not been damaged beyond repair. The CSW and client are both best served by the CSW seeking to understand and correct her personal biases while continuing to treat.*

b. **Incorrect.** Seek consultation and refer the client to a therapist who does not share the CSW's weight bias. *A therapist bias does not always require a referral. In some instances it is better to continue treatment while managing the bias and repairing the relationship. In this case, the client's continued efforts suggest that the relationship can be preserved.*

c. **Incorrect.** Refer the client out and seek additional training to recognize and not blame the client for common correlates to depression. *A therapist bias does not always require a referral. In some instances it is better to continue treatment while managing the bias and repairing the relationship. In this case, the client's continued efforts suggest that the relationship can be preserved.*

d. **Incorrect.** Refer the client out as it does not appear that therapy has a reasonable likelihood of success. *Nothing in the question stem suggests that therapy is hopeless. It is possible that the CSW's efforts to address her own biases and repair the therapeutic relationship could lead to meaningful gains.*

23. An LCSW in private practice has a new adult client, who describes a variety of troubling experiences in prior therapy with another local LCSW. As the client describes it, the prior therapist pressured the client for advance payment for sessions, raised the client's fees frequently and without warning, and at one point asked the client for a significant loan. To address their ethical responsibilities, the LCSW now seeing this client should:

   a. **Incorrect.** Report the colleague to the BBS based on the client description
   b. **Incorrect.** Confront the colleague on their behavior, without revealing how they learned about it
   c. **Incorrect.** Inform the client that descriptions of unethical or unprofessional behavior are an exception to confidentiality
   d. **CORRECT.** Inform the client of the process for reporting the prior therapist's behavior

Unprofessional conduct does not qualify as an exception to confidentiality under California law. While social workers are ethically obligated to take appropriate action to expose and prevent the unethical conduct of colleagues, here, that must be done by informing the client of the reporting process. Reporting the colleague directly, or confronting the colleague on their behavior, would be a violation of confidentiality in this instance.

24. A military family in treatment with a CSW for four months comes into session appearing dazed, as the mother has learned she will be deployed to Germany in a matter of weeks. The family will be moving with her and will need to discontinue treatment upon their moving date, they say, even though the treatment is incomplete. The CSW should:

   a. **CORRECT.** Discuss the transition, consider increasing the frequency of sessions in the remaining weeks, and encourage the family to continue therapy with a local provider during the deployment. *Given that their treatment is incomplete, it would be better for them to continue it with a local provider during the deployment than to simply wait out the deployment while family problems continue.*

   b. **Incorrect.** Empower the mother to delay the deployment, discuss the possibility of transition, and consider adding individual sessions with the mother. *It is unlikely that the mother could delay the deployment; even if she could, adding individual sessions while family sessions continue would be a potential conflict of interests.*

   c. **Incorrect.** Assess for substance abuse, discuss the transition, and offer to provide online therapy during the deployment. *There is nothing in the vignette to indicate heightened risk of substance abuse.*

   d. **Incorrect.** Consider the deployment a "pause" rather than an ending of therapy, and encourage the family to continue treatment once they return. *Given that their treatment is incomplete, it would be better for them to continue it with a local provider during the deployment than to simply wait out the deployment while family problems continue.*

25. A clinical social worker in a cash-pay private practice notices that several clients have unpaid balances. Some of those with unpaid balances attend the same religious service as the CSW. As the CSW considers how to resolve the unpaid balances, how can the CSW best address their legal responsibilities?

   a. **Incorrect.** Forgive the balances of those in the religious group, and consider it a donation to that group.
   b. **Incorrect.** Terminate the clients with unpaid balances above $250, refusing to release records or provide other documentation or referrals until the balance is paid.
   c. **CORRECT.** Work with each client with an unpaid balance to develop a payment plan.
   d. **Incorrect.** Charge fees for unpaid balances, to discourage clients from carrying balances in the future. Inform all clients of the new fee and how much, if any, they additionally owe.

Forgiving the balances of those who share the CSW's religious practice, while not forgiving the balances of others (A), would likely be considered discrimination based on religion. Terminating clients for lack of payment (B) can be ethically acceptable, but the CSW cannot legally refuse to release records on the basis of an unpaid balance. While it is legal to charge fees for unpaid balances (D), such fees need to be spelled out to clients *before* they are implemented -- typically in the initial informed consent agreement. Imposing them before informing clients of them would be a violation.

How did you do? If you struggled a bit with these, don't worry. They're designed to help you understand the mechanics of this kind of multiple-choice test. If you've reviewed the rationales carefully, and understand *why* you missed any questions you answered incorrectly, then the mini-mock has done its job. If you are interested in taking a full-length practice test, well, that's up next.

You've got this.

Good luck!

Practice Test: Information

Instructions

There are two answer sheets on the next two pages, which you can tear out of the book and fill in as you are taking the practice test. There are *two* sheets there to give you two attempts at the test. Hopefully if you take the practice test a second time, your score increases. However, you should interpret such increases carefully: It's better if your score improved because you deepened your understanding of the material than if your score improved simply because you memorized some of the correct answers.

Use the practice test here as you see fit! There are a number of different ways you could use it to help you prepare:

1. **Focus on understanding.** In this study method, you would take a practice test untimed, focusing on carefully examining the question and thinking through the available responses. You would then spend a fair amount of time with the *rationale* for each correct answer, making sure that you are deeply understanding the underlying concepts. While of course you hope to get a good score, your scores on the practice exams are not terribly important when understanding is your goal. Any question you answer incorrectly is simply a chance to expand your knowledge and better prepare you for the real test. After all, while the actual test will cover the same content areas as these practice exams, it is unlikely they will ask the same questions in the same ways. You need to be able to understand and apply the key legal and ethical concepts across different clinical situations.

2. **Focus on timing.** In this study method, you would time yourself on each test, making sure you finish within the 90-minute time limit. This also gives you an opportunity to practice any anxiety management techniques you may need, and to practice time management skills like skipping questions you may want to come back to later. Many examinees have reported that they spent more time on the actual test than they did on practice tests, so it's good if you have at least some amount of time left over when you complete the test here.

3. **Focus on performance.** In this study method, a good score is the only goal. As is the case in method 1 above, you still want to make sure you understand why you answered incorrectly on any items you got wrong, but this method is more about confidence-building leading up to your test day. One thing to note if you're focused on your score: Because the real exam varies in difficulty with each exam cycle, it is not safe to presume that a score on any given practice test equates with the same score on the real thing. If you're getting a significant majority of the items on a practice test right, your scores have been steadily improving, and you can understand why any incorrect answers you gave were incorrect, that is probably a better measure of preparedness than any specific score.

There are other, more creative ways you can use the material here as well, such as dividing the questions into three "mini-exams" of 25 questions each, or going through questions and rationales one at a time, flash-card style. I'm a big believer in being pragmatic where studying for an exam is concerned. Do what you know works best for you.

A few cautionary notes

While these questions and responses are written to help prepare you for the California CSW Law and Ethics Exam, it is important to bear in mind that the practice test here (like all practice tests) is an *approximation* of the style and format of the exam itself. The actual exam changes with each 90-day test cycle; some exam cycles have a more difficult exam, while others have an easier exam. This is why the passing score cutoff changes with each cycle, to ensure that examinees aren't disadvantaged by happening into a tougher cycle of the test.

It's also worth noting that, while every effort has been made here to tie these questions with specific and identifiable legal and ethical principles, ethical decision-making isn't always clear-cut. Even on questions where there is a clear correct answer, reasonable arguments can sometimes be made for some of the other response choices. If you find yourself arguing with the rationale on a question, focus your efforts on understanding why the correct response was identified as such.

If you are using multiple practice tests from different sources (for example, if you are using this book alongside practice tests provided by a test prep company), you may find that in some instances, the different sources suggest different answers for similar questions. That can be confusing and anxiety-provoking, but usually has a good explanation. You may be able to find that even minor, technical differences between the questions account for the differences in the best answers. You may also find that one source or another has something wrong – either because the law or ethical standard has changed, or because it has been misinterpreted. All of us (myself included) make mistakes on occasion. Rest assured that for the actual exam, every item must be keyed to an objective standard, so there will always be a current, justifiable best answer. If you find yourself disagreeing with a practice item from any source, and you have a clear legal or ethical rationale supporting your response choice, you're probably in good shape for the actual test. And of course, if you'd like to discuss anything in this book that you think I may have incorrect, please email my team at support@bencaldwelllabs.com and let us know.

Finally, as a reminder of the disclaimer from the beginning of this book, you may find that some questions here resemble situations that you have actually encountered in your practice. However, real clinical situations are by nature more complex than what is typically captured in a multiple-choice exam question. For that reason, nothing here should be construed as legal advice or as a substitute for consulting with a qualified attorney.

Practice Test:
Answer Sheets

California LCSW Law & Ethics Practice Exam

1. ____	21. ____	41. ____	61. ____
2. ____	22. ____	42. ____	62. ____
3. ____	23. ____	43. ____	63. ____
4. ____	24. ____	44. ____	64. ____
5. ____	25. ____	45. ____	65. ____
6. ____	26. ____	46. ____	66. ____
7. ____	27. ____	47. ____	67. ____
8. ____	28. ____	48. ____	68. ____
9. ____	29. ____	49. ____	69. ____
10. ____	30. ____	50. ____	70. ____
11. ____	31. ____	51. ____	71. ____
12. ____	32. ____	52. ____	72. ____
13. ____	33. ____	53. ____	73. ____
14. ____	34. ____	54. ____	74. ____
15. ____	35. ____	55. ____	75. ____
16. ____	36. ____	56. ____	
17. ____	37. ____	57. ____	
18. ____	38. ____	58. ____	
19. ____	39. ____	59. ____	
20. ____	40. ____	60. ____	

California LCSW Law & Ethics Practice Exam

1. ____	21. ____	41. ____	61. ____
2. ____	22. ____	42. ____	62. ____
3. ____	23. ____	43. ____	63. ____
4. ____	24. ____	44. ____	64. ____
5. ____	25. ____	45. ____	65. ____
6. ____	26. ____	46. ____	66. ____
7. ____	27. ____	47. ____	67. ____
8. ____	28. ____	48. ____	68. ____
9. ____	29. ____	49. ____	69. ____
10. ____	30. ____	50. ____	70. ____
11. ____	31. ____	51. ____	71. ____
12. ____	32. ____	52. ____	72. ____
13. ____	33. ____	53. ____	73. ____
14. ____	34. ____	54. ____	74. ____
15. ____	35. ____	55. ____	75. ____
16. ____	36. ____	56. ____	
17. ____	37. ____	57. ____	
18. ____	38. ____	58. ____	
19. ____	39. ____	59. ____	
20. ____	40. ____	60. ____	

Practice Test

1. A client who has expressed great concern about anyone knowing she is in therapy passes out in the middle of a session. The CSW the client was seeing is able to wake her long enough to learn that she has recently been struggling with illness and has pain from a neck injury, and the CSW knows from the client's intake paperwork that she has a blood disorder. The CSW should:

   a. Stay with the client and continue attempting to wake her
   b. Call 911 and transport the client outside of the office into a public area to protect her privacy
   c. Call 911 and summon paramedics without providing any information about the client or her illness
   d. Call 911, summon paramedics, and inform them of the client's medical issues

2. With the client's permission, an LCSW contacts another California psychotherapist who had previously been involved in the client's treatment. The client reported to the LCSW that about a year ago, the other therapist had become confrontational with the client in several sessions, challenging the client with statements like, "Why are you acting like such a baby?" and "Drinking is the coward's way of coping, and you're a coward, so I'm sure you're going to go drink as soon as we're done here." The client reported to the LCSW that these sessions left the client struggling to get out of bed each day, and contributed to the client getting fired for missing work. During their call, the other therapist becomes defensive, and tells the LCSW that the client was unresponsive to more empathetic approaches, and so these confrontations were "I guess, my way of pushing [the client] to take some accountability. That's not a crime." How should the LCSW proceed?

   a. Inform the client of their ability to report the prior therapist to the BBS
   b. Inform the other therapist that their conduct was harmful and is indeed a crime
   c. Ask the client to provide documentation of their decline in functioning and their job loss in response to the prior therapy
   d. Seek to better understand the other therapist's clinical approach

3. A CSW who is new to the community seeks to build her referral base so that she can grow her practice. For those colleagues who refer clients to her, she calls the colleague (without revealing any information about the client) and offers to buy the colleague lunch to say thanks and engage in professional networking. An established CSW in the community receives such an offer from the new CSW after referring a client to the new CSW. How should the established CSW respond?

    a.   Accept the invitation under the condition that they each agree to pay their own bill
    b.   Decline the invitation and report the new CSW to the BBS
    c.   Accept the invitation under the condition that no client information will be discussed
    d.   Accept the invitation and request a release of information from the client allowing the established CSW to discuss the case with the new CSW

4. An LCSW learns that his individual client, who is being seen for symptoms of Bipolar Disorder, is also interested in attending couple therapy with her spouse. The client asks the LCSW whether the couple could see the LCSW together for couple therapy separately from her individual sessions, and says she is willing to sign a release form such that information from her individual sessions could be discussed in couple therapy and vice versa. Ethically, the LCSW should:

    a.   Continue individual treatment with the client and refer out for the couple therapy
    b.   Continue individual treatment with the client and begin concurrent couple therapy, utilizing a separate file with a separate treatment plan
    c.   Inform the client that it would be better to complete individual treatment before engaging in couple therapy, regardless of whether the couple therapy is with the LCSW or another provider
    d.   Discontinue the individual treatment in order to begin couple treatment, with the client's release in place to allow for material from the individual sessions to be discussed in couple work

5. An LCSW is working with a family where the parents are in the process of getting a divorce and are arguing over custody of their two children. Therapy has focused on maintaining effective co-parenting, as neither parent wants an extended court battle. Because the LCSW knows the family well and has seen both parents interacting with the children, the parents ask the LCSW to submit a letter to the court with the LCSW's clinical evaluation of each of their parenting skills. The best course of action for the LCSW would be to:

    a. Obtain a release from all family members, and send the letter to the court, emphasizing that the evaluative statements should not be used to draw conclusions about custody

    b. Obtain a release from all family members, and send the letter to the court, offering specific recommendations for custody based on the LCSW's work with the family and based on the LCSW's knowledge of the wishes of the children

    c. Obtain a release from all family members, and engage in a process of testing and evaluation to draw objective conclusions before completing the letter

    d. Refuse to send the letter

6. The director of an afterschool program contacts an LCSW by phone to refer a 14-year-old girl to the social worker for psychotherapy. The director says that the girl is a participant in the program and has been struggling with extreme shyness. The director further says that the program will be happy to pay for the therapy. The girl, who is with the director in an office, gets on the phone to provide the LCSW with more information. She says she does not want her parents to know she is seeking help. How should the LCSW proceed?

    a. Allow the program director to consent for treatment on the minor's behalf and accept financial responsibility

    b. Inform the minor that one parent must consent to her receiving treatment regardless of how it is being paid for

    c. Assess the maturity of the minor

    d. Allow the minor to consent for treatment on her own, and have her complete a Release of Information so that the program can be billed

7. A young adult client with a history of severe childhood trauma begins weeping in session as she connects her traumatic experiences with her current struggles in building trusting relationships. An LCSW has been providing the client with individual sessions for more than two years, and the client has only even begun to trust the therapist in the past few months. The LCSW notices that the client is having difficulty calming herself, and is shaking in her seat. The client turns to the social worker and softly asks, "Will you please just hold me for a moment, so I can catch my breath?" The client has never made such a request before. Considering her ethical responsibilities, how should the social worker proceed?

    a. Briefly hold the client, and immediately afterward, discuss it in order to reinforce a strong clinical boundary

    b. Briefly hold the client, to support their autonomy. Since the client has not made such a request in more than two years of treatment, it is unlikely that a clarifying conversation is needed

    c. Decline the client's request, while offering a blanket or other means the client can use for calming

    d. Decline the client's request, and when appropriate, re-evaluate the clinical relationship in light of the client's efforts toward dependence

8. A 23-year-old client whose family immigrated to California from Indonesia calls her LCSW to inform the therapist that the client cannot attend therapy for the next three weeks, as the client's sister just had a baby and the client is going to be helping the sister and the sister's partner. The LCSW has been treating the client for post-traumatic stress disorder and wonders whether the treatment has simply been overwhelming for the client. What steps should the LCSW take to fulfill their ethical duties?

    a. Ensure crisis needs are met and a safety plan is in place if needed; schedule a next session for three weeks from now

    b. Offer to reduce the intensity of sessions in exchange for the client remaining consistent in treatment

    c. Seek to understand the client's behavior from a cultural perspective; treat the interruption of therapy as a crisis and intervene accordingly

    d. Wish the client well for the upcoming three weeks; hold the client's usual spot on the LCSW's calendar; ask to see photos of the baby upon the client's return

9. Following a contentious presidential election, an LCSW in private practice is interested in providing care for supporters of the losing candidate. The LCSW advertises short-term grief therapy for the losing candidate's supporters at a 50% reduced rate. A man who was a supporter of the winning candidate asks the LCSW whether he, too, can have the reduced rate, as he is struggling with grief following the retirement of the man's mentor at work. The LCSW should:

    a. Agree to the reduced rate for this client, and alter their advertising to remove mention of the election
    b. Agree to the reduced rate for this client, and for anyone else who asks for it
    c. Agree to the reduced rate for this client, and alter their advertising to clarify that the grief treatment must be focused on the election to qualify for a reduced rate
    d. Cite the language in the LCSW's advertising and inform the client that they do not qualify for the specific rate reduction, but consider their income in setting a fee

10. A CSW is working with an individual client who is employed in the movie industry. The client is emotionally unstable following a breakup. The client informs the CSW that the client will be travelling out of state for the next three weeks to work on a film, and asks whether the CSW can continue to work with the client by phone during that time. The CSW should first:

    a. Assess the severity of the client's symptoms to determine whether phone therapy is appropriate, and if so, proceed with phone sessions
    b. Determine whether they have the requisite qualifications to practice in the state to which the client is travelling
    c. Determine the client's state of residency
    d. Inquire with the BBS as to the appropriateness and legality of phone sessions for this client

11. A social worker who is part of a multidisciplinary treatment team becomes concerned when the team decides to contact the mother of an adult client and ask her to become more involved in treatment. The team made this decision based on the client's worsening symptoms, out of concern that the client may soon need to be hospitalized. The social worker notes that there is not a release in place allowing them to share information with the mother. The social worker should:

    a. Respect the treatment team's decision, and not be personally involved in the efforts to contact the mother

    b. Respect the treatment team's decision, and be prepared to address the client's possible feelings of betrayal

    c. Contact the treatment team and ask to meet with them as soon as possible in an effort to change their decision

    d. Contact the treatment team and inform them that if the team's decision goes forward, the social worker will encourage the client to report a confidentiality violation

12. The individual client of a CSW tells the CSW that he recently took his 94-year-old grandfather, who has been suffering from dementia, on a fishing trip to a nearby lake in a California State Park. He had grown frustrated with the quality of care the grandfather had been receiving at his nursing home, which he said was not adequate to the grandfather's medical needs. He also wanted to give his grandfather "one last hurrah," as he was concerned the grandfather's death was just weeks away. He was angry that the nursing home staff had berated him upon their return for not notifying them he was taking the grandfather for the weekend. Considering the CSW's legal obligations, the CSW should:

    a. Report the nursing home for inadequate care, and the client for abduction

    b. Report the nursing home for inadequate care

    c. Report the client for abduction

    d. Ask the client to clarify how the nursing home's care is inadequate

13. An LCSW in private practice grows frustrated with a client who seems to be frequently in crisis, and determines that the client needs a higher level of care than what the LCSW can provide. The LCSW informs the client in person and in writing that in 30 days the LCSW will no longer provide treatment, and offers referrals to inpatient and partial-hospitalization programs as well as other local crisis resources. As the 30 days approach their end, the client has a scheduled termination session with the LCSW. The client reports that they have not even attempted to contact any of the provided referrals, they don't feel capable of doing so, and they are feeling moderately suicidal but without a specific plan or intent. Ethically, the LCSW should:

    a. Offer to assist the client during session in contacting other service providers to create a warm handoff
    b. Extend the termination deadline by 30 days and encourage the client to contact the referrals previously offered
    c. Terminate as scheduled, and ask the client to sign a release granting the LCSW permission to follow up with a close friend or family member to ensure the client is receiving ongoing care
    d. Terminate as scheduled, and ask the client to sign a release once they are connected with a new treatment provider, so that the new provider and the LCSW can communicate

14. A CSW with a full-time caseload finds herself on the edge of burnout. She notices she is becoming less empathetic and more combative with clients, and frequently arrives at the office in the morning still tired from the day before. A colleague she greatly respects refers her a complex case. The CSW should:

    a. Discontinue or temporarily pause treatment with some of her better-functioning clients in order to take the referral
    b. Take the referral without changing any aspects of treatment for her other clients, and take other steps to manage her burnout
    c. Decline the referral, and consider reducing her overall caseload
    d. Accept the referral on a short-term basis, agreeing only to two sessions with the client in order to better assess their needs

15. A CSW works across the street from a major software company's offices. The CSW begins advertising specifically to employees of the company, using the company's logo on the CSW's website and business cards to say that the CSW is "now proudly serving employees of" that company. One client, who works for the software company and had found the CSW through the website, asks about the relationship between the CSW and the software company. The CSW should:

    a.   Clarify for the client that there is no formal relationship, and that the CSW simply enjoys working with employees of the company

    b.   Clarify for the client that there is no formal relationship, and change the website and business cards to not use the company's logo

    c.   Seek to develop a more formal relationship with the company, including a contract to treat their employees

    d.   Change the website and business cards to indicate that the company's logo is a registered trademark used with permission

16. A client with a history of eating disorder schedules an intake session with an LCSW to discuss the client's current emotional struggles. In the intake, the client reports that prior treatment has been helpful in reducing disordered eating, but that the client still struggles with body image concerns. Referring to prior treatment, the client says, "I learned a lot about monitoring and responding to my body, but not so much about how to prepare food or specifically what to eat." Ethically, the LCSW should:

    a.   Diagnose the client as having an active eating disorder

    b.   Collaborate with the client to determine whether a referral to a dietitian is appropriate

    c.   Request that the client sign a Release of Information for all prior eating disorder treatment providers, allowing the LCSW to request treatment records

    d.   Educate the client about the typical course of eating disorder over the life span

17. A CSW learns that her client's adopted son was recently involved in a series of hit-and-run accidents. At present, law enforcement is investigating but does not know who is responsible. The client expresses fear of all possible outcomes; if the police determine it was her son, the son will likely go to jail. If the police do not determine it was her son, the son may continue with his risky and damaging behavior. The client says she does not want to turn her son in. Considering her legal and ethical obligations, the CSW should:

   a. Report the son to law enforcement as a potential danger to others
   b. Anonymously report the son's actions to law enforcement, without revealing the name of the therapist or the client, and without revealing how the CSW came to know the information
   c. Encourage the client to report the son to law enforcement to reduce the risk that he will harm others in the future
   d. Discuss the client's feelings in greater detail and examine the risks and benefits of various possible courses of action while maintaining the client's confidentiality

18. A polyamorous couple experiencing difficulty in their sexual relationship presents for therapy with a CSW who believes sexual activity outside of a monogamous relationship is inappropriate and harmful. The couple does not believe that their sexual relationships outside of their own relationship are causing their sexual problems with each other. Ethically, the CSW should:

   a. Seek to address underlying emotional issues that may be impacting the couple's sexual relationship, so as to improve the relationship without directly discussing the couple's other partners
   b. Refer the couple to a therapist who does not share the CSW's belief
   c. Inform the clients in advance of her belief, allowing the clients to determine whether they would like to continue therapy with her
   d. Begin therapy by explaining her belief and the underlying research, and explaining that the couple's theory that their polyamory is not related to their own sexual difficulty is unlikely to be true

19. A mother arrives late for her therapy session and is enraged. She reports that she just spent an hour dealing with police, who came to the grocery store where her car was parked and were about to break a window when she returned to the car and stopped them. The police, she said, rudely lectured her about the infant son she had left in the car while she was grocery shopping. While the car was in sunlight, it was only about 80 degrees out at the time and she had been away from the car for less than 20 minutes, she said. The CSW should:

   a. Explore the mother's feelings of anger and shame
   b. Assess whether the son had suffered any harm
   c. Ask for a Release of Information and offer to contact police directly to follow up
   d. Report suspected child neglect

20. A CSW is close to successful termination with a father who has been in treatment for 15 sessions. The father expresses his gratitude to the CSW, and says he would like to find a way to help families with similar needs. The CSW is aware of an online discussion group where the father could share his experience in therapy, steering potential clients toward the CSW and offering hope to families experiencing similar problems to the ones his own family had experienced at the beginning of therapy. Ethically, the CSW should:

   a. Encourage the father to share his experience in the discussion group, including both positive and negative components, and including the CSW's name so that other participants know where they can receive confidential help
   b. Thank the father for his work in therapy, and discuss potential benefits and risks of several potential means by which the father could help similar families
   c. Thank the father for his work in therapy, and discourage him from publicly sharing his experience in the interest of confidentiality
   d. Encourage the father to share his experience in the discussion group but to do so anonymously, only naming the CSW if he chooses to do so

21. A 70-year-old client tells a CSW that the client had been under-medicated for several months while living at a nursing home in Florida the prior year. The CSW asks how the client knows this, and the client says that her prescription specifically noted that her medication should be given twice a day, but she received it only once each day. The CSW believes the client has good cognitive functioning. The CSW should:

    a.   Report suspected elder abuse to the CSW's local adult protective service agency
    b.   Report suspected elder abuse to the adult protective service agency local to the nursing home in Florida
    c.   Encourage the client to report what happened to the appropriate adult protective service agency in Florida
    d.   Encourage the client to document the events for a possible civil lawsuit against the nursing home in Florida

22. A Latina CSW receives a phone call from a prospective new client couple. The couple reports that they moved to the US from India three years ago, and they would like to come to therapy to work on communication difficulty in their marriage. The CSW strives to maintain strong awareness of cultural issues, but has never worked with anyone from India before. The best course of action for the CSW would be to:

    a.   Refer the couple to a therapist of Indian descent
    b.   Encourage the clients to educate the CSW about Indian culture and customs
    c.   Seek resources and consultation to become familiar with Indian culture and customs, and to understand how Indian clients typically present in therapy
    d.   Wait until the clients come in for an initial assessment to determine whether meaningful cultural differences exist

23. A client tells an LCSW that she left her previous therapist after the therapist became erratic and unfocused. The previous therapist's father died six months ago, and the client wonders whether the therapist had been drinking to cope with the loss. The client's previous therapist is also a clinical social worker, and is someone the current LCSW knows personally. The LCSW should:

    a. Apologize on behalf of the colleague. Report the previous therapist to the BBS, as she appears to be unable to provide quality clinical care

    b. Without disclosing what the client said, reach out to the colleague and offer to provide confidential therapy to the colleague to protect clients

    c. Without disclosing what the client said, check in with the colleague. If she volunteers any information about her grief process, encourage the colleague to enter treatment

    d. Directly confront the colleague with what the LCSW knows. Inform the colleague's employer that she may not be healthy enough to provide services

24. Partway through an emotionally difficult session, a client tells their social worker, "My psychic said this was going to get worse before it got better. I guess this what they meant." The LCSW is initially startled, and asks the client more about the psychic. The client notes that they have been going to the same psychic weekly for more than five years, and find the process valuable and reassuring, especially when discussing issues of grief. The LCSW should:

    a. Ask the client's permission to contact the psychic to develop a professional relationship

    b. Discuss the LCSW's concern that the psychic is exploiting the client's fragile emotional state

    c. Express to the client that while the services of the psychic may be helpful, they are not grounded in science

    d. Explore the client's relationship with the psychic to determine whether the psychic has attempted to diagnose or treat mental illness

25. Three months before a local election, a social worker is meeting with a client who serves as campaign director for a prominent local politician. The politician is facing a close race, and the social worker supports the politician in light of the politician's policies related to social and economic justice. The client appears exhausted in session, largely due to the demands of their role. The social worker decides to contact the client after the session to offer encouragement. What message should the social worker send to the client?

    a. I'll be tuning in to the debate next week. Good luck.
    b. Let me know how I and everyone who is on your side can make your job easier.
    c. Keep your head up. I know it's hard. You can do this.
    d. I've just donated $100 to your campaign. It's a small gesture, but I want you to know how much I support the campaign.

26. A couple seeks counseling from an LCSW to address conflict in their relationship. One partner in the couple identifies as asexual, while the other partner angrily suggests that "asexual" is a "cop-out" the first partner is using to avoid taking action on the first partner's lack of sexual desire, which has been a source of conflict for the couple since the birth of their child four years ago. The first partner has been medically evaluated, and was determined to be in good physical health. Considering the LCSW's ethical responsibilities, how should the LCSW proceed?

    a. Gather information to determine whether the first partner qualifies as asexual
    b. Treat this conflict as being no different from other forms of couple conflict, and seek to determine and address the root cause
    c. Assess whether changes in the couple's diet, exercise, or sleep hygiene may lead to changes in sexual desire
    d. Gather the couple's history, including information about the first partner's history of how they identify

27. A new Latina client informs her social worker that the client has more than 2 million followers on a video-based social media platform, where she talks daily about her struggles with mental health. The client has come to therapy to address symptoms of depression and concerns about body image, and tells the LCSW, "It's getting harder and harder to put an optimistic voice out into the world. Everyone can see what I'm going through." The client asks whether the social worker has heard of the client before; the social worker says no. The session leaves the social worker concerned about the possibility that the client may be heading into crisis, considering that the client has a history of suicide attempts, though the client has made no directly threatening statements. The client does not show for her next session. Considering the social worker's ethical responsibilities, how should they proceed?

    a. Search online for the client's social media posts, without becoming a follower or subscriber

    b. Search online for the client's social media posts only if the social worker can do so anonymously

    c. Search online for the client's social media posts and consider other steps to address potential crisis

    d. Contact the client to request their permission to review the client's social media posts

28. An elder client tells a CSW working in hospice care that the client was recently taken to a local religious gathering against her will by her 50-year-old daughter. The daughter is a member of the religious group. By the client's report, the daughter told her mother that "this might be good for you, being around people with good values" and did not bring the mother home when the mother said she was uncomfortable there. Furthermore, the daughter donated the cash in the client's purse to the religious group, despite the client's repeated statements to her daughter that the client did not support the group. How should the CSW respond to their legal obligations in this case?

    a. Report suspected elder abuse (specifically, abduction)

    b. Report suspected elder abuse (specifically, financial abuse)

    c. Report suspected elder abuse (specifically, emotional abuse)

    d. Report suspected elder abuse (specifically, isolation)

29. An LCSW has been treating a 38-year-old woman who has been abusing substances. The woman has experienced a series of health problems, and lost the debit card that she uses to buy food through a state program. She leaves the social worker a voicemail one morning, saying that she is "tired of people messing with me" and that "the next person who tries to put me down or take something from me is getting dead." The social worker knows that the client carries a gun and a knife with her in most places. What should the LCSW do next?

    a. Invoke *Tarasoff* and begin the process of notifying law enforcement and the client's neighbors of the potential risk
    b. Notify law enforcement and attempt to contact and locate the client to initiate the process of hospitalization
    c. Invoke *Tarasoff* and attempt to contact and locate the client to initiate the process of hospitalization
    d. Notify law enforcement as a precautionary measure, and assume the client's statements reflect substance intoxication rather than actual physical danger

30. A private university contracts with a group practice to provide long-term therapy to university students in need of such services. The university agrees to pay the group practice for up to 20 sessions per student per year at a discounted rate. The practice owner, an LCSW, receives the first request from the university for records that will allow the university to issue payment to the practice. The university requests a list of client names, session dates, and procedure codes for all sessions held with the university's students in the past month. Legally, how should the LCSW respond?

    a. Request that each client who attends the university provide a Release of Information allowing the practice to share complete records with the university for billing purposes
    b. Provide the university with all data requested except for client names, which can be replaced with ID numbers
    c. Provide the university with all of the requested data
    d. Ask that all clients who are students of the university pay for sessions at the time of the session, and then submit receipts to the university for reimbursement

31. To battle her flu symptoms, an LCSW working via telehealth takes an over-the-counter medication. Despite the medication containing caffeine, the LCSW soon finds herself drowsy and struggling to maintain focus in session. A couple of clients notice this and express their empathy, as well as their gratitude for the LCSW working with them via telehealth so that there is no risk of the clients becoming infected. Considering the LCSW's ethical responsibilities, the LCSW should:

    a. Consult their physician and cancel remaining sessions for the day, ensuring available backup care for any clients who may be in or may go into crisis

    b. Ask a colleague to monitor their work for the rest of the day to ensure they are not missing anything clinically important

    c. No action is called for, as the LCSW is providing services via telehealth

    d. Seek out additional training on working effectively in the presence of illness

32. The parents of a developmentally delayed 16-year-old bring the teenager to therapy and provide consent for the teenager's individual therapy. The LCSW providing therapy finds the teenager to be witty and charming. The LCSW also finds the teenager to be emotionally immature and believes her intelligence to be around a second-grade level. After a few sessions where the client appears to be making limited progress, the parents express their dissatisfaction with the LCSW and inform the LCSW that they are pulling their child out of therapy. Considering the LCSW's ethical responsibilities, the LCSW should:

    a. Offer to assist with continuity of care to another provider or referrals for additional services

    b. Inform the parents that because the child is older than 12, the child can make their own decisions about consent for treatment

    c. Advocate on behalf of the client for continuing as the client's therapist

    d. Ask the client directly, in the presence of the parents, about the client's desire to remain in treatment

33. An LCSW's former client threatens a licensing board complaint after the former client requested their records be shared with their new therapist. The records were forwarded as requested, and the new therapist then informed their client that the client had been diagnosed by the LCSW with Post-Traumatic Stress Disorder. The client was surprised by the news, as they had not been previously informed of the diagnosis; treatment with the LCSW had focused on the client's social and relational functioning. The former client demands the LCSW apologize and explain why the LCSW believes the client is, as the client describes it, "broken and unfixable." The LCSW should:

   a. Retract the release of the client's record, as its release has caused the client harm
   b. Contact the new therapist to explain the diagnosis
   c. Explain to the former client what the diagnosis means and how the LCSW determined it
   d. Inform the former client of the process for filing a board complaint, and remind them of their ability to provide an addendum that would be added to the treatment record

34. An LCSW is nearing termination with a family the social worker has helped through multiple crises, including the unexpected death of a family member. The family has frequently expressed their gratitude to the social worker, saying things like "you saved us. We're still a family because of you." The LCSW is interested in using one specific, touching statement of gratitude the family shared in session on the LCSW's web site. Ethically, the LCSW should:

   a. Ask the clients for their permission, and if granted, post the statement without attaching the clients' names to it
   b. Wait until therapy has ended, and then post the statement without attaching the clients' names to it
   c. Not post the statement, regardless of timing or client permission
   d. Wait until two years after therapy has ended, and then seek the clients' permission to post the statement

35. An LCSW is providing individual counseling to a 14-year-old at the center of a custody dispute. The mother currently has primary custody, but the father is able to provide independent consent for health care, and was the one to bring the child to treatment and provide consent. The LCSW receives a subpoena to testify at the next custody hearing. The LCSW believes the child is comfortable with the LCSW testifying. The LCSW can best demonstrate understanding of the law by:

    a. Contacting the mother to ask her wishes in relation to claiming privilege
    b. Asserting privilege on behalf of the client, and asking that the court make a determination about whether the LCSW should testify
    c. Contacting the father to ask his wishes in relation to claiming privilege
    d. Refusing to testify as the LCSW is not serving as a custody evaluator

36. An LCSW has been treating a 16-year-old under consent from the child's father. The child's parents are divorced, and under the terms of their joint custody agreement, either parent has the authority to consent to health care on behalf of any of the couple's three children. The mother contacts the LCSW to say that she objects to the therapy and is concerned that the LCSW has not prevented the 16-year-old from using marijuana. Consistent with the LCSW's legal responsibilities, the LCSW should:

    a. Explain to the mother that the LCSW's role is not to prevent the 16-year-old from engaging in marijuana use, but rather to openly discuss such choices and support the 16-year-old's autonomy
    b. Inform the client and the father of the mother's objection, and let them and the mother know that going forward, both parents' consent will be necessary to continue therapy
    c. Inform the mother that unless the custody agreement allows her specifically to revoke the father's consent, the LCSW will continue treating the minor as they have been
    d. Say nothing to the mother, and review the custody agreement

37. In a hospital setting, an LCSW works with patients who are involuntarily hospitalized for being a danger to themselves or others. One such patient is preparing for discharge after one night in the hospital. The treating psychiatrist interrupts the process, and insists that the patient be held for at least another 24 hours. The LCSW brings together the psychiatrist, a member of the nursing team, and a hospital administrator to discuss the case. The psychiatrist is insistent, based on their view of the patient's symptoms. While the others say they are not sure the extended hospitalization is needed, they express willingness to defer to the psychiatrist. The LCSW strongly believes that the additional night is not needed, and explains why, but the psychiatrist is unmoved. The team plans to keep the patient in the hospital for one more night. How should the LCSW proceed?

    a. Accept the decision of the team, and seek to better understand the others' perspectives
    b. Insist that the perspective of the LCSW be given equal weight to that of the psychiatrist
    c. Re-convene the treatment team in an effort to change their minds
    d. Refuse to participate in the ongoing care of this specific patient, without allowing it to impact the quality of care provided to others

[Item #38 is on the next page.]

38. An LCSW is serving as a consultant for a software company that is developing a platform where prospective clients can connect with licensed mental health treatment providers, and where providers can make referrals to one another by securely sharing client data when clients have given permission to do so. The company proposes several different pricing models for therapists who wish to participate on the platform. Which of these models could social workers participate in under state law?

    a. Therapist listings are free; when the prospective client matches with a therapist on specified criteria, the therapist pays a fee to view the prospective client's full information and reach out to them

    b. Therapists buy credits that are not assigned to any specific client; when a prospective client matches with a therapist on specified criteria, the therapist can spend one credit to view the prospective client's full information and reach out to them

    c. Referrals, whether from clients referring themselves or from colleagues, are on a dynamic pricing model; depending on demand in the therapist's area, the therapist may need to pay a fee for a prospective referral, or may get paid a small amount to accept the referral

    d. Therapists subscribe to the service to be included in its directory; for an added subscription fee, they can be notified each time a prospective client who matches with them on specified criteria joins the platform and allows clinicians to reach out to them

[Item #39 is on the next page.]

39. Following an arrest for assault, a 20-year-old man has been seeing an LCSW for private anger management and substance use counseling on orders from the court. Three months into the therapy process, and one month prior to the client's next court date, he reveals to the social worker that he recently had a relapse with methamphetamine. He asks the LCSW to keep this information private. As the court date approaches, the LCSW receives a subpoena from the court demanding all records from the client's treatment. The LCSW is obligated to:

    a. Provide full and complete records to the court
    b. Provide the court a treatment summary, outlining in general terms the client's participation but without specific information on recent substance use
    c. Claim privilege on behalf of the client
    d. Provide the court with the client's clinical file, and withhold psychotherapy notes, where the client's recent substance use are noted

40. A family from Cambodia is seeing an LCSW for family therapy. During a family session, the father tells the therapist that he sometimes disciplines his 15-year-old son the same way the father had been disciplined in Cambodia when he was young: With lashes across his back, using a stick. The mother voices her objection to this form of discipline, and notes that on multiple occasions the son was left bleeding and crying. The most appropriate action for the LCSW would be to:

    a. Consider the cultural elements involved and inform the clients that such discipline may not be accepted in the US
    b. Report suspected physical abuse to the local child protective service agency
    c. Remind the family of the limits of confidentiality and ask whether there are any photos of the son's injuries
    d. Consider the cultural elements involved and research common Cambodian disciplinary practices to determine whether the behavior is consistent with cultural norms

41. A client diagnosed with a moderate Anxiety Disorder calls her therapist, who is an LCSW, at the client's scheduled session time. The client informs the therapist that the client will be unable to attend today's scheduled session and asks the LCSW whether they could do a phone session instead. Which step is a necessary part of the LCSW addressing their legal responsibilities?

    a. Inform the client that the LCSW must have certification in telehealth to engage in phone sessions

    b. Go forward with the session as scheduled, and assess for potential crisis

    c. Determine and document the client's specific location

    d. Inform the client that while a phone session is not allowed, they can have a session through telehealth if the client can meet using a HIPAA-compliant videoconference platform

42. A client sees an LCSW at a local community clinic for court-mandated anger management groups. The client comes to dislike the LCSW and becomes disruptive, frequently comparing the group to jail, and saying "I'm not free when I'm here." In considering her ethical responsibilities, the LCSW should:

    a. Empathize and validate the client's feeling of disempowerment

    b. Terminate therapy with the client and refer them back to court

    c. Remind the client that he is free to attend any anger management group he wishes, or none at all

    d. Tell the client the LCSW will inform the court of his statements if he continues, and encourage him to become more open to the group process

43. An LCSW is working as the Director for a non-profit agency serving the LGBTQIA+ community. As part of her role, the LCSW occasionally sits in on treatment sessions to observe the work of clinicians at the agency. In a session the LCSW is observing, the client informs the treating therapist that the client is in the process of coming out as bisexual, and is unsure of what to reveal to her parents, or when. The client notices that the Director is older than the treating therapist, and asks the Director, "what would you do in my shoes?" The Director should:

    a.   Clarify the Director's role and defer to the treating clinician
    b.   Avoid speaking, so as to reinforce that the treating clinician is running the session
    c.   Answer the question, and then leave the session in order to support the treating clinician in their role
    d.   Inform the client that it is inappropriate to ask such a question of the Director, and redirect the question to the treating clinician

44. A client on probation comes to a scheduled session with an LCSW appearing angry. The client confronts the LCSW on a report the LCSW recently filed with the probation officer, updating the probation officer on the client's attendance in therapy. (There is a release in place allowing for the report to be sent directly.) The client had been making good progress in therapy, and is disappointed that the probation officer "didn't seem to know or care." To manage their ethical responsibilities, the LCSW should:

    a.   Review with the client what information is sent to the probation officer, and how that information can be used
    b.   Review with the client their progress to date in therapy
    c.   Remind the client that legally, the LCSW can only inform the probation officer about their attendance in therapy, not about specific therapy content
    d.   Remind the client that the role of the probation officer is not to provide support or encouragement, but to ensure compliance

45. A 14-year-old girl presents for therapy at a local mental health clinic, where a CSW is assigned to her case. During a screening interview, the girl tells the CSW that she is struggling with anxiety around her schoolwork and social relationships. She goes on to say that she plans to pay for therapy on her own and would prefer that her parents not know she is in therapy. The CSW should:

   a. Assess the girl's ability to participate intelligently in therapy and determine whether notifying the parents would be damaging
   b. Determine whether notifying the parents would be damaging and determine what adult can consent for the girl's therapy
   c. Assess the girl's ability to participate intelligently in treatment and inform her that even when seen under her own consent, her parents may have the right to access her records if they become aware she is in therapy
   d. Determine whether notifying the parents would be damaging and determine whether notifying the girl's school would be damaging

46. A CSW provided therapy to a 16-year-old boy for several months with his parents' consent. A few months later, the CSW receives a subpoena from the attorney for a classmate of the boy. The classmate accused the client of physical assault, and the classmate's family is suing to recover medical expenses. The subpoena requests complete records of the boy's treatment. The CSW attempts to contact the client and his parents but is unsuccessful. The CSW should:

   a. Wait to respond to the subpoena until the CSW is able to determine how the client would like the CSW to respond
   b. Wait to respond to the subpoena until the CSW is able to determine how the parents would like the CSW to respond
   c. Respond to the subpoena by asserting privilege, and continue attempts to contact the client and his parents
   d. Acknowledge the exception to privilege, turn over the client's records, and inform the client and his family as soon as possible

47. An LCSW is working with a Latina mother and her 7-year-old son in therapy, when the LCSW observes unusual bruises on the boy's face and arms. The bruises seem to be in several different stages of healing. When the LCSW asks how he got the bruises, the boy does not answer. His mother says, "He's a normal boy, he likes to play rough" and refuses to discuss the matter further. The LCSW should:

    a. Report suspected child abuse
    b. Consider whether physical discipline is common in Latin cultures
    c. Remind the mother of the limits of confidentiality
    d. Ask the child to remove his shirt to inspect his torso for additional injuries

48. A CSW worked with a woman in individual therapy for six months, focusing on treatment of depression symptoms following the client's messy divorce. The client improved significantly in therapy and terminated successfully. One year later, the CSW has been dating a man for two months when the CSW realizes the man is the ex-husband of the former client. The CSW should:

    a. Discontinue the romantic relationship
    b. Contact the former client to determine her wishes. Given the amount of time that has passed and the success of treatment, she is likely to give her blessing
    c. Self-report to the BBS to seek their guidance on the most appropriate way to proceed
    d. No action is called for

49. With the client's consent, a CSW working with an adolescent client encourages one of the client's teachers to attend sessions that will focus on the adolescent's behavior in school. While the teacher's presence is at first helpful, the teacher asks to continue coming to the sessions, and it is clear to the CSW that the client is finding the teacher's presence gradually more intrusive and uncomfortable. The CSW should:

    a.   Clarify the teacher's role in treatment, and ask the client whether they would like to continue having the teacher in session

    b.   Ask the client whether they would like to continue having the teacher in session, and remind the teacher of the limits to confidentiality

    c.   Ask the client to contact the school and request that the teacher be removed from the therapy sessions

    d.   Remind the client of the goals of therapy and the reasons for the teacher's presence in session

50. An older woman who has been seeing a CSW for seven months storms out of session after her therapist started the session some 30 minutes late. The CSW attempted to explain that another client had been in crisis, but the woman cut off the CSW, saying that the delay was disrespectful of her time. A few days later the client calls the CSW saying she will not come back for future sessions and requesting a copy of the treatment record be sent to her. The CSW should:

    a.   Insist that the client come in for an additional session to discuss her hurt feelings, and provide a copy of the treatment record

    b.   Apologize for the delay, offer to discuss it further, provide options for other treatment providers, and provide a copy of the treatment record

    c.   Provide a copy of the treatment record, and consider whether the client's display was simply a way of resolving cognitive dissonance about the need to end treatment

    d.   Provide options for other treatment providers, and inform the client that the CSW will forward the treatment record to the new provider of the client's choosing, in order to ensure that the client does remain in therapy

51. An LCSW with strong religious beliefs is talking with a trans male client about the client's family history. The client reveals that his parents had strong religious beliefs, but the client describes himself as atheist and says, "I just never understood why people buy into those fairy tales." The client says he has never found comfort or strength in religious or spiritual activity, and has judgment toward those who do. The LCSW should:

   a. Mention the LCSW's beliefs briefly, without challenging the client's experience
   b. Inform the client that religion is a source of comfort for many people, and encourage the client to keep an open mind toward it for the future
   c. Connect the client's beliefs about religion with their history of family trauma
   d. Show understanding of the client's beliefs and inquire further about their family history

52. A CSW is consulting with the physician who sent a young couple to the CSW for couple therapy. Both partners in the couple are struggling with symptoms of anxiety. The physician provides the CSW with useful information on the couple's medications and their possible side effects. The CSW offers the physician useful information on the progression of the couple's symptoms. Toward the end of the conversation, the physician asks whether the older partner in the couple is "still wearing that same brown sweater twice a week." The CSW should:

   a. Answer the question
   b. Politely decline to answer the question, as it is not relevant to the consultation
   c. Request a release from both partners to provide this type of information
   d. Gently note that the physician is asking a question outside of their scope of practice

53. A middle-aged woman struggling with panic disorder asks an LCSW whether her brother can come with her to therapy, and the LCSW approves. In the intake session, the woman describes her panic symptoms, as well as the strain that her panic has caused in her relationship with her brother. She relies on him to feel safe in public situations, and becomes angry with him when he cannot be with her due to his job or other obligations. The brother agrees, saying that while he wants to help his sister as much as he can and is glad that she is seeking treatment, he is growing resentful of being her main source of support. The LCSW should:

    a. Clarify whether the woman and her brother are seeking conjoint treatment to address their relationship, or whether treatment is to focus on the woman's panic

    b. Ask the brother to leave the session so that the LCSW can assess the woman for possible dependent adult abuse

    c. Ask the client to sign a release of information allowing for discussion of her symptoms in therapy sessions where her brother is also present

    d. Provide the client with referrals to co-occurring disorder treatment

54. An LCSW has a client who lives on a boat three months of the year, as a commercial fisherman. During that time, he comes back to shore one day a week, and sees the LCSW on that day. The client is relatively poor, and asks the LCSW whether he can pay for services in fresh salmon. The client says he may need to discontinue treatment otherwise. The LCSW frequently eats salmon, and so is familiar with the fair market value of the fish. Which of the following statements of the LCSW's responsibilities is correct?

    a. The LCSW should provide services pro bono, rather than accepting payment in fish

    b. If the LCSW chooses to go ahead with the barter agreement, the value of the fish should approximate the fee generally charged for therapy, and there should be a clear contract

    c. The LCSW should refer the client to a low-fee or no-fee clinic rather than accepting salmon as payment

    d. The LCSW should consider whether other clients would also want to pay for therapy through the products they make or services they provide

55. An LCSW suffers a serious illness, and a colleague steps in to take over the LCSW's ongoing clients until the LCSW can return to practice. The LCSW agrees to continue handling billing and to review the colleague's session notes to keep up with what is happening while she is recovering. Some of the LCSW's ongoing clients pay for sessions through their health insurance. However, the colleague (who is also a licensed LCSW in private practice) is not on any insurance panels. The ill LCSW should:

    a. Continue to submit insurance billing listing herself as the treatment provider

    b. Continue to submit insurance billing listing the colleague as the treatment provider and herself as the supervisor

    c. Either directly or through the colleague, inform clients of the difference in panel status and arrange alternate payment or referrals as needed

    d. Defer to the colleague to negotiate fees independently, and otherwise presume that the LCSW's typical business practices will be followed

56. An adult client who has been seeing a CSW in therapy for six months asks the CSW for a copy of her treatment record. Because the CSW has documented that she suspects the client is being dishonest in her denials of recent drug use, the CSW worries that sharing the file would harm the therapeutic relationship. The most appropriate course of action for the CSW would be to:

    a. Turn over the records as required by law, and use it as an opportunity to address the client's possible substance use

    b. Provide the client with a partial copy of the file, leaving out the suspicion of recent drug use

    c. Refuse to turn over the records, offer a treatment summary instead, and inform the client that if she wishes, she can select a neutral therapist to review the file

    d. Submit the client's request, and the CSW's reason for refusing, to a district judge for review

57. An individual client acknowledges to her therapist (a CSW) that she lied on the CSW's intake form and actually does have several past suicide attempts in her history. She says she is not feeling suicidal now, though she has recently experienced the ending of a romantic relationship and the death of a distant relative. Legally, the CSW should:

   a. Complete a No Harm Contract with the client
   b. Discontinue therapy and refer the client to a higher level of care, as she is high risk
   c. Initiate the process of involuntary hospitalization
   d. Assess further and break confidentiality if required to resolve any threat of suicide

58. A client reports to her therapist, a CSW, that the client's antidepressant medication does not appear to be having a positive effect even after eight weeks of her taking the prescribed dosage. The client complains that the office staff for the prescribing physician is disorganized, and the doctor is sometimes hard to reach. The CSW should:

   a. Encourage the client to request a medication change
   b. Encourage the client to request a higher dosage to achieve the intended effect
   c. Encourage the client to consult with her physician
   d. Encourage the client to consider discontinuing the medication and focusing on efforts to improve her depressive symptoms through therapy

59. An LCSW in an outpatient group practice setting has fallen behind on their documentation. The owner of the practice expresses concern that the delays will impact insurance billing and, ultimately, the practice's financial health. To ethically resolve this issue, the LCSW should:

    a. Create at least cursory progress notes for all sessions more than 7 days in the past, even if such notes are a single sentence each, to allow billing to move forward

    b. Transfer their clients to other clinicians in the group, allowing the other clinicians to create documentation of past sessions establishing themselves as the service providers and to properly submit insurance claims

    c. Work diligently to catch up

    d. Consider reducing their client load or, if necessary, leaving the practice

60. An LCSW is serving as the family therapist for a family where the father is also engaged in individual therapy with another provider. The family has only attended one session so far, and while the father informed the LCSW of his individual therapy, he did not provide information about the other therapist or sign a release of information. The LCSW receives a voicemail message from a local therapist, identifying themselves as the individual therapist for the father, and asking the LCSW to provide any information the LCSW may have regarding the father's history of psychosis, as the individual therapist is attempting to determine a proper diagnosis. Considering the LCSW's ethical responsibilities, the LCSW should:

    a. Provide the colleague with the minimum information necessary to aid them in diagnosis

    b. Provide the colleague with the client's full medical and mental health history

    c. Contact the father to assess his wishes and ask him to sign a release of information

    d. Contact the father to inform him that his information will be disclosed; remind him of the limits of confidentiality

61. In a mid-size college town, an LCSW is the only local mental health provider who speaks fluent Farsi. She routinely receives referrals from other providers when the other provider discovers that their client identifies as Persian or speaks Farsi, even if the client is also fluent in English. Given her ties to the local Persian community, the LCSW often finds that she is at least somewhat familiar with the new clients being referred to her. Considering her ethical responsibilities, the LCSW should:

   a. Refer out clients who could effectively receive services from other providers, retaining those who speak only Farsi, unless her familiarity makes her incapable of providing unbiased care
   b. Refer out clients she has any form of prior knowledge about
   c. Refer out clients she has personally interacted with in the last two years, retaining the rest
   d. Reach out to referring providers and let them know she cannot accept additional Farsi-speaking clients

62. A single LCSW finds herself sometimes flirting with one particular group therapy client at the end of each week's session, as the other group members are making their way outside. The group member is also single, and appears to be interested in the therapist, but is careful to not cross boundaries during session or in other situations where other group members could see. One evening, the client sends the social worker an email to express gratitude for all she has done in the group, and attaches a couple of racy photos. The LCSW should:

   a. Ignore the photos, respond to the gratitude, and encourage continued growth in group
   b. Do not respond via email, engage the client in a phone discussion, warn the client that the email cannot remain confidential, and consider termination from the group
   c. Acknowledge the email, inform the client that they are violating the LCSW's boundaries, and inform the client that sexually explicit communications must be reported
   d. Acknowledge the email, inform the client that including the photos was inappropriate, apologize for any misunderstanding about the nature of their relationship, and monitor both the LCSW's and the client's future behavior

63. A social worker at a private nonprofit outpatient clinic is surprised to learn that the clinic has a policy of neutrality on political matters. The social worker had hoped to get the clinic to support a proposed local law that would raise sales taxes to improve local services and accessibility for those with disabilities. The clinic asks the social worker to stay out of political discussion about the proposed law, which the social worker believes would advance social justice. The director of the clinic says that she also believes the proposal is good, but is committed to the clinic policy. How should the social worker proceed?

    a. Respect the wishes of the employer, and support the proposal by voting for it and potentially donating money to groups that are advocating for its passage
    b. Engage in public discussion of the proposal, and describe the clinic as being in favor of it
    c. Engage in public discussion of the proposal, and criticize the clinic's unwillingness to take a public stance as likely an effort to preserve their grants and contracts
    d. Engage in public discussion of the proposal, but as an individual and not as a representative of the clinic

[Question 64 is on the next page.]

64. A group practice specializing in working with depression is considering implementing a new policy to build awareness of their work: As part of the consent process, all clients must agree to post at least once on social media about their experience in therapy, making specific mention of the group practice when they do. The policy specifies that the post does not need to be an endorsement or testimonial; even negative discussion is allowed, so long as it is truthful. Clients who have no social media presence would be exempt. Considering the LCSW's ethical responsibilities, what should the LCSW do around this policy?

    a.   Clarify to clients that since it is part of the consent process, they are free to go to a different provider who does not have such a policy if they wish

    b.   Clarify to all clients that such posts are strongly encouraged, but are not required, regardless of what the official policy may say

    c.   Clarify with the practice owners what the consequence would be for clients who agree to the policy but ultimately do not post about their experience

    d.   Refuse to implement the policy, and ask the group practice to withdraw it

[Question 65 is on the next page.]

65. In a large public mental health clinic, a social worker (Social Worker A) becomes aware of a colleague in the clinic (Social Worker B) who describes all trans, queer, nonbinary, or otherwise gender-nonconforming clients as mentally ill, and refuses to work with such clients. Supervisors are aware of the issue and make sure that the colleague is only assigned cisgender clients. A different colleague (Social Worker C), who complained about Social Worker B's behavior, was then told that Social Worker B had accused them of religious discrimination, a charge that Social Worker A believes to be false. What ethical responsibility does Social Worker A have in this circumstance?

    a.   Assist in Social Worker C's defense; bring Social Worker B's behavior to the attention of administrators; file a formal ethical complaint against Social Worker B if needed

    b.   Assist in Social Worker C's defense; demand supervisors explain why they did not take additional action

    c.   Because all potentially problematic behavior has been reported, allow the administrative processes of resolving all complaints to reach their conclusions; evaluate options at that point

    d.   File an ethics complaint against Social Worker B and their supervisor with the NASW Ethics Committee

[Question 66 is on the next page.]

66. An LCSW is working in a community clinic in a city where most residents identify themselves as religious. The LCSW is sometimes asked about their own beliefs, and answers the question briefly when asked, before moving on with the conversation. An individual client presses the LCSW for more detail, noting that the LCSW seems confident and well-grounded, while the client has experienced a great deal of upheaval. The client asks the LCSW where they attend services, and how the client might learn more about or even convert to the LCSW's religion. The LCSW is a leader in their religious group. Ethically, how should the LCSW proceed?

   a. Inform the client that there are many ways by which they could find peace and comfort, and that religion does not necessarily need to be one of them
   b. Considering that the client is initiating the conversation, the LCSW can inform the client about the LCSW's religious group, as doing so is in the client's best interests
   c. Seek to understand more about the client's suffering and their spiritual beliefs and preferences, so as to guide them more appropriately
   d. Refuse to address religious or spiritual belief in the context of secular treatment

[Question 67 is on the next page.]

67. A 15-year-old girl is seeing a CSW individually for issues related to body image and self-esteem. Her parents provided consent for the therapy and pay for her sessions, but do not participate. The girl tells the CSW that she has been exploring her sexuality. While her parents were out of town, she had sexual intercourse with a friend's 19-year-old brother. A few days later, she had intercourse with another boy, an 18-year-old senior at her high school. The CSW should manage their legal responsibilities by:

   a. Reporting child abuse to the local child protective service agency
   b. Investigating to ensure that the sexual activity was not coerced or while under the influence of drugs or alcohol
   c. Notifying the parents of their daughter's high-risk sexual behavior
   d. Maintaining confidentiality

68. A client has cancelled three of the last seven scheduled sessions with an LCSW, and been a no-show for the other four. Each time, the client has promised to pay any balance charged, and to come in for a session the following week. The LCSW finds herself irritated with the client's behavior, going so far as to warn the client two weeks ago that she would simply close the client's case and refer out if the client didn't come in. The client was a no-show for the next two scheduled weekly sessions. Even before this long series of missed appointments, the LCSW found herself personally disliking the client. How should the LCSW manage her ethical responsibilities in this case?

   a. Meaningfully assess for crisis, and continue as the client's treatment provider if necessary
   b. Close the case, providing the client with appropriate referrals to other providers
   c. Provide the client at least two additional warnings, one of which must be in writing, prior to terminating therapy
   d. Seek consultation to address countertransference, and continue to work toward the client more regularly attending therapy

69. As a client leaves a CSW's office, the CSW believes the client poses a serious danger to the client's spouse. (The client had been making threats in session about what he would do to her.) The CSW, knowing the couple lives roughly 30 minutes from the CSW's office, calls the client immediately, and is able to resolve the danger. The client disavows any continued plan to harm his spouse, and apologizes to the CSW for "getting so out of hand." What does the CSW need to do to resolve the CSW's legal responsibility?

    a. Notify the spouse and law enforcement immediately
    b. Notify the spouse immediately
    c. Notify law enforcement within 24 hours
    d. Notify the local child protective services agency

70. A CSW has a new client who explains during the intake session that she had a hard time coming into therapy. The client says that her previous therapist asked her to go on a date with him immediately after their termination session ended. She refused, and has not spoken with the former therapist again, but the experience left her skeptical of therapists generally. Legally, the CSW must:

    a. Report the other therapist's actions to the BBS
    b. Confront the other therapist on their behavior
    c. Provide the client a copy of the brochure "Therapy Never Includes Sexual Behavior"
    d. Maintain the client's confidentiality

71. A CSW is interested in conducting research on her clients, in an effort to determine whether a new form of treatment developed by the CSW is superior to existing treatments. Because the CSW already has access to the client files and would be reporting statistics on her recent treatment results, without specifics of any individual cases, she prepares to conduct an analysis of cases she has closed over the prior year. She hopes to publish the results of her research in a prominent journal. Ethically, the CSW should:

    a. Contact those former clients, inform them of the risks and benefits of involvement in the research, and determine their willingness to have their file included as one of those analyzed
    b. Take steps to protect the confidentiality of individual cases, but include all cases from the prior year in her analysis to eliminate possible selection bias
    c. Contact those former clients to let them know that their files have been included in her research
    d. Because she is working with archival data that will be reported in aggregate, no action is required

72. A 27-year-old trans female client has been receiving services from an LCSW at a reduced-fee clinic. The client has been unable to pay even her reduced fee, and over 8 weeks has built up an unpaid balance of more than $100. The client is apologetic and has reassured the LCSW that she will pay the overdue fees once her aging mother dies and she can collect her inheritance. The LCSW has informed the client while she empathizes with the client's struggles, a balance that goes unpaid for more than 30 days will result in the termination of services. This policy also appears in the informed consent document the client signed at the beginning of services. The client does not have stable food, work, or shelter, but is typically able to engage public services and shelter space when needed. How should the social worker proceed?

    a. Assess whether the client poses imminent danger to self or others
    b. Terminate the client for nonpayment and provide at least three community referrals
    c. Pay the client's balance on the client's behalf
    d. Set a specific deadline by which the full balance must be paid off to retain services

73. An LCSW is supervising an associate clinical social worker from a different cultural background. Early in their supervision relationship, they discover that they both are part of a small social media group for health care professionals in their city who suffered abuse as children. How should the supervisor proceed?

    a. Ask the supervisee to set a boundary on their social media interactions that is comfortable for the supervisee, based on the supervisee's cultural background and expectations

    b. Meet with the supervisee to establish that the supervisor will not discuss their professional relationship in the social media group or interact with the supervisee's posts in that group; discuss what other limitations may be necessary

    c. Acknowledge their professional relationship in the group, in the interest of transparency; discuss what other limitations may be necessary

    d. Inform the supervisee that if they are going to work together, neither the supervisor nor the supervisee can participate in the social media group

[Question 74 is on the next page.]

74. A white family has been attending family therapy to address conflict among the three siblings: A 16-year-old girl, a 13-year-old girl, and a 10-year-old who identifies as nonbinary. In session, the 16-year-old admits that she and the 10-year-old sometimes wake up before the 13-year-old, and then wake the 13-year-old by climbing on top of her, slapping, and punching her. The 13-year-old has shown her parents the bruises on her face and arms that have resulted, but the parents say they did not take photos of the bruises, and the LCSW providing family therapy has not observed any bruising. The 13-year-old says she has tried to "get back" at her siblings by stealing and giving away their belongings. The parents say they feel helpless to stop the siblings' behavior toward one another. How should the LCSW proceed?

   a. File a report of suspected child abuse, naming all three siblings as both victims and perpetrators
   b. File a report of suspected child abuse, naming the 16-year-old and 10-year-old as perpetrators
   c. File a report of suspected child neglect, naming the parents as perpetrators for failing to protect the 13-year-old
   d. File a report of suspected child abuse, naming only the 16-year-old as a perpetrator

[Question 75 is on the next page.]

75. A 56-year-old male client is seeing a social worker to address the client's substance use. The client also regularly sees a psychiatrist. The client provided the social worker with the psychiatrist's name, contact information, and date of most recent visit during the intake process. When discussing the psychiatrist in session, the client asks the social worker not to contact the psychiatrist. The client says the psychiatrist "isn't real big on therapy. I don't know if they would like that I'm here." Considering the social worker's ethical responsibilities, how should the social worker proceed?

    a.   Contact the psychiatrist to coordinate care, as the psychiatrist is an active member of the client's treatment team

    b.   Inform the client that coordinated care is necessary for effective treatment, and reassure the client that only a minimal amount of information will be shared

    c.   Inform the client that coordinated care is necessary for effective treatment, and direct the client to sign a Release of Information form allowing the social worker to coordinate with the psychiatrist

    d.   Do not contact the psychiatrist, and discuss the implications of the client coming to therapy against the psychiatrist's guidance

- STOP HERE -
END OF TEST

Practice Test:
Quick Answer Key

Quick Answer Key

1. D	21. C	41. C	61. A
2. A	22. C	42. C	62. D
3. A	23. C	43. A	63. D
4. A	24. A	44. A	64. D
5. D	25. C	45. A	65. A
6. C	26. D	46. C	66. C
7. C	27. C	47. A	67. D
8. A	28. B	48. D	68. B
9. A	29. B	49. A	69. C
10. B	30. C	50. B	70. D
11. C	31. A	51. D	71. A
12. D	32. A	52. B	72. A
13. A	33. C	53. A	73. B
14. C	34. C	54. B	74. B
15. B	35. B	55. C	75. D
16. B	36. D	56. C	
17. D	37. A	57. D	
18. B	38. D	58. C	
19. D	39. A	59. C	
20. B	40. B	60. C	

Subscale scoring

The numbers below refer to **question numbers** aligned with each of the major content areas in the exam. You can use these subscale scores to assess your strengths and weaknesses and guide additional study.

Law			Ethics		
Confidentiality, privilege, and consent	Limits to confidentiality, including mandated reporting	Legal standards for professional practice	Professional competence and preventing harm	Therapeutic relationship	Business practices and policies
6	1	2	5	4	15
10	19	3	7	8	25
17	21	38	13	9	27
20	28	54	14	11	33
30	29	55	16	12	34
35	39	58	18	23	43
36	40	70	22	24	59
41	47		31	26	65
45	57		48	32	71
46	67		51	37	72
56	69		61	42	73
	74		62	44	
			64	49	
			66	50	
				52	
				53	
				60	
				63	
				68	
				75	
Total: _____ out of 11	Total: _____ out of 12	Total: _____ out of 7	Total: _____ out of 14	Total: _____ out of 20	Total: _____ out of 11
Law Total: _____ out of 30			Ethics Total: _____ out of 45		

Practice Test:
Answers and Rationales

1. A client who has expressed great concern about anyone knowing she is in therapy passes out in the middle of a session. The CSW the client was seeing is able to wake her long enough to learn that she has recently been struggling with illness and has pain from a neck injury, and the CSW knows from the client's intake paperwork that she has a blood disorder. The CSW should:

    a. **Incorrect.** Stay with the client and continue attempting to wake her. *Passing out mid-session may be indicative of a medical emergency. Absent other information, it should be treated as an emergency.*

    b. **Incorrect.** Call 911 and transport the client outside of the office into a public area to protect her privacy. *Calling 911 is appropriate, but attempting to transport the client is not, particularly given her known neck injury. Further, it is difficult to argue that moving the client to a public area from a private one would protect her privacy.*

    c. **Incorrect.** Call 911 and summon paramedics without providing any information about the client or her illness. *Paramedics may need information on the woman's recent illness, neck injury, and blood disorder in order to treat her appropriately. It is acceptable to share this information with other health care providers in an emergency, and the CSW can do so without revealing anything about the woman's therapy.*

    d. **CORRECT.** Call 911, summon paramedics, and inform them of the client's medical issues. *CSWs are allowed to share medical information in an emergency situation, and the CSW in this instance can do so without revealing any information about the client's therapy.*

2. With the client's permission, an LCSW contacts another California psychotherapist who had previously been involved in the client's treatment. The client reported to the LCSW that about a year ago, the other therapist had become confrontational with the client in several sessions, challenging the client with statements like, "Why are you acting like such a baby?" and "Drinking is the coward's way of coping, and you're a coward, so I'm sure you're going to go drink as soon as we're done here." The client reported to the LCSW that these sessions left the client struggling to get out of bed each day, and contributed to the client getting fired for missing work. During their call, the other therapist becomes defensive, and tells the LCSW that the client was unresponsive to more empathetic approaches, and so these confrontations were "I guess, my way of pushing [the client] to take some accountability. That's not a crime." How should the LCSW proceed?

    a. **CORRECT.** Inform the client of their ability to report the prior therapist to the BBS

    b. **Incorrect.** Inform the other therapist that their conduct was harmful and is indeed a crime

    c. **Incorrect.** Ask the client to provide documentation of their decline in functioning and their job loss in response to the prior therapy

    d. **Incorrect.** Seek to better understand the other therapist's clinical approach

No accepted form of psychotherapy involves the clinician directly insulting their client in this manner. It is reckless and caused harm, which is a violation of unprofessional conduct standards. The LCSW does not need to further investigate, either by attempting to learn more about the other clinician's approach or demanding supporting documentation from the client. The LCSW should empower the client to make a report of unprofessional conduct to the BBS if the client chooses to do so. While there may be utility in informing the other therapist of the harm their actions caused to the client, the LCSW cannot determine on their own that the other therapist's actions violated the law (and even if they did, the other therapist's actions technically would have violated administrative, not criminal, law).

3. A CSW who is new to the community seeks to build her referral base so that she can grow her practice. For those colleagues who refer clients to her, she calls the colleague (without revealing any information about the client) and offers to buy the colleague lunch to say thanks and engage in professional networking. An established CSW in the community receives such an offer from the new CSW after referring a client to the new CSW. How should the established CSW respond?

    a. **CORRECT.** Accept the invitation under the condition that they each agree to pay their own bill. *As long as the established CSW is not receiving any form of payment, it would be acceptable to join the new CSW for lunch or coffee.*

    b. **Incorrect.** Decline the invitation and report the new CSW to the BBS. *It would be acceptable to decline the invitation, but reporting to the BBS is not justified. Ethical obligations include assisting colleagues and respecting their confidences; it would be better to discuss with the new CSW the risks inherent in their offer.*

    c. **Incorrect.** Accept the invitation under the condition that no client information will be discussed. *Having the new CSW pay for her lunch would amount to receiving payment for referrals, which is specifically prohibited by state law and the NASW Code of Ethics.*

    d. **Incorrect.** Accept the invitation and request a release of information from the client allowing the established CSW to discuss the case with the new CSW. *Having the new CSW pay for her lunch would amount to receiving payment for referrals, which is specifically prohibited by state law and the NASW Code of Ethics.*

4. An LCSW learns that his individual client, who is being seen for symptoms of Bipolar Disorder, is also interested in attending couple therapy with her spouse. The client asks the LCSW whether the couple could see the LCSW together for couple therapy separately from her individual sessions, and says she is willing to sign a release form such that information from her individual sessions could be discussed in couple therapy and vice versa. Ethically, the LCSW should:

- a. **CORRECT.** Continue individual treatment with the client and refer out for the couple therapy. *This preserves continuity of care for individual treatment and keeps the LCSW out of a potential conflict of interests that would result from serving the client in multiple roles.*
- b. **Incorrect.** Continue individual treatment with the client and begin concurrent couple therapy, utilizing a separate file with a separate treatment plan. *Even with a release in place and a clearly different treatment plan, the therapist is likely to be more aligned with the partner being seen individually as well. Better to refer out for couple therapy to a therapist who will be more neutral.*
- c. **Incorrect.** Inform the client that it would be better to complete individual treatment before engaging in couple therapy, regardless of whether the couple therapy is with the LCSW or another provider. *Concurrent treatment carries some risks, but also some potential benefits. It should not simply be dismissed as an option.*
- d. **Incorrect.** Discontinue the individual treatment in order to begin couple treatment, with the client's release in place to allow for material from the individual sessions to be discussed in couple work. *Discontinuing individual treatment prematurely does not appear likely to be in the best interests of the client.*

5. An LCSW is working with a family where the parents are in the process of getting a divorce and are arguing over custody of their two children. Therapy has focused on maintaining effective co-parenting, as neither parent wants an extended court battle. Because the LCSW knows the family well and has seen both parents interacting with the children, the parents ask the LCSW to submit a letter to the court with the LCSW's clinical evaluation of each of their parenting skills. The best course of action for the LCSW would be to:

   a. **Incorrect.** Obtain a release from all family members, and send the letter to the court, emphasizing that the evaluative statements should not be used to draw conclusions about custody.
   b. **Incorrect.** Obtain a release from all family members, and send the letter to the court, offering specific recommendations for custody based on the LCSW's work with the family and based on the LCSW's knowledge of the wishes of the children.
   c. **Incorrect.** Obtain a release from all family members, and engage in a process of testing and evaluation to draw objective conclusions before completing the letter.
   d. **CORRECT.** Refuse to send the letter.

The NASW Code of Ethics requires social workers to clarify their role and avoid conflicts of interest. The parents in this case are asking the LCSW, who has been in the treatment provider role, to also take on an evaluative stance. If the LCSW were to do so, the parents would likely be less forthcoming in the future about any struggles they experienced in parenting. Options (A), (B), and (C) all place the LCSW in an evaluator position that should be avoided if the LCSW has provided clinical treatment.

6. The director of an afterschool program contacts an LCSW by phone to refer a 14-year-old girl to the social worker for psychotherapy. The director says that the girl is a participant in the program and has been struggling with extreme shyness. The director further says that the program will be happy to pay for the therapy. The girl, who is with the director in an office, gets on the phone to provide the LCSW with more information. She says she does not want her parents to know she is seeking help. How should the LCSW proceed?

a. **Incorrect.** Allow the program director to consent for treatment on the minor's behalf and accept financial responsibility
b. **Incorrect.** Inform the minor that one parent must consent to her receiving treatment regardless of how it is being paid for
c. **CORRECT.** Assess the maturity of the minor
d. **Incorrect.** Allow the minor to consent for treatment on her own, and have her complete a Release of Information so that the program can be billed

While minors as young as 12 can consent for their own treatment, this is conditioned upon the clinician determining that the minor is mature enough to participate intelligently in treatment. The LCSW should assess the minor's maturity level to determine whether the minor can consent on her own, or whether she will need the consent of a parent or guardian.

7. A young adult client with a history of severe childhood trauma begins weeping in session as she connects her traumatic experiences with her current struggles in building trusting relationships. An LCSW has been providing the client with individual sessions for more than two years, and the client has only even begun to trust the therapist in the past few months. The LCSW notices that the client is having difficulty calming herself, and is shaking in her seat. The client turns to the social worker and softly asks, "Will you please just hold me for a moment, so I can catch my breath?" The client has never made such a request before. Considering her ethical responsibilities, how should the social worker proceed?

    a. **Incorrect.** Briefly hold the client, and immediately afterward, discuss it in order to reinforce a strong clinical boundary

    b. **Incorrect.** Briefly hold the client, to support their autonomy. Since the client has not made such a request in more than two years of treatment, it is unlikely that a clarifying conversation is needed

    c. **CORRECT.** Decline the client's request, while offering a blanket or other means the client can use for calming

    d. **Incorrect.** Decline the client's request, and when appropriate, re-evaluate the clinical relationship in light of the client's efforts toward dependence

The NASW Code of Ethics requires social workers to avoid physical contact when that contact includes the possibility of causing psychological harm to the client. Here, that possibility exists; the client might become dependent on the social worker, or might experience their relationship in a different way. The social worker can be soothing to the client without physically holding them, and that is the most appropriate course of action.

8. A 23-year-old client whose family immigrated to California from Indonesia calls her LCSW to inform the therapist that the client cannot attend therapy for the next three weeks, as the client's sister just had a baby and the client is going to be helping the sister and the sister's partner. The LCSW has been treating the client for post-traumatic stress disorder and wonders whether the treatment has simply been overwhelming for the client. What steps should the LCSW take to fulfill their ethical duties?

    a. **CORRECT.** Ensure crisis needs are met and a safety plan is in place if needed; schedule a next session for three weeks from now

    b. **Incorrect.** Offer to reduce the intensity of sessions in exchange for the client remaining consistent in treatment

    c. **Incorrect.** Seek to understand the client's behavior from a cultural perspective; treat the interruption of therapy as a crisis and intervene accordingly

    d. **Incorrect.** Wish the client well for the upcoming three weeks; hold the client's usual spot on the LCSW's calendar; ask to see photos of the baby upon the client's return

When treatment needs to be interrupted, regardless of the reason why, it is the responsibility of the social worker to ensure that any crisis needs are met. Option B is not correct as the question does not establish any reason why a three-week break in treatment may be detrimental to the point where continuity would become more important than the client's other wishes and obligations. Option C treats the break itself as a crisis, which is not established in the question. Option D is a supportive response but does not provide appropriate protection in the event that a crisis emerges.

9. Following a contentious presidential election, an LCSW in private practice is interested in providing care for supporters of the losing candidate. The LCSW advertises short-term grief therapy for the losing candidate's supporters at a 50% reduced rate. A man who was a supporter of the winning candidate asks the LCSW whether he, too, can have the reduced rate, as he is struggling with grief following the retirement of the man's mentor at work. The LCSW should:

    a. **CORRECT.** Agree to the reduced rate for this client, and alter their advertising to remove mention of the election
    b. **Incorrect.** Agree to the reduced rate for this client, and for anyone else who asks for it
    c. **Incorrect.** Agree to the reduced rate for this client, and alter their advertising to clarify that the grief treatment must be focused on the election to qualify for a reduced rate
    d. **Incorrect.** Cite the language in the LCSW's advertising and inform the client that they do not qualify for the specific rate reduction, but consider their income in setting a fee

The NASW Code of Ethics non-discrimination standard prohibits discrimination on the basis of political belief, and providing a reduced rate to those who have one set of political beliefs while denying it to others would be discriminatory. Providing the reduced rate upon request (B or C) does little good if the LCSW's advertising continues to suggest discriminatory rate-setting; prospective clients who do not share the LCSW's political preferences would not know to ask. Refusing to provide this client the reduced rate but offering a different kind of rate reduction (D) also does nothing to resolve the apparent discrimination in the LCSW's advertising.

10. A CSW is working with an individual client who is employed in the movie industry. The client is emotionally unstable following a breakup. The client informs the CSW that the client will be travelling out of state for the next three weeks to work on a film, and asks whether the CSW can continue to work with the client by phone during that time. The CSW should first:

   a. **Incorrect.** Assess the severity of the client's symptoms to determine whether phone therapy is appropriate, and if so, proceed with phone sessions. *There is no point in doing the assessment if the CSW is not legally authorized to provide services in the state where the client will be.*

   b. **CORRECT.** Determine whether they have the requisite qualifications to practice in the state to which the client is travelling. *Phone sessions are only an option if the therapist is legally authorized to provide services in the state to which the client will be travelling. If the therapist is also licensed in that state, or if the state has a carve-out in their licensure law allowing for short-term continuation of care with an out-of-state therapist, then the phone sessions requested here are a possibility, pending further assessment.*

   c. **Incorrect.** Determine the client's state of residency. *Residency does not matter. The BBS, like most state licensure boards, considers the physical location of the client at the time of service as where the therapy takes place (and, thus, where the therapist needs to be licensed or otherwise authorized to provide care).*

   d. **Incorrect.** Inquire with the BBS as to the appropriateness and legality of phone sessions for this client. *The BBS cannot provide legal advice and may not know current licensing requirements for all other states. It would be a more appropriate step to check with the licensing board of the state where the client will be, to see what the rules there are.*

11. A social worker who is part of a multidisciplinary treatment team becomes concerned when the team decides to contact the mother of an adult client and ask her to become more involved in treatment. The team made this decision based on the client's worsening symptoms, out of concern that the client may soon need to be hospitalized. The social worker notes that there is not a release in place allowing them to share information with the mother. The social worker should:

a. **Incorrect.** Respect the treatment team's decision, and not be personally involved in the efforts to contact the mother
b. **Incorrect.** Respect the treatment team's decision, and be prepared to address the client's possible feelings of betrayal
c. **CORRECT.** Contact the treatment team and ask to meet with them as soon as possible in an effort to change their decision
d. **Incorrect.** Contact the treatment team and inform them that if the team's decision goes forward, the social worker will encourage the client to report a confidentiality violation

When a treatment team makes a decision that a social worker believes raises ethical concerns, as is the case here, the social worker should seek to resolve the disagreement through appropriate channels – not just defer to the team. However, such challenges should be addressed in ways *consistent with the client's well-being*. Threatening the team, or encouraging the client to report a violation, makes the client a pawn in the dispute and is likely to be counter to their best interests.

12. The individual client of a CSW tells the CSW that he recently took his 94-year-old grandfather, who has been suffering from dementia, on a fishing trip to a nearby lake in a California State Park. He had grown frustrated with the quality of care the grandfather had been receiving at his nursing home, which he said was not adequate to the grandfather's medical needs. He also wanted to give his grandfather "one last hurrah," as he was concerned the grandfather's death was just weeks away. He was angry that the nursing home staff had berated him upon their return for not notifying them he was taking the grandfather for the weekend. Considering the CSW's legal obligations, the CSW should:

   a. **Incorrect.** Report the nursing home for inadequate care, and the client for abduction. *While the nursing home care may be inadequate, the simple fact that a family member describes it as such does not mean it is so, and it certainly does not mean the problems in care rise to the level of being abusive or neglectful. (Note that a direct report of suspected abuse* from the victim *generally triggers reporting responsibility for elder or dependent adult abuse.) Also see the rationale for response C below.*

   b. **Incorrect.** Report the nursing home for inadequate care. *While the nursing home care may be inadequate, the simple fact that a family member describes it as such does not mean it is so, and it certainly does not mean the problems in care rise to the level of being abusive or neglectful.*

   c. **Incorrect.** Report the client for abduction. *The simple fact that the client took his grandfather on a fishing trip does not mean the grandfather was abducted. The definition of abduction in elder abuse reporting law specifically requires that the victim have been taken outside of California.*

   d. **CORRECT.** Ask the client to clarify how the nursing home's care is inadequate. *There is nothing reportable in this vignette. While the nursing home care may be inadequate, the simple fact that a family member describes it as such does not mean it is so, and it certainly does not mean the problems in care rise to the level of being abusive or neglectful. While the CSW does not want to take on the role of investigator, inquiring about the client's frustrations with his grandfather's care is clinically appropriate, and this is the only response option that is consistent with the CSW's legal obligations.*

13. An LCSW in private practice grows frustrated with a client who seems to be frequently in crisis, and determines that the client needs a higher level of care than what the LCSW can provide. The LCSW informs the client in person and in writing that in 30 days the LCSW will no longer provide treatment, and offers referrals to inpatient and partial-hospitalization programs as well as other local crisis resources. As the 30 days approach their end, the client has a scheduled termination session with the LCSW. The client reports that they have not even attempted to contact any of the provided referrals, they don't feel capable of doing so, and they are feeling moderately suicidal but without a specific plan or intent. Ethically, the LCSW should:

    a. **CORRECT.** Offer to assist the client during session in contacting other service providers to create a warm handoff

    b. **Incorrect.** Extend the termination deadline by 30 days and encourage the client to contact the referrals previously offered

    c. **Incorrect.** Terminate as scheduled, and ask the client to sign a release granting the LCSW permission to follow up with a close friend or family member to ensure the client is receiving ongoing care

    d. **Incorrect.** Terminate as scheduled, and ask the client to sign a release once they are connected with a new treatment provider, so that the new provider and the LCSW can communicate

This question assesses your knowledge of the ethical requirement to prevent client abandonment. While extending the termination deadline does prevent abandonment in the immediate term, it does little more than kick the can down the road – and may have the result of encouraging future client crises if the client feels that voicing a crisis is necessary to keep the LCSW involved. (The client's voicing of a new crisis may actually support the notion that the client needs a higher level of care than the LCSW can provide.) A better answer is to take necessary steps in session to assist the client in connecting with appropriate providers, ensuring that a transition occurs without crisis needs falling through the cracks.

14. A CSW with a full-time caseload finds herself on the edge of burnout. She notices she is becoming less empathetic and more combative with clients, and frequently arrives at the office in the morning still tired from the day before. A colleague she greatly respects refers her a complex case. The CSW should:

    a. **Incorrect.** Discontinue or temporarily pause treatment with some of her better-functioning clients in order to take the referral.

    b. **Incorrect.** Take the referral without changing any aspects of treatment for her other clients, and take other steps to manage her burnout.

    c. **CORRECT.** Decline the referral, and consider reducing her overall caseload.

    d. **Incorrect.** Accept the referral on a short-term basis, agreeing only to two sessions with the client in order to better assess their needs.

Interrupting treatment with other clients in order to take a new referral (A) may be considered abandonment of those existing clients, and is putting the therapist's needs above those of the clients. Maintaining the same caseload while adding a complex case (B) is likely to only worsen the CSW's burnout; she needs to recognize her impairment and not add to her workload. Accepting the referral on a short-term basis (D) is not likely to be in the best interests of a complex case, and does nothing to move toward resolving the burnout that may be impacting *all* of the CSW's caseload.

15. A CSW works across the street from a major software company's offices. The CSW begins advertising specifically to employees of the company, using the company's logo on the CSW's website and business cards to say that the CSW is "now proudly serving employees of" that company. One client, who works for the software company and had found the CSW through the website, asks about the relationship between the CSW and the software company. The CSW should:

    a. **Incorrect.** Clarify for the client that there is no formal relationship, and that the CSW simply enjoys working with employees of the company. *Clarifying this for one client who has been misled, while helpful, does not prevent others from being similarly misled by the CSW's advertising.*

    b. **CORRECT.** Clarify for the client that there is no formal relationship, and change the website and business cards to not use the company's logo. *Use of the company's logo suggests an affiliation with the company that does not exist.*

    c. **Incorrect.** Seek to develop a more formal relationship with the company, including a contract to treat their employees. *The possible development of a more formal relationship with the company in the future does not make the CSW's advertising any less misleading in the present.*

    d. **Incorrect.** Change the website and business cards to indicate that the company's logo is a registered trademark used with permission. *Providing an indication that the company logo is trademarked does not solve the problem of the marketing material being misleading. Also note that this response did not include the CSW actually obtaining that permission.*

16. A client with a history of eating disorder schedules an intake session with an LCSW to discuss the client's current emotional struggles. In the intake, the client reports that prior treatment has been helpful in reducing disordered eating, but that the client still struggles with body image concerns. Referring to prior treatment, the client says, "I learned a lot about monitoring and responding to my body, but not so much about how to prepare food or specifically what to eat." Ethically, the LCSW should:

   a. **Incorrect.** Diagnose the client as having an active eating disorder
   b. **CORRECT.** Collaborate with the client to determine whether a referral to a dietitian is appropriate
   c. **Incorrect.** Request that the client sign a Release of Information for all prior eating disorder treatment providers, allowing the LCSW to request treatment records
   d. **Incorrect.** Educate the client about the typical course of eating disorder over the life span

Providing a diagnosis or specific education may prove to be wise, but this would be a clinical decision, not an ethical one. The question asks for your ethical judgment. Social workers are expected to refer clients to other professionals when specialized knowledge is necessary to more fully meet the client's needs.

17. A CSW learns that her client's adopted son was recently involved in a series of hit-and-run accidents. At present, law enforcement is investigating but does not know who is responsible. The client expresses fear of all possible outcomes; if the police determine it was her son, the son will likely go to jail. If the police do not determine it was her son, the son may continue with his risky and damaging behavior. The client says she does not want to turn her son in. Considering her legal and ethical obligations, the CSW should:

 a.   **Incorrect.** Report the son to law enforcement as a potential danger to others. *The CSW does not have enough information to justify such a report. There is nothing to indicate that the son's behavior represents an imminent danger.*

 b.   **Incorrect.** Anonymously report the son's actions to law enforcement, without revealing the name of the therapist or the client, and without revealing how the CSW came to know the information. *For the CSW to decide to report would be to breach confidentiality; even if the CSW does not reveal the source of the information, she would be sharing confidential information learned from the client in therapy.*

 c.   **Incorrect.** Encourage the client to report the son to law enforcement to reduce the risk that he will harm others in the future. *Encouraging the client to report the son could be seen as interfering with the client's autonomy, placing the therapist's values above the client's.*

 d.   **CORRECT.** Discuss the client's feelings in greater detail and examine the risks and benefits of various possible courses of action while maintaining the client's confidentiality. *There is no reason here for the therapist to break confidentiality. The focus then becomes addressing how the client should handle the information she has.*

18. A polyamorous couple experiencing difficulty in their sexual relationship presents for therapy with a CSW who believes sexual activity outside of a monogamous relationship is inappropriate and harmful. The couple does not believe that their sexual relationships outside of their own relationship are causing their sexual problems with each other. Ethically, the CSW should:

a. **Incorrect.** Seek to address underlying emotional issues that may be impacting the couple's sexual relationship, so as to improve the relationship without directly discussing the couple's other partners. *While the couple certainly may be correct in their reporting that polyamory is not a problem for them, avoiding discussion of it in therapy is likely to quickly become awkward given that they are there to address couple relationship issues.*

b. **CORRECT.** Refer the couple to a therapist who does not share the CSW's belief. *The therapist's belief is closely related to the issue for which the couple is seeking treatment, and is likely to interfere with that treatment.*

c. **Incorrect.** Inform the clients in advance of her belief, allowing the clients to determine whether they would like to continue therapy with her. *It is the therapist's responsibility, not the client's, to determine when the therapist's values are likely to interfere with effective care.*

d. **Incorrect.** Begin therapy by explaining her belief and the underlying research, and explaining that the couple's theory that their polyamory is not related to their own sexual difficulty is unlikely to be true. *This explanation serves only to defend the therapist's belief and presupposes the cause of the couple's problems.*

19. A mother arrives late for her therapy session and is enraged. She reports that she just spent an hour dealing with police, who came to the grocery store where her car was parked and were about to break a window when she returned to the car and stopped them. The police, she said, rudely lectured her about the infant son she had left in the car while she was grocery shopping. While the car was in sunlight, it was only about 80 degrees out at the time and she had been away from the car for less than 20 minutes, she said. The CSW should:

a. **Incorrect.** Explore the mother's feelings of anger and shame. *Exploring her feelings may be clinically useful, but is not required; a report of suspected child neglect is required.*

b. **Incorrect.** Assess whether the son had suffered any harm. *Unlike with other forms of child abuse, children do not need to have suffered any actual injuries to qualify as having been neglected.*

c. **Incorrect.** Ask for a Release of Information and offer to contact police directly to follow up. *Contacting police to follow up on the incident is offered here without a rationale, so it is unclear whether this would serve any meaningful clinical purpose. To the degree that it may help with the decision of reporting, it places the CSW in an investigator role.*

d. **CORRECT.** Report suspected child neglect. *Leaving an infant alone in a car in direct sunlight, on a warm day with the windows up, presents significant danger to the child. Even if the child did not suffer actual harm, a report is justified.*

20. A CSW is close to successful termination with a father who has been in treatment for 15 sessions. The father expresses his gratitude to the CSW, and says he would like to find a way to help families with similar needs. The CSW is aware of an online discussion group where the father could share his experience in therapy, steering potential clients toward the CSW and offering hope to families experiencing similar problems to the ones his own family had experienced at the beginning of therapy. Ethically, the CSW should:

    a. **Incorrect.** Encourage the father to share his experience in the discussion group, including both positive and negative components, and including the CSW's name so that other participants know where they can receive confidential help. *Asking for the CSW's name to be included would amount to solicitation of a testimonial from a current client, which is ethically prohibited.*

    b. **CORRECT.** Thank the father for his work in therapy, and discuss potential benefits and risks of several potential means by which the father could help similar families. *Confidentiality is the client's right, and they are free to share information from the therapy as they see fit.*

    c. **Incorrect.** Thank the father for his work in therapy, and discourage him from publicly sharing his experience in the interest of confidentiality. *Since the father would like to use the family's experience to help others, it does not make sense to discourage him from doing so. This would arguably interfere with his autonomy.*

    d. **Incorrect.** Encourage the father to share his experience in the discussion group but to do so anonymously, only naming the CSW if he chooses to do so. *Unless the therapist can foresee a specific harm to the client from doing so, it does not make sense to discourage the client from using his own name if he wishes.*

21. A 70-year-old client tells a CSW that the client had been under-medicated for several months while living at a nursing home in Florida the prior year. The CSW asks how the client knows this, and the client says that her prescription specifically noted that her medication should be given twice a day, but she received it only once each day. The CSW believes the client has good cognitive functioning. The CSW should:

 a. **Incorrect.** Report suspected elder abuse to the CSW's local adult protective service agency. *Because she was living in Florida at the time the under-medication occurred, she was not an elder adult as California defines it.*

 b. **Incorrect.** Report suspected elder abuse to the adult protective service agency local to the nursing home in Florida. *Because she was living in Florida at the time the under-medication occurred, she was not an elder adult as California defines it.*

 c. **CORRECT.** Encourage the client to report what happened to the appropriate adult protective service agency in Florida. *The therapist is not obligated to report this under California law, which includes California residency in the definition of an elder adult.*

 d. **Incorrect.** Encourage the client to document the events for a possible civil lawsuit against the nursing home in Florida. *This amounts to providing legal advice to the client, which is outside the CSW scope of practice.*

22. A Latina CSW receives a phone call from a prospective new client couple. The couple reports that they moved to the US from India three years ago, and they would like to come to therapy to work on communication difficulty in their marriage. The CSW strives to maintain strong awareness of cultural issues, but has never worked with anyone from India before. The best course of action for the CSW would be to:

a. **Incorrect.** Refer the couple to a therapist of Indian descent. *Referring the couple out would be discrimination based on national origin.*

b. **Incorrect.** Encourage the clients to educate the CSW about Indian culture and customs. *Relying solely on the clients to educate the therapist on cultural issues is not sufficient; the CSW is expected to do additional work on their own to develop competence where it is lacking.*

c. **CORRECT.** Seek resources and consultation to become familiar with Indian culture and customs, and to understand how Indian clients typically present in therapy. *This best summarizes the CSW's responsibilities. Understanding typical client presentation based on the client culture does not mean the CSW should or would assume that the particular case will match cultural norms, but at least provides a useful reference point for assessment.*

d. **Incorrect.** Wait until the clients come in for an initial assessment to determine whether meaningful cultural differences exist. *Waiting until the clients come in leaves the CSW vulnerable to their own blind spots related to cultural difference, and may lead to incorrect assessment of the couple.*

23. A client tells an LCSW that she left her previous therapist after the therapist became erratic and unfocused. The previous therapist's father died six months ago, and the client wonders whether the therapist had been drinking to cope with the loss. The client's previous therapist is also a clinical social worker, and is someone the current LCSW knows personally. The LCSW should:

   a. **Incorrect.** Apologize on behalf of the colleague. Report the previous therapist to the BBS, as she appears to be unable to provide quality clinical care.
   b. **Incorrect.** Without disclosing what the client said, reach out to the colleague and offer to provide confidential therapy to the colleague to protect clients.
   c. **CORRECT.** Without disclosing what the client said, check in with the colleague. If she volunteers any information about her grief process, encourage the colleague to enter treatment.
   d. **Incorrect.** Directly confront the colleague with what the LCSW knows. Inform the colleague's employer that she may not be healthy enough to provide services.

The NASW Code of Ethics guides CSWs to assist struggling colleagues in obtaining help for issues that interfere with clinical care. Social workers cannot, however, share this information with the BBS or the employer – or with the colleague, for that matter – without permission, as this would be a breach of client confidentiality. Providing direct treatment to the friend would be an improper dual relationship.

24. Partway through an emotionally difficult session, a client tells their social worker, "My psychic said this was going to get worse before it got better. I guess this what they meant." The LCSW is initially startled, and asks the client more about the psychic. The client notes that they have been going to the same psychic weekly for more than five years, and find the process valuable and reassuring, especially when discussing issues of grief. The LCSW should:

    a. **CORRECT.** Ask the client's permission to contact the psychic to develop a professional relationship
    b. **Incorrect.** Discuss the LCSW's concern that the psychic is exploiting the client's fragile emotional state
    c. **Incorrect.** Express to the client that while the services of the psychic may be helpful, they are not grounded in science
    d. **Incorrect.** Explore the client's relationship with the psychic to determine whether the psychic has attempted to diagnose or treat mental illness

Social workers are ethically obligated to develop positive working relationships with other professionals when doing so serves the client. Whatever the LCSW's personal beliefs about the psychic may be, the client clearly finds the interactions with the psychic comforting. The simple fact that the client has been seeing the psychic regularly for five years does not suggest inappropriate behavior on the part of the psychic, either in terms of exploitation or stepping beyond their appropriate scope.

25. Three months before a local election, a social worker is meeting with a client who serves as campaign director for a prominent local politician. The politician is facing a close race, and the social worker supports the politician in light of the politician's policies related to social and economic justice. The client appears exhausted in session, largely due to the demands of their role. The social worker decides to contact the client after the session to offer encouragement. What message should the social worker send to the client?

    a.   **Incorrect.** I'll be tuning in to the debate next week. Good luck.
    b.   **Incorrect.** Let me know how I and everyone who is on your side can make your job easier.
    c.   **CORRECT.** Keep your head up. I know it's hard. You can do this.
    d.   **Incorrect.** I've just donated $100 to your campaign. It's a small gesture, but I want you to know how much I support the campaign.

Since this is a clinical relationship, contacts that are political rather than clinical in nature would be considered non-work-related. All of the options here suggest support for the candidate or the campaign, rather than the client, except for option C. This option is most clearly and specifically clinical support for the client, making it the best choice.

26. A couple seeks counseling from an LCSW to address conflict in their relationship. One partner in the couple identifies as asexual, while the other partner angrily suggests that "asexual" is a "cop-out" the first partner is using to avoid taking action on the first partner's lack of sexual desire, which has been a source of conflict for the couple since the birth of their child four years ago. The first partner has been medically evaluated, and was determined to be in good physical health. Considering the LCSW's ethical responsibilities, how should the LCSW proceed?

a. **Incorrect.** Gather information to determine whether the first partner qualifies as asexual

b. **Incorrect.** Treat this conflict as being no different from other forms of couple conflict, and seek to determine and address the root cause

c. **Incorrect.** Assess whether changes in the couple's diet, exercise, or sleep hygiene may lead to changes in sexual desire

d. **CORRECT.** Gather the couple's history, including information about the first partner's change in how they identify

"Asexual" is generally understood to be a sexual orientation, and sexual orientation is an element of identity determined by the individual, not by the clinician. Conflict over sexual orientation should not be treated the same way as conflict over housework; to do so would likely bring forth a range of oppressive and discriminatory clinical acts. Assessing diet, exercise, and sleep suggest that the first partner's asexuality is a problem to be solved, rather than a sexual orientation to be accepted and affirmed. The clinician should gather the couple's history as part of the assessment process. Gathering information about the first partner's history of how they identify is consistent with that process, and can be done in an affirming manner.

27. A new Latina client informs her social worker that the client has more than 2 million followers on a video-based social media platform, where she talks daily about her struggles with mental health. The client has come to therapy to address symptoms of depression and concerns about body image, and tells the LCSW, "It's getting harder and harder to put an optimistic voice out into the world. Everyone can see what I'm going through." The client asks whether the social worker has heard of the client before; the social worker says no. The session leaves the social worker concerned about the possibility that the client may be heading into crisis, considering that the client has a history of suicide attempts, though the client has made no directly threatening statements. The client does not show for her next session. Considering the social worker's ethical responsibilities, how should they proceed?

    a. **Incorrect.** Search online for the client's social media posts, without becoming a follower or subscriber

    b. **Incorrect.** Search online for the client's social media posts only if the social worker can do so anonymously

    c. **CORRECT.** Search online for the client's social media posts and consider other steps to address potential crisis

    d. **Incorrect.** Contact the client to request their permission to review the client's social media posts

The NASW Code of Ethics generally requires that social workers obtain client consent before searching for them online, making exceptions only when there is imminent danger or other "compelling professional reasons." Here, the client's potential crisis would be considered a compelling professional reason even in the absence of directly threatening statements. Contrast this question with question #8 from the mini-mock exam, where there were not compelling professional reasons to conduct such a search prior to obtaining the client's permission.

28. An elder client tells a CSW working in hospice care that the client was recently taken to a local religious gathering against her will by her 50-year-old daughter. The daughter is a member of the religious group. By the client's report, the daughter told her mother that "this might be good for you, being around people with good values" and did not bring the mother home when the mother said she was uncomfortable there. Furthermore, the daughter donated the cash in the client's purse to the religious group, despite the client's repeated statements to her daughter that the client did not support the group. How should the CSW respond to their legal obligations in this case?

    a. **Incorrect.** Report suspected elder abuse (specifically, abduction)
    b. **CORRECT.** Report suspected elder abuse (specifically, financial abuse)
    c. **Incorrect.** Report suspected elder abuse (specifically, emotional abuse)
    d. **Incorrect.** Report suspected elder abuse (specifically, isolation)

All four options share reporting, so it is safe to presume that reporting is a requirement here. The differences relate to the *type* of abuse being reported. The law surrounding abduction (a) requires that the elder have been taken across state lines, which is not stated in the question. Emotional abuse (c) is not a specific category of elder abuse in statute, though the elder abuse rules do provide wide latitude for therapists to report anything they find to be abusive to an elder. Isolation (d) is perhaps most clearly not appropriate here, as the daughter took the client to a social event. Financial abuse (b) is most appropriate here, given that the client states her daughter took her money against her will and spent it on a cause she would not have supported on her own.

29. An LCSW has been treating a 38-year-old woman who has been abusing substances. The woman has experienced a series of health problems, and lost the debit card that she uses to buy food through a state program. She leaves the social worker a voicemail one morning, saying that she is "tired of people messing with me" and that "the next person who tries to put me down or take something from me is getting dead." The social worker knows that the client carries a gun and a knife with her in most places. What should the LCSW do next?

a. **Incorrect.** Invoke *Tarasoff* and begin the process of notifying law enforcement and the client's neighbors of the potential risk
b. **CORRECT.** Notify law enforcement and attempt to contact and locate the client to initiate the process of hospitalization
c. **Incorrect.** Invoke *Tarasoff* and attempt to contact and locate the client to initiate the process of hospitalization
d. **Incorrect.** Notify law enforcement as a precautionary measure, and assume the client's statements reflect substance intoxication rather than actual physical danger

While the client is potentially dangerous, this is not a *Tarasoff* situation as the client poses a general danger to others, and not a specific danger to reasonably identifiable others. As a result, we can immediately rule out response choices that involve *Tarasoff*. Notifying law enforcement is appropriate, as is attempting to contact and locate the client. Depending on the client's history, their statements may or may not be a result of intoxication; with only the information in the question, the LCSW would err on the side of caution and take steps to protect public safety.

30. A private university contracts with a group practice to provide long-term therapy to university students in need of such services. The university agrees to pay the group practice for up to 20 sessions per student per year at a discounted rate. The practice owner, an LCSW, receives the first request from the university for records that will allow the university to issue payment to the practice. The university requests a list of client names, session dates, and procedure codes for all sessions held with the university's students in the past month. Legally, how should the LCSW respond?

    a. **Incorrect.** Request that each client who attends the university provide a Release of Information allowing the practice to share complete records with the university for billing purposes

    b. **Incorrect.** Provide the university with all data requested except for client names, which can be replaced with ID numbers

    c. **CORRECT.** Provide the university with all of the requested data

    d. **Incorrect.** Ask that all clients who are students of the university pay for sessions at the time of the session, and then submit receipts to the university for reimbursement

The law creates a clear and specific exception to confidentiality for information that is necessary for billing purposes. In this case, it is reasonable for the university to request client names, so that the university can verify that each client is indeed a student. The university is not asking for diagnoses or other treatment details beyond the scope of what is necessary to facilitate billing. The LCSW is free to provide the information requested, understanding that they should only provide the minimum information necessary to achieve the purposes of the disclosure.

31. To battle her flu symptoms, an LCSW working via telehealth takes an over-the-counter medication. Despite the medication containing caffeine, the LCSW soon finds herself drowsy and struggling to maintain focus in session. A couple of clients notice this and express their empathy, as well as their gratitude for the LCSW working with them via telehealth so that there is no risk of the clients becoming infected. Considering the LCSW's ethical responsibilities, the LCSW should:

   a. **CORRECT.** Consult their physician and cancel remaining sessions for the day, ensuring available backup care for any clients who may be in or may go into crisis
   b. **Incorrect.** Ask a colleague to monitor their work for the rest of the day to ensure they are not missing anything clinically important
   c. **Incorrect.** No action is called for, as the LCSW is providing services via telehealth
   d. **Incorrect.** Seek out additional training on working effectively in the presence of illness

While it may not fit into the same mental framework as a clinician abusing substances or struggling with a mental illness, this question is asking about a form of impairment. Clients are noticing the LCSW's difficulty, indicating that it is obvious in – and likely interfering with – sessions. This doesn't reasonably require additional training for the clinician or an outside monitor (which would raise confidentiality concerns); the LCSW should get the treatment they need to resolve the impairment, which likely means resting and focusing on getting healthy.

32. The parents of a developmentally delayed 16-year-old bring the teenager to therapy and provide consent for the teenager's individual therapy. The LCSW providing therapy finds the teenager to be witty and charming. The LCSW also finds the teenager to be emotionally immature and believes her intelligence to be around a second-grade level. After a few sessions where the client appears to be making limited progress, the parents express their dissatisfaction with the LCSW and inform the LCSW that they are pulling their child out of therapy. Considering the LCSW's ethical responsibilities, the LCSW should:

a. **CORRECT.** Offer to assist with continuity of care to another provider or referrals for additional services
b. **Incorrect.** Inform the parents that because the child is older than 12, the child can make their own decisions about consent for treatment
c. **Incorrect.** Advocate on behalf of the client for continuing as the client's therapist
d. **Incorrect.** Ask the client directly, in the presence of the parents, about the client's desire to remain in treatment

It's arguably problematic that the LCSW even took on someone with a second-grade level of intelligence as an individual client, as children at this maturity level are often better served with family-based care. However, that is not what the question asks about, and it is entirely possible that the LCSW has been regularly involving the parents in treatment up to this point. The question assesses whether you understand parents' rights and responsibilities when their child does not have the ability to make effective choices on their own. While social workers "should seek to ensure that the third party [here, the parents] acts in a manner consistent with clients' wishes and interests" (Standard 1.03(c)), asking the child their wishes in the presence of the parents puts the child in a difficult and stressful position. Social workers honor the rights of clients' guardians and representatives to make treatment decisions on behalf of those in their care who are unable to make decisions for themselves.

33. An LCSW's former client threatens a licensing board complaint after the former client requested their records be shared with their new therapist. The records were forwarded as requested, and the new therapist then informed their client that the client had been diagnosed by the LCSW with Post-Traumatic Stress Disorder. The client was surprised by the news, as they had not been previously informed of the diagnosis; treatment with the LCSW had focused on the client's social and relational functioning. The former client demands the LCSW apologize and explain why the LCSW believes the client is, as the client describes it, "broken and unfixable." The LCSW should:

   a. **Incorrect.** Retract the release of the client's record, as its release has caused the client harm
   b. **Incorrect.** Contact the new therapist to explain the diagnosis
   c. **CORRECT.** Explain to the former client what the diagnosis means and how the LCSW determined it
   d. **Incorrect.** Inform the former client of the process for filing a board complaint, and remind them of their ability to provide an addendum that would be added to the treatment record

Social workers are ethically obligated to assist clients in understanding information in their records. In this instance, the client's description of themselves as "broken and unfixable" does not align with current professional thinking about PTSD, which is understood as being both understandable and treatable. The client's description suggests they may not understand what the PTSD diagnosis means.

34. An LCSW is nearing termination with a family the social worker has helped through multiple crises, including the unexpected death of a family member. The family has frequently expressed their gratitude to the social worker, saying things like "you saved us. We're still a family because of you." The LCSW is interested in using one specific, touching statement of gratitude the family shared in session on the LCSW's web site. Ethically, the LCSW should:

   a. **Incorrect.** Ask the clients for their permission, and if granted, post the statement without attaching the clients' names to it
   b. **Incorrect.** Wait until therapy has ended, and then post the statement without attaching the clients' names to it
   c. **CORRECT.** Not post the statement, regardless of timing or client permission
   d. **Incorrect.** Wait until two years after therapy has ended, and then seek the clients' permission to post the statement

The NASW Code of Ethics prohibits the solicitation of testimonials from current clients, and also specifically prohibits solicitation of consent to use a client's prior statement as a testimonial endorsement. Any client statements made in the context of therapy should remain in the context of therapy.

35. An LCSW is providing individual counseling to a 14-year-old at the center of a custody dispute. The mother currently has primary custody, but the father is able to provide independent consent for health care, and was the one to bring the child to treatment and provide consent. The LCSW receives a subpoena to testify at the next custody hearing. The LCSW believes the child is comfortable with the LCSW testifying. The LCSW can best demonstrate understanding of the law by:

   a. **Incorrect.** Contacting the mother to ask her wishes in relation to claiming privilege.
   b. **CORRECT.** Asserting privilege on behalf of the client, and asking that the court make a determination about whether the LCSW should testify.
   c. **Incorrect.** Contacting the father to ask his wishes in relation to claiming privilege.
   d. **Incorrect.** Refusing to testify as the LCSW is not serving as a custody evaluator.

Even minors are typically holders of their own privilege, though they may not be able to waive it on their own. In this instance, given the nature of the case, a judge should determine whether the minor wishes to waive privilege, and if so, whether the court will honor that request. As for option D, the LCSW is allowed to testify as to the facts of the services being provided to the teenager. The LCSW simply could not offer an opinion as to custody, given the nature of the LCSW's role in this case.

36. An LCSW has been treating a 16-year-old under consent from the child's father. The child's parents are divorced, and under the terms of their joint custody agreement, either parent has the authority to consent to health care on behalf of any of the couple's three children. The mother contacts the LCSW to say that she objects to the therapy and is concerned that the LCSW has not prevented the 16-year-old from using marijuana. Consistent with the LCSW's legal responsibilities, the LCSW should:

a. **Incorrect.** Explain to the mother that the LCSW's role is not to prevent the 16-year-old from engaging in marijuana use, but rather to openly discuss such choices and support the 16-year-old's autonomy

b. **Incorrect.** Inform the client and the father of the mother's objection, and let them and the mother know that going forward, both parents' consent will be necessary to continue therapy

c. **Incorrect.** Inform the mother that unless the custody agreement allows her specifically to revoke the father's consent, the LCSW will continue treating the minor as they have been

d. **CORRECT.** Say nothing to the mother, and review the custody agreement

In the absence of a release of information, the mother has no right to any information about the minor's treatment – including even that the minor is a client of the LCSW. Any response to the mother that acknowledges the minor is a client could be seen as a breach of confidentiality. Further, the question stem specifically notes that either parent can consent for treatment, so the LCSW does not need to establish a rule that both parents must consent. (The LCSW *can* establish such a rule, but they are not required to do so.) The best option is to say nothing to the mother in order to protect confidentiality, and to review the custody agreement to determine whether the mother has the right to revoke consent provided by the father. Such a scenario is unlikely, but possible, and the agreement may also include other language that is instructive to the LCSW.

37. In a hospital setting, an LCSW works with patients who are involuntarily hospitalized for being a danger to themselves or others. One such patient is preparing for discharge after one night in the hospital. The treating psychiatrist interrupts the process, and insists that the patient be held for at least another 24 hours. The LCSW brings together the psychiatrist, a member of the nursing team, and a hospital administrator to discuss the case. The psychiatrist is insistent, based on their view of the patient's symptoms. While the others say they are not sure the extended hospitalization is needed, they express willingness to defer to the psychiatrist. The LCSW strongly believes that the additional night is not needed, and explains why, but the psychiatrist is unmoved. The team plans to keep the patient in the hospital for one more night. How should the LCSW proceed?

    a. **CORRECT.** Accept the decision of the team, and seek to better understand the others' perspectives
    b. **Incorrect.** Insist that the perspective of the LCSW be given equal weight to that of the psychiatrist
    c. **Incorrect.** Re-convene the treatment team in an effort to change their minds
    d. **Incorrect.** Refuse to participate in the ongoing care of this specific patient, without allowing it to impact the quality of care provided to others

The team made a clinical decision that appears to be based on clinical factors. The social worker fulfilled their responsibility in contributing to the team's process, and was outvoted. This happens, and is not indicative of an ethical violation or problem. The social worker should continue to work collaboratively with colleagues, appreciating the perspective of each of their professions.

38. An LCSW is serving as a consultant for a software company that is developing a platform where prospective clients can connect with licensed mental health treatment providers, and where providers can make referrals to one another by securely sharing client data when clients have given permission to do so. The company proposes several different pricing models for therapists who wish to participate on the platform. Which of these models could social workers participate in under state law?

   a.   **Incorrect.** Therapist listings are free; when the prospective client matches with a therapist on specified criteria, the therapist pays a fee to view the prospective client's full information and reach out to them

   b.   **Incorrect.** Therapists buy credits that are not assigned to any specific client; when a prospective client matches with a therapist on specified criteria, the therapist can spend one credit to view the prospective client's full information and reach out to them

   c.   **Incorrect.** Referrals, whether from clients referring themselves or from colleagues, are on a dynamic pricing model; depending on demand in the therapist's area, the therapist may need to pay a fee for a prospective referral, or may get paid a small amount to accept the referral

   d.   **CORRECT.** Therapists subscribe to the service to be included in its directory; for an added subscription fee, they can be notified each time a prospective client who matches with them on specified criteria joins the platform and allows clinicians to reach out to them

Each of the first three options amounts to paying for referrals, which is specifically prohibited by law. (In the third case, therapists might also get paid for accepting referrals; that is also legally prohibited.) The final option operates like traditional advertising, which LCSWs can legally pay for.

39. Following an arrest for assault, a 20-year-old man has been seeing an LCSW for private anger management and substance use counseling on orders from the court. Three months into the therapy process, and one month prior to the client's next court date, he reveals to the social worker that he recently had a relapse with methamphetamine. He asks the LCSW to keep this information private. As the court date approaches, the LCSW receives a subpoena from the court demanding all records from the client's treatment. The LCSW is obligated to:

    a. **CORRECT.** Provide full and complete records to the court
    b. **Incorrect.** Provide the court a treatment summary, outlining in general terms the client's participation but without specific information on recent substance use
    c. **Incorrect.** Claim privilege on behalf of the client
    d. **Incorrect.** Provide the court with the client's clinical file, and withhold psychotherapy notes, where the client's recent substance use are noted

When therapy is taking place by court order, privilege does not apply. The social worker should provide the court with complete records. California does not protect psychotherapy notes from subpoena, so if the LCSW was keeping separate psychotherapy notes for this client, those too would need to be provided.

40. A family from Cambodia is seeing an LCSW for family therapy. During a family session, the father tells the therapist that he sometimes disciplines his 15-year-old son the same way the father had been disciplined in Cambodia when he was young: With lashes across his back, using a stick. The mother voices her objection to this form of discipline, and notes that on multiple occasions the son was left bleeding and crying. The most appropriate action for the LCSW would be to:

a. **Incorrect.** Consider the cultural elements involved and inform the clients that such discipline may not be accepted in the US. *While LCSWs must consider cultural influences when designing and implementing treatment, the reporting standards for physical abuse are written to be as objective as possible: If the intentional striking of a child leaves an injury, it is reportable as physical abuse. Failing to report suspected abuse is a legal violation.*

b. **CORRECT.** Report suspected physical abuse to the local child protective service agency. *If the intentional striking of a child leaves an injury, it is reportable as physical abuse. It is up to the local child protective service agency to determine whether and how to involve cultural factors in their response to the abuse.*

c. **Incorrect.** Remind the family of the limits of confidentiality and ask whether there are any photos of the son's injuries. *Asking for photos places the LCSW in the role of investigator rather than treating clinician.*

d. **Incorrect.** Consider the cultural elements involved and research common Cambodian disciplinary practices to determine whether the behavior is consistent with cultural norms. *While LCSWs should consider cultural influences when designing and implementing treatment, the reporting standards for physical abuse are written to be as objective as possible: If the intentional striking of a child leaves an injury, it is reportable as physical abuse. Failing to report suspected abuse is a legal violation.*

41. A client diagnosed with a moderate Anxiety Disorder calls her therapist, who is an LCSW, at the client's scheduled session time. The client informs the therapist that the client will be unable to attend today's scheduled session and asks the LCSW whether they could do a phone session instead. Which step is a necessary part of the LCSW addressing their legal responsibilities?

    a. **Incorrect.** Inform the client that the LCSW must have certification in telehealth to engage in phone sessions.
    b. **Incorrect.** Go forward with the session as scheduled, and assess for potential crisis.
    c. **CORRECT.** Determine and document the client's specific location.
    d. **Incorrect.** Inform the client that while a phone session is not allowed, they can have a session through telehealth if the client can meet using a HIPAA-compliant videoconference platform.

Phone sessions are legal (ruling out option D), and are considered telehealth. Telehealth has its own set of legal requirements established in state regulation. Among those requirements is that the CSW must document the client's specific location (C) at every instance of telehealth. This serves in part to ensure that the therapist is not accidentally practicing across state lines. The LCSW is not obligated to carry on with the session (B), and would be violating the law to go forward with the session without fulfilling their other telehealth responsibilities first. The LCSW does not need specific telehealth certification (A) to engage in telehealth.

42. A client sees an LCSW at a local community clinic for court-mandated anger management groups. The client comes to dislike the LCSW and becomes disruptive, frequently comparing the group to jail, and saying "I'm not free when I'm here." In considering her ethical responsibilities, the LCSW should:

   a. **Incorrect.** Empathize and validate the client's feeling of disempowerment.
   b. **Incorrect.** Terminate therapy with the client and refer them back to court.
   c. **CORRECT.** Remind the client that he is free to attend any anger management group he wishes, or none at all.
   d. **Incorrect.** Tell the client the LCSW will inform the court of his statements if he continues, and encourage him to become more open to the group process.

Empathy and validation (A) may be clinically appropriate but do not address any legal or ethical responsibilities. Termination (B) is premature, given that client frustration with mandated treatment is relatively normal and often can be resolved. While repeated disclosures of the limits of confidentiality are encouraged, using those limits as threats (D) undermines efforts to work collaboratively with the court system. Option C supports client autonomy and maximizes client choice. While failure to attend groups may have legal consequences for the client, they do have the right to make that choice. The client can attend any group, or none; the social worker is not holding the client against their will.

43. An LCSW is working as the Director for a non-profit agency serving the LGBTQIA+ community. As part of her role, the LCSW occasionally sits in on treatment sessions to observe the work of clinicians at the agency. In a session the LCSW is observing, the client informs the treating therapist that the client is in the process of coming out as bisexual, and is unsure of what to reveal to her parents, or when. The client notices that the Director is older than the treating therapist, and asks the Director, "what would you do in my shoes?" The Director should:

a. **CORRECT.** Clarify the Director's role and defer to the treating clinician
b. **Incorrect.** Avoid speaking, so as to reinforce that the treating clinician is running the session
c. **Incorrect.** Answer the question, and then leave the session in order to support the treating clinician in their role
d. **Incorrect.** Inform the client that it is inappropriate to ask such a question of the Director, and redirect the question to the treating clinician

Unless the client had been previously instructed not to engage with the Director, they haven't done anything wrong by asking the question. The Director is also not required to take an extreme stance here, such as avoiding speaking entirely or leaving the room immediately after they respond. The Director's ethical obligation, since they are an LCSW but not serving in a direct treatment role, is to clarify the Director role.

44. A client on probation comes to a scheduled session with an LCSW appearing angry. The client confronts the LCSW on a report the LCSW recently filed with the probation officer, updating the probation officer on the client's attendance in therapy. (There is a release in place allowing for the report to be sent directly.) The client had been making good progress in therapy, and is disappointed that the probation officer "didn't seem to know or care." To manage their ethical responsibilities, the LCSW should:

a. **CORRECT.** Review with the client what information is sent to the probation officer, and how that information can be used
b. **Incorrect.** Review with the client their progress to date in therapy
c. **Incorrect.** Remind the client that legally, the LCSW can only inform the probation officer about their attendance in therapy, not about specific therapy content
d. **Incorrect.** Remind the client that the role of the probation officer is not to provide support or encouragement, but to ensure compliance

While roles within a treatment team should be clarified among the professionals involved, it is generally not the LCSW's place to describe the roles of others (D). A release of information can request or allow whatever information the client wishes to be sent, and is not limited to attendance (C). Reviewing client progress (B) may be helpful, but would be a clinical determination and not an ethical one. The ethical responsibility here is to review confidentiality and its limitations as needed throughout the therapeutic process. That reasonably includes what information is sent and how it can be used (or, as in this case, not used).

45. A 14-year-old girl presents for therapy at a local mental health clinic, where a CSW is assigned to her case. During a screening interview, the girl tells the CSW that she is struggling with anxiety around her schoolwork and social relationships. She goes on to say that she plans to pay for therapy on her own and would prefer that her parents not know she is in therapy. The CSW should:

a. **CORRECT.** Assess the girl's ability to participate intelligently in therapy and determine whether notifying the parents would be damaging. *Minors 12 and older can independently consent for treatment if the therapist considers them mature enough to participate intelligently. No adult needs to consent on their behalf. This law also requires therapists to contact the parents unless doing so would be damaging.*

b. **Incorrect.** Determine whether notifying the parents would be damaging and determine what adult can consent for the girl's therapy. *Minors 12 and older can independently consent for treatment if the therapist considers them mature enough to participate intelligently. No adult needs to consent on their behalf.*

c. **Incorrect.** Assess the girl's ability to participate intelligently in treatment and inform her that even when seen under her own consent, her parents may have the right to access her records if they become aware she is in therapy. *When a minor consents for their own therapy, the parents do not have a right to records of treatment.*

d. **Incorrect.** Determine whether notifying the parents would be damaging and determine whether notifying the girl's school would be damaging. *Notifying the school without the client's permission could be a breach of confidentiality.*

46. A CSW provided therapy to a 16-year-old boy for several months with his parents' consent. A few months later, the CSW receives a subpoena from the attorney for a classmate of the boy. The classmate accused the client of physical assault, and the classmate's family is suing to recover medical expenses. The subpoena requests complete records of the boy's treatment. The CSW attempts to contact the client and his parents but is unsuccessful. The CSW should:

a. **Incorrect.** Wait to respond to the subpoena until the CSW is able to determine how the client would like the CSW to respond. *Failing to respond to a subpoena may land the CSW in trouble with the court.*

b. **Incorrect.** Wait to respond to the subpoena until the CSW is able to determine how the parents would like the CSW to respond. *Failing to respond to a subpoena may land the CSW in trouble with the court.*

c. **CORRECT.** Respond to the subpoena by asserting privilege, and continue attempts to contact the client and his parents. *When clients cannot be reached to determine their preferred response to a subpoena, asserting privilege on their behalf is a reasonable default position to take.*

d. **Incorrect.** Acknowledge the exception to privilege, turn over the client's records, and inform the client and his family as soon as possible. *It is up to a judge, and not the therapist, to determine whether an exception to privilege applies.*

47. An LCSW is working with a Latina mother and her 7-year-old son in therapy, when the LCSW observes unusual bruises on the boy's face and arms. The bruises seem to be in several different stages of healing. When the LCSW asks how he got the bruises, the boy does not answer. His mother says, "He's a normal boy, he likes to play rough" and refuses to discuss the matter further. The LCSW should:

    a. **CORRECT.** Report suspected child abuse.
    b. **Incorrect.** Consider whether physical discipline is common in Latin cultures.
    c. **Incorrect.** Remind the mother of the limits of confidentiality.
    d. **Incorrect.** Ask the child to remove his shirt to inspect his torso for additional injuries.

While the injuries, and both clients' response to the therapist's inquiries, are not a guarantee that abuse has taken place, remember that the therapist does not need to be certain. They just need to reasonably suspect abuse. The location of the injuries, the fact that they are in multiple stages of healing, and the refusal to explain them would amount to reasonable suspicion in almost any CSW's mind. B would not be correct because the abuse reporting standards do not change on the basis of client culture. C is not correct because it would be an insufficient response to what appears to be abuse. D is not correct because this would place the CSW in the role of an investigator, which is not the proper role of a therapist.

48. A CSW worked with a woman in individual therapy for six months, focusing on treatment of depression symptoms following the client's messy divorce. The client improved significantly in therapy and terminated successfully. One year later, the CSW has been dating a man for two months when the CSW realizes the man is the ex-husband of the former client. The CSW should:

    a. **Incorrect.** Discontinue the romantic relationship. *The ex-husband is not a current or former client. The client terminated successfully. None of the standards surrounding social workers' sexual partners appear to apply here. There is reason to wonder whether the former client may wish to return to therapy in the future, and what the CSW should do in that instance. But that is not part of the question at hand.*

    b. **Incorrect.** Contact the former client to determine her wishes. Given the amount of time that has passed and the success of treatment, she is likely to give her blessing. *Contacting the former client inappropriately places the therapist's interests ahead of the former client's, and makes the former client responsible to some degree for the CSW's ethical decision-making.*

    c. **Incorrect.** Self-report to the BBS to seek their guidance on the most appropriate way to proceed. *The BBS does not serve in the role of ethics consultant. They enforce the legal standards of the profession. If the CSW is interested in an ethical opinion, they should contact NASW or other professional and legal resources.*

    d. **CORRECT.** No action is called for. *Because none of the ethical prohibitions regarding sexual relationships appear to apply here, the CSW is not obligated to any specific course of action.*

49. With the client's consent, a CSW working with an adolescent client encourages one of the client's teachers to attend sessions that will focus on the adolescent's behavior in school. While the teacher's presence is at first helpful, the teacher asks to continue coming to the sessions, and it is clear to the CSW that the client is finding the teacher's presence gradually more intrusive and uncomfortable. The CSW should:

a. **CORRECT.** Clarify the teacher's role in treatment, and ask the client whether they would like to continue having the teacher in session. *When third parties are brought into treatment, that does not mean that the presence of these third parties is permanent or unmanageable. Clarifying roles on an ongoing basis in helpful and expected. Permission for third parties to be involved in therapy can be revoked in many circumstances.*

b. **Incorrect.** Ask the client whether they would like to continue having the teacher in session, and remind the teacher of the limits to confidentiality. *Reminding the teacher of the limits of confidentiality may or may not alleviate the client's concern about the teacher's presence.*

c. **Incorrect.** Ask the client to contact the school and request that the teacher be removed from the therapy sessions. *Having the client contact the school about the teacher's presence in therapy places an undue burden of responsibility on both the client and the school; if the client wants the teacher removed and the therapist believes the teacher's presence is harmful, the therapist should take responsibility for ensuring that the teacher is removed.*

d. **Incorrect.** Remind the client of the goals of therapy and the reasons for the teacher's presence in session. *Reminding the adolescent of the goals of treatment may or may not alleviate the client's concern about the teacher's presence.*

50. An older woman who has been seeing a CSW for seven months storms out of session after her therapist started the session some 30 minutes late. The CSW attempted to explain that another client had been in crisis, but the woman cut off the CSW, saying that the delay was disrespectful of her time. A few days later the client calls the CSW saying she will not come back for future sessions and requesting a copy of the treatment record be sent to her. The CSW should:

a. **Incorrect.** Insist that the client come in for an additional session to discuss her hurt feelings, and provide a copy of the treatment record. *The client cannot be forced to come back in, and making the discussion about the client's hurt feelings suggests that the client is to blame for feeling hurt. This is not likely to improve the fractured therapeutic relationship.*

b. **CORRECT.** Apologize for the delay, offer to discuss it further, provide options for other treatment providers, and provide a copy of the treatment record. *When treatment is terminated, even if the termination is conflictual, CSWs are obligated to provide additional treatment options for continuity of care, and this response option includes this key step.*

c. **Incorrect.** Provide a copy of the treatment record, and consider whether the client's display was simply a way of resolving cognitive dissonance about the need to end treatment. *Even if the client's departure was a way of resolving dissonance around leaving therapy -- a big leap from the information in the vignette -- referrals still must be provided to ensure continuity of care.*

d. **Incorrect.** Provide options for other treatment providers, and inform the client that the CSW will forward the treatment record to the new provider of the client's choosing, in order to ensure that the client does remain in therapy. *The CSW cannot hold records hostage and demand that the client continue treatment. Doing so violates the client's autonomy. The client requested that records be sent to her, so the CSW should either take steps to provide those records or establish why doing so would be harmful.*

51. An LCSW with strong religious beliefs is talking with a trans male client about the client's family history. The client reveals that his parents had strong religious beliefs, but the client describes himself as atheist and says, "I just never understood why people buy into those fairy tales." The client says he has never found comfort or strength in religious or spiritual activity, and has judgment toward those who do. The LCSW should:

   a. **Incorrect.** Mention the LCSW's beliefs briefly, without challenging the client's experience
   b. **Incorrect.** Inform the client that religion is a source of comfort for many people, and encourage the client to keep an open mind toward it for the future
   c. **Incorrect.** Connect the client's beliefs about religion with their history of family trauma
   d. **CORRECT.** Show understanding of the client's beliefs and inquire further about their family history

There is nothing in the question to indicate that the client's beliefs are causing him suffering. There's no obligation or evidence of likely clinical benefit for the LCSW to raise their own beliefs. For the social worker to mention their own beliefs, to try to change the client to a position of openness for future changes in belief, or to conclude that the client's beliefs must be related to trauma *in the absence of any evidence of trauma*, would be inappropriate.

52. A CSW is consulting with the physician who sent a young couple to the CSW for couple therapy. Both partners in the couple are struggling with symptoms of anxiety. The physician provides the CSW with useful information on the couple's medications and their possible side effects. The CSW offers the physician useful information on the progression of the couple's symptoms. Toward the end of the conversation, the physician asks whether the older partner in the couple is "still wearing that same brown sweater twice a week." The CSW should:

    a. **Incorrect.** Answer the question. *Even without a release, the CSW could answer questions directly related to diagnosis or treatment planning; however, since this question does not appear to fall in either category, it falls outside of that allowance in HIPAA.*

    b. **CORRECT.** Politely decline to answer the question, as it is not relevant to the consultation. *When taking part in a consultation, a CSW only provides information relevant to the purposes of that consultation.*

    c. **Incorrect.** Request a release from both partners to provide this type of information. *While the CSW could get a release from the clients allowing the CSW to discuss whatever the clients want the CSW to discuss, this does not change the CSW's ethical responsibilities around consultations, which include refusing to share information that is not relevant to the reason for the consult.*

    d. **Incorrect.** Gently note that the physician is asking a question outside of their scope of practice. *It is not the CSW's proper role to inform a physician of their own scope. The physician may have reasons for asking the question that relate to the partner's physical symptoms or mental health.*

53. A middle-aged woman struggling with panic disorder asks an LCSW whether her brother can come with her to therapy, and the LCSW approves. In the intake session, the woman describes her panic symptoms, as well as the strain that her panic has caused in her relationship with her brother. She relies on him to feel safe in public situations, and becomes angry with him when he cannot be with her due to his job or other obligations. The brother agrees, saying that while he wants to help his sister as much as he can and is glad that she is seeking treatment, he is growing resentful of being her main source of support. The LCSW should:

   a. **CORRECT.** Clarify whether the woman and her brother are seeking conjoint treatment to address their relationship, or whether treatment is to focus on the woman's panic
   b. **Incorrect.** Ask the brother to leave the session so that the LCSW can assess the woman for possible dependent adult abuse
   c. **Incorrect.** Ask the client to sign a release of information allowing for discussion of her symptoms in therapy sessions where her brother is also present
   d. **Incorrect.** Provide the client with referrals to co-occurring disorder treatment

There is no evidence here of substance use (co-occurring disorder) or dependent adult abuse (while the brother's resentment is a potential risk factor warranting assessment for violence, panic disorder alone does not make someone a dependent adult). A release of information may be warranted if treatment is to go forward as individual treatment. But the first thing the LCSW needs to do here is determine who exactly is the "client," and asking about the focus of treatment is a good way to get there.

54. An LCSW has a client who lives on a boat three months of the year, as a commercial fisherman. During that time, he comes back to shore one day a week, and sees the LCSW on that day. The client is relatively poor, and asks the LCSW whether he can pay for services in fresh salmon. The client says he may need to discontinue treatment otherwise. The LCSW frequently eats salmon, and so is familiar with the fair market value of the fish. Which of the following statements of the LCSW's responsibilities is correct?

a. **Incorrect.** The LCSW should provide services pro bono, rather than accepting payment in fish. *Reducing fees is an acceptable resolution to the dilemma, but this response uses the word "should," suggesting that this solution is better than bartering. The carve-out in the ethics code for bartering appears to be made for precisely this type of situation.*

b. **CORRECT.** If the LCSW chooses to go ahead with the barter agreement, the value of the fish should approximate the fee generally charged for therapy, and there should be a clear contract. *While LCSWs ordinarily do not accept goods or services as payment, in limited circumstances it can be acceptable. In this case, the client has specifically requested the barter arrangement, a fair value for the salmon can be easily determined, and there does not appear to be any distortion to the professional relationship that would occur. As the alternative is discontinuation of treatment, it would be ethically appropriate to at least consider the barter arrangement.*

c. **Incorrect.** The LCSW should refer the client to a low-fee or no-fee clinic rather than accepting salmon as payment. *Referring out is an acceptable resolution to the dilemma, but this option uses the word "should," suggesting that this solution is better than bartering. The carve-out in the ethics codes for bartering appear to be made for precisely this type of situation.*

d. **Incorrect.** The LCSW should consider whether other clients would also want to pay for therapy through the products they make or services they provide. *Whether a barter agreement would be appropriate for another client is not relevant to the consideration of appropriateness for this specific client.*

55. An LCSW suffers a serious illness, and a colleague steps in to take over the LCSW's ongoing clients until the LCSW can return to practice. The LCSW agrees to continue handling billing and to review the colleague's session notes to keep up with what is happening while she is recovering. Some of the LCSW's ongoing clients pay for sessions through their health insurance. However, the colleague (who is also a licensed LCSW in private practice) is not on any insurance panels. The ill LCSW should:

    a.   **Incorrect.** Continue to submit insurance billing listing herself as the treatment provider. *This would be a misrepresentation and may be considered insurance fraud.*

    b.   **Incorrect.** Continue to submit insurance billing listing the colleague as the treatment provider and herself as the supervisor. *Because the colleague is taking over treatment, the colleague is indeed the treatment provider. Listing herself as the supervisor, however, is problematic as the colleague is apparently neither employed nor supervised by the LCSW. This would be a misrepresentation and may be considered insurance fraud.*

    c.   **CORRECT.** Either directly or through the colleague, inform clients of the difference in panel status and arrange alternate payment or referrals as needed.

    d.   **Incorrect.** Defer to the colleague to negotiate fees independently, and otherwise presume that the LCSW's typical business practices will be followed. *Each of these issues help establish why a professional will is so important. It should clarify whether the colleague can change client fees, and what business practices the LCSW expects the colleague to follow. It is not safe to simply presume that the colleague's business practices will be the same as the LCSW's.*

56. An adult client who has been seeing a CSW in therapy for six months asks the CSW for a copy of her treatment record. Because the CSW has documented that she suspects the client is being dishonest in her denials of recent drug use, the CSW worries that sharing the file would harm the therapeutic relationship. The most appropriate course of action for the CSW would be to:

a. **Incorrect.** Turn over the records as required by law, and use it as an opportunity to address the client's possible substance use. *CSWs are not required to turn over requested records if the CSW believes the release would be harmful to the client.*

b. **Incorrect.** Provide the client with a partial copy of the file, leaving out the suspicion of recent drug use. *While providing a treatment summary is legal and often appropriate, simply providing a partial copy of the file and leaving out the suspicion of drug use is not an option under the law. It may even be considered fraudulent if it is presented as if it were the complete record.*

c. **CORRECT.** Refuse to turn over the records, offer a treatment summary instead, and inform the client that if she wishes, she can select a neutral therapist to review the file. *The CSW has good reason to believe that releasing the full treatment record could harm the therapeutic relationship and thus harm the client. Under the law, the CSW is allowed to offer a treatment summary instead. Further, when a CSW refuses to release records due to the risk of harm, the CSW must also inform the client of their right to a third-party review of the record by another therapist.*

d. **Incorrect.** Submit the client's request, and the CSW's reason for refusing, to a district judge for review. *Turning over the records to a judge in the absence of a release of information from the client would be a breach of confidentiality.*

57. An individual client acknowledges to her therapist (a CSW) that she lied on the CSW's intake form and actually does have several past suicide attempts in her history. She says she is not feeling suicidal now, though she has recently experienced the ending of a romantic relationship and the death of a distant relative. Legally, the CSW should:

a. **Incorrect.** Complete a No Harm Contract with the client. *No Harm Contracts have largely fallen out of favor, replaced by safety plans; either way, such a response here would likely be considered inadequate to the client's level of risk.*

b. **Incorrect.** Discontinue therapy and refer the client to a higher level of care, as she is high risk. *Discontinuing therapy is not a legal requirement and may be clinically harmful, leaving the client with the lesson that they will be punished if they openly discuss their history of suicidality.*

c. **Incorrect.** Initiate the process of involuntary hospitalization. *While the client does pose an elevated level of risk, the fact that she denies current suicidality means that an attempt to initiate involuntary hospitalization would likely be considered a breach of confidentiality - - and that hospitals would likely turn her away to keep room available for higher-risk patients who are more actively suicidal.*

d. **CORRECT.** Assess further and break confidentiality if required to resolve any threat of suicide. *CSWs are legally obligated to take steps necessary to prevent a threatened suicide, and may break confidentiality if necessary as part of that process.*

58. A client reports to her therapist, a CSW, that the client's antidepressant medication does not appear to be having a positive effect even after eight weeks of her taking the prescribed dosage. The client complains that the office staff for the prescribing physician is disorganized, and the doctor is sometimes hard to reach. The CSW should:

a. **Incorrect.** Encourage the client to request a medication change
b. **Incorrect.** Encourage the client to request a higher dosage to achieve the intended effect
c. **CORRECT.** Encourage the client to consult with her physician
d. **Incorrect.** Encourage the client to consider discontinuing the medication and focusing on efforts to improve her depressive symptoms through therapy

All responses other than option C would be advising on medication, which is outside of the CSW scope of practice. While CSWs should maintain awareness of potential drug side effects to know when a referral is appropriate, CSWs can ultimately only guide clients back to their physician to address medication-related concerns. The physician being difficult to reach does not change any of the CSW's legal obligations in this scenario.

59. An LCSW in an outpatient group practice setting has fallen behind on their documentation. The owner of the practice expresses concern that the delays will impact insurance billing and, ultimately, the practice's financial health. To ethically resolve this issue, the LCSW should:

    a. **Incorrect.** Create at least cursory progress notes for all sessions more than 7 days in the past, even if such notes are a single sentence each, to allow billing to move forward

    b. **Incorrect.** Transfer their clients to other clinicians in the group, allowing the other clinicians to create documentation of past sessions establishing themselves as the service providers and to properly submit insurance claims

    c. **CORRECT.** Work diligently to catch up

    d. **Incorrect.** Consider reducing their client load or, if necessary, leaving the practice

The NASW Code of Ethics demands that social workers produce accurate and timely documentation that adequately reflects the services provided. One-sentence progress notes (A) likely would not be sufficient (they would not meaningfully reflect the services provided, and they would not be useful if a need for continuity of service with another clinician emerged), having other clinicians present themselves as the service providers for past sessions (B) would not be accurate, and reducing client load or leaving the practice (D) does nothing to resolve the issues related to the notes for sessions already conducted. There's also no other evidence in the question to suggest that the LCSW is impaired in such a way that would support reducing their client load or potentially leaving the practice. The most ethical thing for the social worker to do here is make a priority of catching up, in accordance with those ethical standards.

60. An LCSW is serving as the family therapist for a family where the father is also engaged in individual therapy with another provider. The family has only attended one session so far, and while the father informed the LCSW of his individual therapy, he did not provide information about the other therapist or sign a release of information. The LCSW receives a voicemail message from a local therapist, identifying themselves as the individual therapist for the father, and asking the LCSW to provide any information the LCSW may have regarding the father's history of psychosis, as the individual therapist is attempting to determine a proper diagnosis. Considering the LCSW's ethical responsibilities, the LCSW should:

    a.   **Incorrect.** Provide the colleague with the minimum information necessary to aid them in diagnosis

    b.   **Incorrect.** Provide the colleague with the client's full medical and mental health history

    c.   **CORRECT.** Contact the father to assess his wishes and ask him to sign a release of information

    d.   **Incorrect.** Contact the father to inform him that his information will be disclosed; remind him of the limits of confidentiality

It's important to note in this question that you are being tested on knowledge of the LCSW's ethical responsibilities, not the laws around disclosure. While it is legally permissible for two active treatment providers to share information without a release when the disclosure is for the purposes of diagnosis or treatment planning, the fact that such releases are *allowed* does not mean they are *required*. So social workers should consider their ethical responsibilities before choosing to disclose such information. One such responsibility is to "inform clients, to the extent possible, about the disclosure of confidential information and the potential consequences, when feasible before the disclosure is made" (Standard 1.07(d)). Since this situation is not an emergency, it would be most appropriate to contact the client prior to any disclosure, to determine his wishes and ask him to formally authorize the release. You can contrast this question with question 30, which asked specifically about the *laws* around disclosure of billing information.

61. In a mid-size college town, an LCSW is the only local mental health provider who speaks fluent Farsi. She routinely receives referrals from other providers when the other provider discovers that their client identifies as Persian or speaks Farsi, even if the client is also fluent in English. Given her ties to the local Persian community, the LCSW often finds that she is at least somewhat familiar with the new clients being referred to her. Considering her ethical responsibilities, the LCSW should:

    a. **CORRECT.** Refer out clients who could effectively receive services from other providers, retaining those who speak only Farsi, unless her familiarity makes her incapable of providing unbiased care

    b. **Incorrect.** Refer out clients she has any form of prior knowledge about

    c. **Incorrect.** Refer out clients she has personally interacted with in the last two years, retaining the rest

    d. **Incorrect.** Reach out to referring providers and let them know she cannot accept additional Farsi-speaking clients

If the LCSW is the only local provider who can provide services in Farsi, this adds complexity to the consideration of how to manage potential dual relationships. The simple fact of familiarity, in and of itself, is not enough for the LCSW to be required to turn away clients (B). Her obligation is to consider whether a dual relationship would impair her clinical judgment or increase the risk of exploitation. This obligation is best balanced with her ability to provide culturally appropriate services in option A. There is no rule related to personal interactions in the past two years (C). And turning away any new Farsi-speaking clients simply because they speak Farsi (D) would leave local Farsi speakers without any local providers.

62. A single LCSW finds herself sometimes flirting with one particular group therapy client at the end of each week's session, as the other group members are making their way outside. The group member is also single, and appears to be interested in the therapist, but is careful to not cross boundaries during session or in other situations where other group members could see. One evening, the client sends the social worker an email to express gratitude for all she has done in the group, and attaches a couple of racy photos. The LCSW should:

    a. **Incorrect.** Ignore the photos, respond to the gratitude, and encourage continued growth in group

    b. **Incorrect.** Do not respond via email, engage the client in a phone discussion, warn the client that the email cannot remain confidential, and consider termination from the group

    c. **Incorrect.** Acknowledge the email, inform the client that they are violating the LCSW's boundaries, and inform the client that sexually explicit communications must be reported

    d. **CORRECT.** Acknowledge the email, inform the client that including the photos was inappropriate, apologize for any misunderstanding about the nature of their relationship, and monitor both the LCSW's and the client's future behavior

There is no legal or ethical standard that requires the social worker to report sexually explicit communications from the client. At the same time, the client's boundary-testing should not be simply ignored, as this may lead the client to believe that their efforts are welcomed. The LCSW should enforce a boundary around sexual contact with clients (sexual communications in this case would be considered sexual contact), and monitor her and her client's behavior closely going forward.

63. A social worker at a private nonprofit outpatient clinic is surprised to learn that the clinic has a policy of neutrality on political matters. The social worker had hoped to get the clinic to support a proposed local law that would raise sales taxes to improve local services and accessibility for those with disabilities. The clinic asks the social worker to stay out of political discussion about the proposed law, which the social worker believes would advance social justice. The director of the clinic says that she also believes the proposal is good, but is committed to the clinic policy. How should the social worker proceed?

   a. **Incorrect.** Respect the wishes of the employer, and support the proposal by voting for it and potentially donating money to groups that are advocating for its passage
   b. **Incorrect.** Engage in public discussion of the proposal, and describe the clinic as being in favor of it
   c. **Incorrect.** Engage in public discussion of the proposal, and criticize the clinic's unwillingness to take a public stance as likely an effort to preserve their grants and contracts
   d. **CORRECT.** Engage in public discussion of the proposal, but as an individual and not as a representative of the clinic

Under the NASW code, social workers should not allow employer policies to prevent them from the ethical practice of social work – including the pursuit of social justice. At the same time, social workers have a responsibility to treat colleagues with fairness and respect; describing the clinic as in favor of the proposal would not be accurate when the clinic has taken no formal position, and criticizing the clinic's non-stance as money-driven in the absence of any evidence of such is not fair to the clinic. The social worker should publicly support the proposal, but should do so on their own.

64. A group practice specializing in working with depression is considering implementing a new policy to build awareness of their work: As part of the consent process, all clients must agree to post at least once on social media about their experience in therapy, making specific mention of the group practice when they do. The policy specifies that the post does not need to be an endorsement or testimonial; even negative discussion is allowed, so long as it is truthful. Clients who have no social media presence would be exempt. Considering the LCSW's ethical responsibilities, what should the LCSW do around this policy?

    a.   **Incorrect.** Clarify to clients that since it is part of the consent process, they are free to go to a different provider who does not have such a policy if they wish

    b.   **Incorrect.** Clarify to all clients that such posts are strongly encouraged, but are not required, regardless of what the official policy may say

    c.   **Incorrect.** Clarify with the practice owners what the consequence would be for clients who agree to the policy but ultimately do not post about their experience

    d.   **CORRECT.** Refuse to implement the policy, and ask the group practice to withdraw it

Such a policy is inherently exploitive, meant to place the business interests of the practice ahead of the clinical needs of clients. The fact that it applies to all clients means that even clients who are deeply depressed or otherwise desperate to receive services would be bound by it. The LCSW should not implement such a policy, and should work with the employer to withdraw it.

65. In a large public mental health clinic, a social worker (Social Worker A) becomes aware of a colleague in the clinic (Social Worker B) who describes all trans, queer, nonbinary, or otherwise gender-nonconforming clients as mentally ill, and refuses to work with such clients. Supervisors are aware of the issue and make sure that the colleague is only assigned cisgender clients. A different colleague (Social Worker C), who complained about Social Worker B's behavior, was then told that Social Worker B had accused them of religious discrimination, a charge that Social Worker A believes to be false. What ethical responsibility does Social Worker A have in this circumstance?

    a.   **CORRECT.** Assist in Social Worker C's defense; bring Social Worker B's behavior to the attention of administrators; file a formal ethical complaint against Social Worker B if needed

    b.   **Incorrect.** Assist in Social Worker C's defense; demand supervisors explain why they did not take additional action

    c.   **Incorrect.** Because all potentially problematic behavior has been reported, allow the administrative processes of resolving all complaints to reach their conclusions; evaluate options at that point

    d.   **Incorrect.** File an ethics complaint against Social Worker B and their supervisor with the NASW Ethics Committee

Social workers are obligated to "defend and assist colleagues who are unjustly charged with unethical conduct" (NASW standard 2.10e), and should not condone or participate in discrimination. They should report unethical or incompetent behavior through proper formal channels; if the supervisors' actions have not addressed the issue, Social Worker A should attempt to address the issue through clinic administration. Social Worker A is not in a position to make demands of supervisors related to their actions surrounding a colleague, but can take additional steps if the problem does not appear to be resolved. However, a complaint to NASW against the supervisor would be premature, without knowing what steps the supervisor had taken in addition to restricting the clients served by Social Worker B.

66. An LCSW is working in a community clinic in a city where most residents identify themselves as religious. The LCSW is sometimes asked about their own beliefs, and answers the question briefly when asked, before moving on with the conversation. An individual client presses the LCSW for more detail, noting that the LCSW seems confident and well-grounded, while the client has experienced a great deal of upheaval. The client asks the LCSW where they attend services, and how the client might learn more about or even convert to the LCSW's religion. The LCSW is a leader in their religious group. Ethically, how should the LCSW proceed?

    a.   **Incorrect.** Inform the client that there are many ways by which they could find peace and comfort, and that religion does not necessarily need to be one of them

    b.   **Incorrect.** Considering that the client is initiating the conversation, the LCSW can inform the client about the LCSW's religious group, as doing so is in the client's best interests

    c.   **CORRECT.** Seek to understand more about the client's suffering and their spiritual beliefs and preferences, so as to guide them more appropriately

    d.   **Incorrect.** Refuse to address religious or spiritual belief in the context of secular treatment

The LCSW should not use this opportunity to recruit for their own religious group. At the same time, avoiding or discouraging the topic of religion or spirituality entirely is not consistent with the client's interests or needs. They may indeed benefit from being part of a like-minded spiritual community. The LCSW can keep the client's needs central by better understanding their beliefs and preferences, and guiding them toward a community aligned with those needs and preferences.

67. A 15-year-old girl is seeing a CSW individually for issues related to body image and self-esteem. Her parents provided consent for the therapy and pay for her sessions, but do not participate. The girl tells the CSW that she has been exploring her sexuality. While her parents were out of town, she had sexual intercourse with a friend's 19-year-old brother. A few days later, she had intercourse with another boy, an 18-year-old senior at her high school. The CSW should manage their legal responsibilities by:

    a.   **Incorrect.** Reporting child abuse to the local child protective service agency

    b.   **Incorrect.** Investigating to ensure that the sexual activity was not coerced or while under the influence of drugs or alcohol

    c.   **Incorrect.** Notifying the parents of their daughter's high-risk sexual behavior

    d.   **CORRECT.** Maintaining confidentiality

The age combination of the partners, in both instances of sexual activity, does not require reporting (A). If either boy were 21 or over, or under 14, these combinations would be reportable. While it may be clinically relevant to explore the context of the sexual activity in more detail, the CSW is not obligated to do so, and in fact should not position themselves as an investigator (B). While the parents may be able to access their daughter's treatment records, the CSW does not have a responsibility to proactively inform them of sexual behavior; further, there is nothing in the question that would necessarily classify this girl's behavior as "high-risk" (C). In the absence of a legal requirement or allowance for disclosure, the CSW is legally obligated to maintain confidentiality.

68. A client has cancelled three of the last seven scheduled sessions with an LCSW, and been a no-show for the other four. Each time, the client has promised to pay any balance charged, and to come in for a session the following week. The LCSW finds herself irritated with the client's behavior, going so far as to warn the client two weeks ago that she would simply close the client's case and refer out if the client didn't come in. The client was a no-show for the next two scheduled weekly sessions. Even before this long series of missed appointments, the LCSW found herself personally disliking the client. How should the LCSW manage her ethical responsibilities in this case?

    a. **Incorrect.** Meaningfully assess for crisis, and continue as the client's treatment provider if necessary.

    b. **CORRECT.** Close the case, providing the client with appropriate referrals to other providers.

    c. **Incorrect.** Provide the client at least two additional warnings, one of which must be in writing, prior to terminating therapy.

    d. **Incorrect.** Seek consultation to address countertransference, and continue to work toward the client more regularly attending therapy.

You can terminate therapy for almost any reason, so long as that reason is not discriminatory in nature, any evident crisis issues are addressed, and the client is provided with appropriate referrals. In this case, the client has a pattern of non-attendance and was warned that this would lead to termination. There is no legal or ethical responsibility to provide redundant warnings (C). While assessing for crisis is generally a good idea (A), even if crisis issues were present (none are noted in the question), this would not necessarily obligate the therapist to remain the client's treatment provider. If anything, evidence of crisis combined with non-attendance in therapy might suggest a need for coordinated transfer to a higher level of care. While the CSW's response to the client may indeed indicate countertransference (D), therapists are not required to continue working with clients they don't like. Termination is appropriate here.

69. As a client leaves a CSW's office, the CSW believes the client poses a serious danger to the client's spouse. (The client had been making threats in session about what he would do to her.) The CSW, knowing the couple lives roughly 30 minutes from the CSW's office, calls the client immediately, and is able to resolve the danger. The client disavows any continued plan to harm his spouse, and apologizes to the CSW for "getting so out of hand." What does the CSW need to do to resolve the CSW's legal responsibility?

a. **Incorrect.** Notify the spouse and law enforcement immediately
b. **Incorrect.** Notify the spouse immediately
c. **CORRECT.** Notify law enforcement within 24 hours
d. **Incorrect.** Notify the local child protective services agency

While warning an intended victim in a *Tarasoff* situation grants the CSW certain additional legal protections, it is not always necessary or appropriate to do so. In this case, the CSW was able to fully resolve the threat on their own, before notifying the intended victim or law enforcement. Still, under state law, the fact that the CSW's *Tarasoff* responsibilities were triggered *at all* means that the CSW must report the threatening person to law enforcement within 24 hours, even if notifying law enforcement was not necessary to resolve the initial threat. As noted in the study guide, the idea of this law is to prevent potentially dangerous individuals from buying guns.

70. A CSW has a new client who explains during the intake session that she had a hard time coming into therapy. The client says that her previous therapist asked her to go on a date with him immediately after their termination session ended. She refused, and has not spoken with the former therapist again, but the experience left her skeptical of therapists generally. Legally, the CSW must:

    a. **Incorrect.** Report the other therapist's actions to the BBS. *The CSW could report the other therapist to the BBS, if the client signed a release of information allowing them to do so – but this is not a legal obligation, and it would be better for the client to report directly.*

    b. **Incorrect.** Confront the other therapist on their behavior. *The CSW has no legal obligation to confront the other therapist, and doing so in the absence of a release of information from the client would be a breach of confidentiality.*

    c. **Incorrect.** Provide the client a copy of the brochure "Therapy Never Includes Sexual Behavior." *Providing the brochure would be a legal obligation if the client reported having had a sexual relationship with the prior therapist. However, such a relationship never began. The CSW can provide the brochure here, but is not required to do so.*

    d. **CORRECT.** Maintain the client's confidentiality. *None of the other options are actual legal obligations in these circumstances. The prior therapist's behavior was romantic but not overtly sexual in nature, and occurred after the psychotherapist-client relationship had been terminated.*

71. A CSW is interested in conducting research on her clients, in an effort to determine whether a new form of treatment developed by the CSW is superior to existing treatments. Because the CSW already has access to the client files and would be reporting statistics on her recent treatment results, without specifics of any individual cases, she prepares to conduct an analysis of cases she has closed over the prior year. She hopes to publish the results of her research in a prominent journal. Ethically, the CSW should:

    a. **CORRECT.** Contact those former clients, inform them of the risks and benefits of involvement in the research, and determine their willingness to have their file included as one of those analyzed. *The NASW Code of Ethics requires that research participants provide informed consent for their participation, including information about risks and benefits and the opportunity to choose not to participate. While the NASW ethics code allows some exceptions to consent for archival research, this is only appropriate when obtaining consent is not feasible. In the situation described in the vignette, it is possible to obtain consent.*

    b. **Incorrect.** Take steps to protect the confidentiality of individual cases, but include all cases from the prior year in her analysis to eliminate possible selection bias. *While there is reasonable concern that those clients who choose not to participate might skew results, participants' rights outweigh concerns about possible selection bias.*

    c. **Incorrect.** Contact those former clients to let them know that their files have been included in her research. *Simply informing them after the fact that they were included would not meet professional standards. It neglects an informed consent process for research and does not give the clients the opportunity to choose against being part of that research.*

    d. **Incorrect.** Because she is working with archival data that will be reported in aggregate, no action is required. *Even though results will be reported in aggregate, the CSW's clients had not been informed that they were also research participants. They must be given the opportunity to choose whether to be involved in the research. While the NASW ethics code allows some exceptions for some types of archival research, this is only appropriate when obtaining consent is not feasible. Here, the clinician presumably has contact information for her former clients, and could obtain consent from prospective participants.*

72. A 27-year-old trans female client has been receiving services from an LCSW at a reduced-fee clinic. The client has been unable to pay even her reduced fee, and over 8 weeks has built up an unpaid balance of more than $100. The client is apologetic and has reassured the LCSW that she will pay the overdue fees once her aging mother dies and she can collect her inheritance. The LCSW has informed the client while she empathizes with the client's struggles, a balance that goes unpaid for more than 30 days will result in the termination of services. This policy also appears in the informed consent document the client signed at the beginning of services. The client does not have stable food, work, or shelter, but is typically able to engage public services and shelter space when needed. How should the social worker proceed?

    a. **CORRECT.** Assess whether the client poses imminent danger to self or others
    b. **Incorrect.** Terminate the client for nonpayment and provide at least three community referrals
    c. **Incorrect.** Pay the client's balance on the client's behalf
    d. **Incorrect.** Set a specific deadline by which the full balance must be paid off to retain services

Under the NASW Code of Ethics, termination for nonpayment of an overdue balance is allowed, but a social worker first needs to engage in a number of specific steps. One of those steps is determining that the client is not an imminent danger to self or others. While nothing in the question suggests such danger, the ethical standard suggests that it should be actively determined prior to terminating with the client. Once such a determination is made, the social worker is free to terminate the client.

73. An LCSW is supervising an associate clinical social worker from a different cultural background. Early in their supervision relationship, they discover that they both are part of a small social media group for health care professionals in their city who suffered abuse as children. How should the supervisor proceed?

    a. **Incorrect.** Ask the supervisee to set a boundary on their social media interactions that is comfortable for the supervisee, based on the supervisee's cultural background and expectations

    b. **CORRECT.** Meet with the supervisee to establish that the supervisor will not discuss their professional relationship in the social media group or interact with the supervisee's posts in that group; discuss what other limitations may be necessary

    c. **Incorrect.** Acknowledge their professional relationship in the group, in the interest of transparency; discuss what other limitations may be necessary

    d. **Incorrect.** Inform the supervisee that if they are going to work together, neither the supervisor nor the supervisee can participate in the social media group

Particular caution around potential multiple relationships is necessary when interacting online. Supervisors, not supervisees (A), are responsible for setting appropriate boundaries around such relationships. In this group, there is risk of potential harm to the supervisee, if the supervisor were to learn more about the supervisee's abuse through the process of supervision. That the supervisor, we hope, would not share this additional information in the social media group does not remove the risk that they could; that risk is reason enough for caution. Simply being transparent about the professional relationship (C) does not do enough to resolve that risk, while declaring that neither the supervisor nor the supervisee can continue to participate in the group (D) is likely an over-reaction. At most, it would seem that one of them, not both, may wish to step away from the online group.

74. A white family has been attending family therapy to address conflict among the three siblings: A 16-year-old girl, a 13-year-old girl, and a 10-year-old who identifies as nonbinary. In session, the 16-year-old admits that she and the 10-year-old sometimes wake up before the 13-year-old, and then wake the 13-year-old by climbing on top of her, slapping, and punching her. The 13-year-old has shown her parents the bruises on her face and arms that have resulted, but the parents say they did not take photos of the bruises, and the LCSW providing family therapy has not observed any bruising. The 13-year-old says she has tried to "get back" at her siblings by stealing and giving away their belongings. The parents say they feel helpless to stop the siblings' behavior toward one another. How should the LCSW proceed?

    a. **Incorrect.** File a report of suspected child abuse, naming all three siblings as both victims and perpetrators

    b. **CORRECT.** File a report of suspected child abuse, naming the 16-year-old and 10-year-old as perpetrators

    c. **Incorrect.** File a report of suspected child neglect, naming the parents as perpetrators for failing to protect the 13-year-old

    d. **Incorrect.** File a report of suspected child abuse, naming only the 16-year-old as a perpetrator

While the child abuse reporting law in California does make an exception to the physical abuse reporting requirement for a "mutual affray" among minors, the violence here is not mutual. It is leaving the 13-year-old with physical injuries. That abuse must be reported, even when the perpetrator is another minor. The 13-year-old's efforts to get back at her siblings are clinically troubling, but do not legally qualify as abuse. A report of suspected physical abuse should be filed, naming the 16-year-old and 10-year-old as perpetrators and the 13-year-old as a victim.

75. A 56-year-old male client is seeing a social worker to address the client's substance use. The client also regularly sees a psychiatrist. The client provided the social worker with the psychiatrist's name, contact information, and date of most recent visit during the intake process. When discussing the psychiatrist in session, the client asks the social worker not to contact the psychiatrist. The client says the psychiatrist "isn't real big on therapy. I don't know if they would like that I'm here." Considering the social worker's ethical responsibilities, how should the social worker proceed?

    a. **Incorrect.** Contact the psychiatrist to coordinate care, as the psychiatrist is an active member of the client's treatment team

    b. **Incorrect.** Inform the client that coordinated care is necessary for effective treatment, and reassure the client that only a minimal amount of information will be shared

    c. **Incorrect.** Inform the client that coordinated care is necessary for effective treatment, and direct the client to sign a Release of Information form allowing the social worker to coordinate with the psychiatrist

    d. **CORRECT.** Do not contact the psychiatrist, and discuss the implications of the client coming to therapy against the psychiatrist's guidance

In this instance, the law allows for the sharing of information between active treatment providers for the purposes of treatment planning, but does not require such sharing. The client may thus make determinations about whether they would like their information to be shared, and the social worker is (with some exceptions) expected to honor those wishes. Here, the social worker can follow both the law and their ethics code by respecting the client's wish not to have information about the therapy shared with the psychiatrist.

Appendix:
Exam Plan with Index

Board of Behavioral Sciences

Licensed Clinical Social Worker

California Law and Ethics Examination Outline

The following document provides detailed information about the LCSW California Law and Ethics Examination, including a description of each content area, subarea and the associated task and knowledge statements. **Each question in the examination is linked to this content.**

Note: The exam outline, including all task and knowledge statements, comes from the BBS outline published online. Page numbers refer to where the relevant information can be found within this text.

I. Law (40%)

This area assesses the candidate's ability to identify and apply legal mandates to clinical social work practice.

IA. Confidentiality, Privilege, and Consent (14%)

Task Statement	Knowledge Statement	Page
T1. Comply with legal requirements regarding the maintenance/dissemination of confidential information to protect the client's privacy.	K1. Knowledge of laws regarding confidential communications within the therapeutic relationship.	39
	K2. Knowledge of laws regarding the disclosure of confidential information to other individuals, professionals, agencies, or authorities.	39
T2. Identify holder of privilege by evaluating client's age, legal status, and/or content of therapy to determine requirements for providing therapeutic services.	K3. Knowledge of laws regarding holder of privilege.	41
	K4. Knowledge of laws regarding privileged communication.	40
T3. Comply with legal requirements regarding the disclosure of privileged information to protect client's privacy in judicial/legal matters.	K4. Knowledge of laws regarding privileged communication.	40
	K5. Knowledge of laws regarding the release of privileged information.	41
	K6. Knowledge of legal requirements for responding to subpoenas and court orders.	41

Preparing for the 2022 California Clinical Social Work Law & Ethics Exam

Task Statement	Knowledge Statement	Page
T4. Comply with legal requirements regarding providing therapeutic services to minor clients.	K1. Knowledge of laws regarding confidential communications within the therapeutic relationship.	39
	K2. Knowledge of laws regarding the disclosure of confidential information to other individuals, professionals, agencies, or authorities.	39
	K3. Knowledge of laws regarding holder of privilege.	41
	K4. Knowledge of laws regarding privileged communication.	40
	K7. Knowledge of legal criteria and requirements for providing therapeutic services to minors.	42
T5. Maintain client records by adhering to legal requirements regarding documentation, storage, and disposal to protect the client's privacy and/or the therapeutic process.	K8. Knowledge of laws regarding documentation of therapeutic services.	42
	K9. Knowledge of laws pertaining to the maintenance/disposal of client records.	43
T6. Respond to requests for records by adhering to applicable laws and regulations to protect client's rights and/or safety.	K10. Knowledge of laws pertaining to client's access to treatment records.	43
	K11. Knowledge of laws pertaining to the release of client records to other individuals, professionals, or third parties.	44
T7. Provide services via information and communication technologies by complying with "telehealth" regulations.	K12. Knowledge of laws regarding the consent to and delivery of services via information and communication technologies.	44
T8. Comply with the Health Information Portability and Accountability Act (HIPAA) regulations as mandated by law.	K13. Knowledge of legal requirements of the Health Information Portability and Accountability Act (HIPAA).	45

IB. Limits to Confidentiality / Mandated Reporting (16%)

Task Statement	Knowledge Statement	Page
T9. Report known or suspected abuse, neglect, or exploitation of dependent adult client(s) to protective authorities.	K14. Knowledge of indicators of abuse, neglect, or exploitation of dependent adults.	57
	K15. Knowledge of laws pertaining to the reporting of known or suspected incidents of abuse, neglect, or exploitation of dependent adults.	55
T10. Report known or suspected abuse, neglect, or exploitation of elderly client(s) to protective authorities.	K16. Knowledge of indicators of abuse, neglect, or exploitation of elderly clients.	57
	K17. Knowledge of laws pertaining to the reporting of known or suspected incidents of abuse, neglect, or exploitation of elderly clients.	55
T11. Report known or suspected abuse or neglect of a child or adolescent to protective authorities.	K18. Knowledge of indicators of abuse/neglect of children and adolescents.	53
	K19. Knowledge of laws pertaining to the reporting of known or suspected incidents of abuse/neglect of children and adolescents.	51
T12. Comply with legal requirements regarding breaking confidentiality to protect the client in the presence of indictors of danger to self/others and/or grave disability.	K20. Knowledge of symptoms of mental impairment that may indicate the need for involuntary hospitalization.	58
	K21. Knowledge of protocols for initiating involuntary hospitalization.	58
	K22. Knowledge of laws regarding confidentiality in situations of client danger to self or others.	59

Preparing for the 2022 California Clinical Social Work Law & Ethics Exam

Task Statement	Knowledge Statement	Page
T13. Comply with legal requirements to report and protect when client expresses intent to cause harm to people or property.	K23. Knowledge of methods/criteria for identifying situations where client poses a danger to others.	60
	K24. Knowledge of laws pertaining to duty to protect when client indicates intent to cause harm.	61
	K25. Knowledge of situations/conditions that constitute reasonable indicators of client's intent to cause harm.	61
T14. Comply with legal requirements regarding privilege exceptions in client litigation or in response to breach of duty accusations.	K26. Knowledge of laws regarding privilege exceptions in litigation involving client's mental or emotional condition as raised by the client or client's representative.	62
	K27. Knowledge of laws regarding privilege exceptions where client alleges breach of duty.	62
T15. Comply with legal requirements regarding privilege exceptions in court-appointed and/or defendant-requested evaluation/therapy.	K28. Knowledge of laws regarding privilege exceptions in court-appointed evaluation or therapy.	62
	K29. Knowledge of laws pertaining to privilege exceptions in defendant-requested evaluation or therapy.	62
T16. Comply with legal requirements regarding reporting instances of crime perpetrated against minor clients.	K30. Knowledge of laws pertaining to the reporting of crimes perpetrated against a minor.	62
	K31. Knowledge of laws regarding privilege exceptions in crime or tort involving minors.	62

IC. Legal Standards for Professional Practice (10%)

Task Statement	Knowledge Statement	Page
T17. Comply with laws regarding sexual contact, conduct, and relations between therapist and client to prevent harm to the client and/or the therapeutic relationship.	K32. Knowledge of laws regarding sexual conduct between therapist and client.	67
	K33. Knowledge of legal requirements for providing client with the brochure *Professional Therapy Never Includes Sex.*	67
T18. Comply with legal parameters regarding scope of practice.	K34. Knowledge of laws that define the scope of clinical practice.	68
T19. Comply with legal parameters regarding professional conduct.	K35. Knowledge of laws that define professional conduct for licensed practitioners.	68
T20. Disclose fee structure prior to initiating therapeutic services.	K36. Knowledge of laws regarding disclosures required prior to initiating therapeutic services.	71
T21. Comply with legal regulations regarding providing treatment when interacting with third-party payers.	K37. Knowledge of laws and regulations regarding third-party reimbursement.	71
	K38. Knowledge of parity laws regarding the provision of mental health services.	72
T22. Comply with laws regarding advertisement of services and professional qualifications.	K39. Knowledge of laws regarding advertisement and dissemination of information of professional qualifications, education, and professional affiliations.	72
T23. Comply with laws pertaining to the payment or acceptance of money or other consideration for referrals.	K40. Knowledge of legal requirements regarding payment or acceptance of money or other considerations for referral of services.	73

II. Ethics (60%)

This area assesses the candidate's ability to identify and apply ethical standards for professional conduct.

IIA. Professional Competence and Preventing Harm (18%)

Task Statement	Knowledge Statement	Page
T24. Consult with other professionals and/or seek additional education, training, and/or supervision to address therapeutic issues that arise outside therapist's scope of competence.	K41. Knowledge of limitations of professional experience, education, and training to determine issues outside scope of competence.	79
	K42. Knowledge of situations that indicate a need for consultation with colleagues or other professionals.	79
	K43. Knowledge of ethical standards regarding the protection of client rights when engaging in consultation/collaboration with other professionals.	80
	K44. Knowledge of ethical methods of developing additional areas of practice or expanding competence.	80
	K45. Knowledge of the ethical responsibility to remain current on developments in the profession.	80
T25. Consult with other professionals to address questions regarding ethical obligations or practice responsibilities that arise during treatment.	K42. Knowledge of situations that indicate a need for consultation with colleagues or other professionals.	79
	K43. Knowledge of ethical standards regarding the protection of client rights when engaging in consultation/collaboration with other professionals.	80

Task Statement	Knowledge Statement	Page
T26. Evaluate therapist's own mental, emotional, or physical problems/impairments to determine impact on ability to provide competent therapeutic services.	K42. Knowledge of situations that indicate a need for consultation with colleagues or other professionals.	79
	K46. Knowledge of problems/impairments that interfere with the process of providing therapeutic services.	81
	K47. Knowledge of referrals and resources to assist in meeting the needs of clients.	81
	K48. Knowledge of methods to facilitate transfer when referrals to other professionals are made.	81
T27. Provide referral(s) to qualified professionals when adjunctive/alternate treatment would benefit the client.	K41. Knowledge of limitations of professional experience, education, and training to determine issues outside scope of competence.	79
	K43. Knowledge of ethical standards regarding the protection of client rights when engaging in consultation/collaboration with other professionals.	80
	K47. Knowledge of referrals and resources to assist in meeting the needs of clients.	81
	K48. Knowledge of methods to facilitate transfer when referrals to other professionals are made.	81
	K49. Knowledge of methods for collaborating with client to determine if referral(s) or other resources are clinically indicated.	79
T28. Manage therapist's personal values, attitudes, and/or beliefs to prevent interference with effective provision of therapeutic services and/or the therapeutic relationship.	K50. Knowledge of the potential impact of therapist's personal values, attitudes, and/or beliefs on the therapeutic relationship.	82
	K51. Knowledge of methods for managing the impact of therapist's personal values, attitudes, and/or beliefs on the client or the therapeutic relationship.	82

Preparing for the 2022 California Clinical Social Work Law & Ethics Exam

Task Statement	Knowledge Statement	Page
T29. Evaluate potential conflict of interest situations to determine the impact on the client or the therapeutic process.	K52. Knowledge of conditions/situations that could potentially exploit or cause harm to the client.	83
	K53. Knowledge of methods for managing boundaries and/or professional relationships with the client.	83
	K54. Knowledge of ethical standards regarding protecting the client's wellbeing in potential conflict of interest situations.	84
T30. Maintain professional boundaries with client to prevent situations or relationships that adversely impact the provision of therapeutic services.	K52. Knowledge of conditions/situations that could potentially exploit or cause harm to the client.	83
	K53. Knowledge of methods for managing boundaries and/or professional relationships with the client.	83
	K55. Knowledge of relationships that can be potentially detrimental to the client and/or therapeutic relationship.	84
	K56. Knowledge of methods to prevent impairment to clinical judgment and/or harm to the client in situations where multiple relationships are unavoidable.	85
T31. Adhere to ethical guidelines regarding sexual activity or contact with prospective, current, or former clients and/or those with whom the client has a personal relationship to avoid causing harm or exploitation of the client.	K57. Knowledge of the potential for client harm or exploitation associated with sexual activity or contact between therapist and client.	85
	K58. Knowledge of ethical standards regarding engaging in sexual activity or contact with client and/or others with whom the client has/had a personal relationship.	86
	K59. Knowledge of ethical standards regarding entering into a therapeutic relationship with former sexual partners.	86

IIB. Therapeutic Relationship/Services (27%)

Task Statement	Knowledge Statement	Page
T32. Obtain informed consent by providing client with information regarding the therapist and the treatment process to facilitate client's ability to make decisions.	K60. Knowledge of the ethical responsibility to provide client with information regarding the therapeutic process.	91
	K61. Knowledge of disclosures that facilitate client's ability to make informed decisions regarding treatment.	91
	K62. Knowledge of client's right to self-determination in making decisions regarding therapeutic services received.	92
	K63. Knowledge of methods for communicating information pertaining to informed consent in a manner consistent with developmental and cultural factors.	92
	K64. Knowledge of the right and responsibility of legal guardian/representative to make decisions on behalf of clients unable to make informed decisions.	93
	K65. Knowledge of methods for protecting client's welfare when client is unable to provide voluntary consent.	93
T33. Evaluate for current relationships with other service providers to determine impact of entering into a relationship with a new service provider.	K66. Knowledge of the effects of concurrent mental health treatments on the provision of therapeutic services.	94
	K67. Knowledge of methods for establishing collaborative professional relationships to improve the welfare of the client.	94
	K68. Knowledge of ethical standards regarding the protection of client rights when engaging in consultation/collaboration with other professionals.	95

321

Preparing for the 2022 California Clinical Social Work Law & Ethics Exam

Task Statement	Knowledge Statement	Page
T34. Address confidentiality and/or therapeutic issues associated with therapist's role, treatment modality, and involvement of third parties to protect the client's rights and/or the therapeutic relationship.	K69. Knowledge of methods for identifying the "client" and the nature of relationships when providing therapeutic services to more than one person.	95
	K70. Knowledge of the impact of client unit, treatment modality, and involvement of multiple systems on confidentiality.	96
	K71. Knowledge of the factors that impact the therapeutic relationship.	96
	K72. Knowledge of methods for managing confidentiality and privacy issues when providing concurrent therapy.	97
	K73. Knowledge of methods for managing confidentiality and privacy issues when treatment involves multiple systems or third parties.	97
T35. Manage the impact of confidentiality/limits of confidentiality on the therapeutic relationship by discussing with the client issues/implications that arise during the therapeutic process.	K74. Knowledge of ethical standards regarding the management of confidentiality issues that arise in the therapeutic process.	98
	K75. Knowledge of methods for managing the impact of confidentiality issues on the therapeutic relationship.	98
T36. Manage the impact of safety and/or crisis situations by evaluating risk factors to protect the client/others.	K76. Knowledge of methods for assessing level of potential danger or harm to client or others.	99
	K77. Knowledge of ethical obligations regarding the management of safety needs.	99
	K78. Knowledge of methods and procedures for managing safety needs.	99

Task Statement	Knowledge Statement	Page
T37. Manage the impact of legal and ethical obligations that arise during the therapeutic process to protect the client/therapist relationship.	K79. Knowledge of the impact of legal and ethical obligations on the therapeutic relationship.	101
	K80. Knowledge of methods for protecting the best interest of the client in situations where legal and ethical obligations conflict.	101
	K81. Knowledge of methods for protecting the best interest of the client in situations where agency and ethical obligations conflict.	102
T38. Manage diversity factors in the therapeutic relationship by applying and/or gaining knowledge and awareness necessary to provide services sensitive to client needs.	K82. Knowledge of diversity factors that potentially impact the therapeutic process.	103
	K83. Knowledge of ethical standards regarding nondiscrimination.	102
	K84. Knowledge of ethical standards for providing therapeutic services congruent with client diversity.	103
	K85. Knowledge of methods to gain knowledge, awareness, sensitivity, and skills necessary for working with clients from diverse populations.	103
T39. Provide treatment that respects the client's inherent dignity and right to self-determination.	K86. Knowledge of the collaborative role between therapist and client in the therapeutic process.	104
	K87. Knowledge of the client's right to make decisions regarding therapeutic services.	104
	K88. Knowledge of methods to assist client to make decisions and clarify goals.	105
T40. Contribute to multidisciplinary team by collaborating with colleagues/other professionals to provide services that promote the wellbeing of the client.	K43. Knowledge of ethical standards regarding the protection of client rights when engaging in consultation/collaboration with other professionals.	80
	K89. Knowledge of methods for establishing collaborative professional relationships to improve welfare of the client.	105
	K90. Knowledge of ethical standards for participating as a member of an interdisciplinary team.	105

Preparing for the 2022 California Clinical Social Work Law & Ethics Exam

Task Statement	Knowledge Statement	Page
T41. Advocate with and/or on behalf of the client by addressing barriers and/or increasing access to assist client in receiving services.	K91. Knowledge of methods for evaluating client's capacity to advocate on own behalf.	106
	K92. Knowledge of ethical standards pertaining to interacting with third-party payers.	106
	K93. Knowledge of ethical standards pertaining to interacting with other service delivery systems.	107
	K94. Knowledge of methods for enhancing client's ability to meet own needs.	107
T42. Maintain practice procedures that provide for consistent care in the event therapeutic services must be interrupted or discontinued.	K95. Knowledge of ethical considerations and conditions for interrupting or terminating therapeutic services.	107
	K96. Knowledge of referrals/resources to provide consistent care in the event therapeutic services must be interrupted or discontinued.	108
	K97. Knowledge of methods to facilitate transfer when referrals to other professionals are made.	109
T43. Terminate therapeutic services when no longer required or no longer benefits the client.	K98. Knowledge of factors and/or conditions that indicate client is ready for termination of therapeutic services.	109
	K99. Knowledge of factors and/or conditions that indicate client is not benefiting from treatment.	110
	K100. Knowledge of methods for managing the termination process.	110
	K101. Knowledge of methods to prevent client abandonment and/or client neglect.	110

IIC. Business Practices and Policies (15%)

Task Statement	Knowledge Statement	Page
T44. Advertise services by adhering to ethical guidelines regarding the use of accurate representations and information to promote services and/or expand practice.	K102. Knowledge of ethical guidelines regarding the use of accurate representation of qualifications and credentials in advertisements and/or solicitation of clients.	115
	K103. Knowledge of ethical guidelines pertaining to the solicitation of testimonials or statements from clients or others.	115
	K104. Knowledge of ethical guidelines regarding the recruitment of clients through employment and/or professional associations.	116
T45. Maintain client records by adhering to ethical guidelines to document services and/or protect the client's confidentiality.	K105. Knowledge of ethical guidelines regarding the documentation of therapeutic services consistent with sound clinical practice.	116
	K106. Knowledge of methods for providing reasonable protection of the confidentiality of client records.	117
	K107. Knowledge of ethical guidelines for releasing client records upon request.	117
	K108. Knowledge of methods to assist client understand/interpret information contained in therapeutic records.	118
T46. Clarify role(s) when acting in a professional capacity other than licensed clinical social worker to avoid confusion and/or inaccurate representation of qualifications.	K109. Knowledge of the ethical responsibility to clarify roles when acting in a professional capacity other than licensed clinical social worker.	118
	K110. Knowledge of ethical guidelines regarding engaging in conflicting and/or dual roles.	118

Preparing for the 2022 California Clinical Social Work Law & Ethics Exam

Task Statement	Knowledge Statement	Page
T47. Implement policies/procedures that address ethical issues associated with the use of electronic media and technology in the course of providing services.	K111. Knowledge of the potential for harm to the client or therapeutic relationship with the use of electronic media in the therapeutic process.	119
	K112. Knowledge of ethical standards for implementing electronic media in the therapeutic process.	119
	K113. Knowledge of the limits and risks associated with electronic means of service delivery.	120
T48. Maintain fee/payment policies that are commensurate with services provided and protect the therapeutic relationship.	K114. Knowledge of methods and conditions for determining fees commensurate with professional services.	120
	K115. Knowledge of prohibited business practices/forms of remuneration for making/accepting client referrals.	121
	K116. Knowledge of the potential for client exploitation or harm that may result from bartering/exchanges for services.	121
	K117. Knowledge of ethical standards pertaining to the collection of unpaid balances.	122
	K118. Knowledge of ethical obligations regarding providing for continuation of treatment to the client.	122
	K119. Knowledge of ethical guidelines regarding the provision of therapeutic services when interacting with third-party payers.	122
	K47. Knowledge of referrals and resources to assist in meeting the needs of clients.	81

Task Statement	Knowledge Statement	Page
T49. Adhere to ethical guidelines regarding the acceptance of gifts and/or tokens of appreciation from clients.	K120. Knowledge of conditions/situations that may interfere with professional judgment or have a detrimental effect on the provision of therapeutic services.	122
	K121. Knowledge of ethical standards regarding the acceptance of gifts from clients.	122
T50. Adhere to ethical guidelines for protecting the welfare and dignity of research participants when conducting research related to the provision of therapeutic services.	K122. Knowledge of procedures to safeguard participants when conducting research projects.	123
	K123. Knowledge of disclosures required to inform participants of the nature and role of research projects.	123
	K124. Knowledge of client's rights regarding participation in research projects.	124
	K125. Knowledge of methods for protecting client confidentiality and data when conducting research projects.	124
T51. Address unethical or incompetent conduct of colleague by taking action to promote the welfare and interests of clients.	K126. Knowledge of conditions/situations that may impair the integrity or efficacy of the therapeutic process.	124
	K127. Knowledge of guidelines for addressing unethical or incompetent conduct of colleagues.	125
T52. Adhere to ethical guidelines for engaging in the supervisor/ prelicensure practitioner relationship.	K128. Knowledge of the ethical guidelines governing the supervisor/ prelicensure practitioner relationship and responsibilities.	125